Branch Banking – Law and Practice

BANKERS WORKBOOK SERIES

Acknowledgement

I should like to thank Paul Cowdell DipFS, FCIB, ACT(Tec) and Jane Cowdell DipFS, ACIB, MCIM for their contributions to this book. Thanks are also given to colleagues and friends for their help. I am also extremely grateful to Renee Hayes and others for their word processing skills in the production of the manuscript. Finally, but by no means least, I must record my appreciation for the encouragement and understanding given to me by my wife Sue and my children Kerry and Robin over the many months spent in writing this book.

Branch Banking–
Law and Practice

BANKERS WORKBOOK SERIES

DEREK HYDE ACIB, Cert Ed (FE)

Published in association with

First published in 1993

BANKERS BOOKS LIMITED
c/o The Chartered Institute of Bankers
10 Lombard Street
London EC3V 9AS

CIB publications are published by The Chartered Institute of Bankers, a non-profit making
registered educational charity, and are distributed exclusively by Bankers Books Limited which
is a wholly owned subsidiary of The Chartered Institute of Bankers.

 British Library Cataloguing in Publication Data

Hyde, D.
  Branch Banking–Law and Practice (Bankers Workbook Series)
  I. Title II. Series
  344.10682

ISBN 0 85297 336 5

Typeset in Times 11/13pt by Commercial Colour Press Ltd, London.
Text printed on 80gsm general purpose, w'free: cover on 240gsm matt coated art.
Printed by Selwood Printing Ltd, Burgess Hill, West Sussex.

BRANCH BANKING – LAW AND PRACTICE

CONTENTS

continued overleaf

INTRODUCTION

Branch Banking – Law and Practice

It is beneficial if students have studied Law Relating to Banking Services before beginning to study Branch Banking – Law and Practice. Law Relating to Banking Services is concerned with the principles of law, whereas Branch Banking – Law and Practice looks at how these principles are applied in practice in the branch situation.

Branch Banking – Law and Practice is a wide-ranging subject. As such, it is imperative that students fully understand each unit before progressing to the next one. Students should therefore ensure that they can tick all the boxes in the summary at the end of each unit to show that they have fully grasped the content. Also, to aid students' understanding of the subject, various student activities are given throughout, together with self-assessment and examination-type questions.

In order to maximise the benefit of this course, students should draw up a study programme which they can adhere to. They should bear in mind that it is far better to study a small amount regularly than to try to cram everything into one session.

In conclusion, remember that the hardest part of study is getting started. You should therefore approach this workbook as if you were meeting a friend. Set a time to meet and be on time!

The Concept of the Course

This workbook has been written for students studying Branch Banking – Law and Practice for the Associateship examinations of The Chartered Institute of Bankers.

The workbook aims to cover all the material contained in the CIB syllabus, although the topics may not be dealt with in exactly the same order. This is simply due to the personal preference of the author, so that knowledge may be built up and developed within the text.

The text consists of two major parts within 22 units: 19 units deal with the main subject matter and three units contain mock examination questions. At the end of each unit dealing with the subject matter there are self-assessment questions, with suggested answers provided at the end of the book in Appendix 2.

This workbook is designed to stand alone, but students must appreciate that changes in law and practice occur all the time. Therefore it is vital to keep abreast of new developments by reading *Banking World* articles, in particular the sections headed 'The Courts' and 'Signposts'. Do not forget to read the 'Updating Notes' for this subject and Law Relating to Banking Services, which are published by the CIB and which can be ordered from the CIB Canterbury office. It is also possible now to obtain summaries of 'Meet the Examiner' meetings which are held prior to the spring examinations. Details of their availability are normally given in *Banking World.*

At the end of each unit, other than those which consist of mock examinations, there is a list of the main cases and statutes covered in that unit. Students are encouraged to add their own notes as regards new developments in the topic area.

The Syllabus

Aim

To develop students' understanding of:

(a) the relationship between banker and customer; banking operations; and the implications arising from different types of accounts and events affecting their conduct;

(b) securities for advances as encountered by bankers/lenders in common situations.

Recent legislation and case law can have a considerable impact on this subject and students should ensure that they keep abreast of current developments.

Section I

(a) *Banker and customer relationships*

The general and special relationships between banker and customer, their respective rights and duties, and resultant practice involved in all features of banking transactions and banking business. The code of banking practice and the role of the Banking Ombudsman. The special relationships arising out of mandates and powers of attorney, appropriation of payments, set-off, confidentiality, status opinions and indemnities given to or by the banker. Safe custody.

(b) *Banking transactions*

Payment and collection of cheques and other instruments. Electronic payment systems such as BACS and CHAPS. Plastic payment cards and the mandatory function of a banker. The respective rights and duties of drawee and drawer and the banker, including statutory and other protection. Debit and credit clearing systems, including the transaction of cheques. The collection of cheques and other instruments. Standing orders and direct debits.

(c) *Types of account holder*

Banking practice in opening and conducting accounts, whether in credit or debit for all customers, viz. personal customers, including minors, joint account customers, executors, administrators and trustees, solicitors, estate agents, insurance brokers, licensed insolvency practitioners, unincorporated clubs and societies, partnerships, limited companies.

(d) *Determination of the banker/customer relationship*
    Action to be taken on the death, mental disorder, insolvency of customers, or upon receipt of garnishee, injunction, sequestration or other legal process.

Section II

A detailed knowledge is required of the suitability of securities, whether by first or subsequent charge, and the appropriate methods of valuation and form of charge. Steps to perfect the security and to enable release on repayment or otherwise, or realisation of the security on default.

— Quoted and unquoted stocks and shares.

— Life policies.

— Land and buildings, domestic and industrial, etc.

— Debentures incorporating fixed and/or floating charges.

— Book debts.

— Assignment of contracts.

— Produce and goods.

— Agricultural charges.

— Guarantees and letters of comfort.

— The use and procedures of solicitors' undertakings.

Knowledge is required of common problems encountered when taking security, and upon the enforcement of securities (including competing interests).

Scheme of Work by Objectives

The following scheme of work by objectives is suggested as an aid to checking coverage of the examination syllabus and your progress in learning/understanding of the various topics. On completion of the scheme of work, students should be fully prepared for this examination.

Syllabus topics – Section I

1 Relationship of banker and customer.

2 Banking operations.

3 Types of account holder.

4 Termination/interference of relationship between banker/customer and how it affects the operation of various types of banking account.

After completion of the Section I scheme of work by objectives, the student should:

1 *Thoroughly understand the nature of the banker/customer relationship*

1.1 Understand the general and special relationships which exist between banker and customer in relation to banking and business activities, and relate and interpret the rights and duties of each as they occur in practical banking situations.

1.2 Comprehend and recognise the effect of the Code of Banking Practice and the role of the Banking Ombudsman on the banker/customer relationship.

1.3 Establish and define what is a customer.

1.4 Examine and understand how the implied and written form of relationship has developed between banker and customer.

1.5 Identify the rights and duties of each party, with special reference to the points established in *Joachimson* v *Swiss Bank Corporation* (1921).

1.6 Identify the practical banking points covering opening and closing of bank accounts.

1.7 Appreciate the special relationships and practical implications involved for bankers in the following: mandates; powers of attorney; appropriation of payments (ensuring a thorough understanding of the points laid down in *Clayton's* case); rules covering the bank's right of set-off; limitation of actions; errors and omissions concerning bank account entries and statements.

1.8 Examine how the Consumer Credit Act 1974 has altered the relationship between banker and customer.

1.9 Examine the need for confidentiality when dealing with customers' affairs and the practical implications arising from the decision in *Tournier* v *National Provincial and Union Bank of England* (1924).

1.10 Analyse the possible liabilities and risks in answering banker's opinions.

1.11 Appreciate the nature, scope and real liability in granting bank indemnities and the need to obtain an effective counter-indemnity.

2 *Be wholly conversant with daily banking operations*

2.1 Examine the mandatory functions of the banker and the respective rights and duties of banker and drawer in paying and collecting cheques and understand how these are affected by statute.

2.2 Understand the potential problems for bankers in dealing with standing orders, direct debits, safe custody, purchase and sale of investments.

2.3 Understand the normal clearing cycle and other procedures for debiting and crediting cheques and payments to customers' accounts including CHAPS, BACS, credit transfers and truncation.

2.4 Be aware of the meaning and implications of transferability, negotiability, forged signatures; holder, holder for value and holder in due course; cheque crossing; overdue, stale, undated and post-dated cheques; the dangers of wrongful dishonour; and alterations and endorsements to cheques.

2.5 Understand the rights and duties of the paying banker and the protection available under section 1 of the Cheques Act 1957 and sections 59, 60 and 80 of Bills of Exchange Act 1882. Appreciate when the authority to pay a customer's cheque is terminated, and have knowledge of the inadvertence rule agreed by members of the London Bankers' Clearing House covering the return of cheques.

2.6　Appreciate the rights and duties of the collecting banker, especially the dangers of conversion, and have a knowledge of the protection available to banks under:

— Holder for value/holder in due course;
— Section 4 Cheques Act 1957;
— Contributory negligence.

Students should be aware of the various circumstances in which a collecting bank will be deemed 'negligent' in its dealings with a customer.

2.7　Identify how the existing relationship between banker and customer is altered through payments made under cheque guarantee cards and credit cards.

3　*Be fully conversant with various types of account holder*

3.1　Understand the practice in opening, conducting and closing accounts in credit and debit for all customers as specified below.

3.2　Appreciate the legal protections available to minors and how this affects the operation of bank accounts.

3.3　Understand how the conduct of married women's accounts is affected by statute, in particular the Sex Discrimination Act 1975, and an understanding of the principle of undue influence and fiduciary relationship.

3.4　Understand the conduct of joint accounts, the rule of survivorship, the implications of joint and several liability and the effect of disputes between parties.

3.5　Understand the conduct for the operation of accounts of executors, administrators and trustees.

3.6　Understand the conduct for the operation of accounts for solicitors, insurance brokers, estate agents and unincorporated clubs and societies.

3.7　Understand the conduct for the operation of accounts for partnerships with special emphasis upon liability on change of constitution of partnership, disputes between partners, bankruptcy of a partner, and dissolution of partnerships.

3.8　Understand the conduct for the operation of accounts of limited companies. This is a key area of the syllabus and students must have a full understanding and knowledge of the following:

The essence of incorporation and the various types of company; account opening formalities; importance of company memorandum and articles of association in establishing objects, borrowing powers, power to give guarantees, directors' powers and how these can be amended and altered; commercial justification – when giving third-party security; the concept of interested directors; the nature of a debenture given to a bank; operation of wages and salaries accounts; deeds of priority; administration orders; winding up and liquidation procedures.

Students must link this section closely with those areas in Section II relevant to limited companies and be aware of how the running of company accounts is governed by the Companies Act 1989 and Insolvency Act 1986.

4   *Thoroughly understand the legal and other factors affecting the operation of various accounts*

4.1   Examine how the relationship between banker and customer is affected by various legal processes, orders and injunctions.

4.2   Assess the action to be taken on notice of death or mental incapacity of a customer.

4.3   Know the effect of garnishee orders/summonses on various accounts, and understand which items are attached and the procedure on receipt of an order.

4.4   Understand the meaning, implication and action to be taken on receipt of a writ of sequestration and a Mareva injunction, with special reference to recent legal decisions.

4.5   Understand the nature of insolvency and bankruptcy procedures and how they affect the running of various classes of account in practical situations.

4.6   Understand the nature, acts and stages of the different forms of administration orders, winding up and liquidation of companies, and how these processes affect the operation of their banking accounts. Particular reference must be made to the Companies Act 1989 and Insolvency Act 1986.

Syllabus topics – Section II, Securities for advances

1   Security – types, valuation, margin, suitability, saleability.

2   Life policies.

3   Stocks and shares (quoted and unquoted).

4   Guarantees.

5   Land and buildings.

6   Solicitors' undertakings.

7   Company securities and debentures.

8   Book debts and assignment of contract moneys, including Milk Marketing Board charges.

9   Produce and goods.

The objectives of Section II are that students should be able: to assess the suitability of the above securities for advances; to pay particular attention to accurate valuations and to choose the correct method of charging. Students should be aware of the precautions to be taken to achieve a good title and the procedure for release on repayment or realisation on default.

After completion of the Section II scheme of work by objectives the student should:

INTRODUCTION

1 *Be aware of the main types of acceptable securities for bankers*

1.1 Assess the advantages and disadvantages of the main types of banking security.

1.2 Understand the different methods of perfecting title to a suitable banking security.

1.3 Distinguish between legal and equitable charges as regards title, rights and remedies.

1.4 Distinguish between direct and collateral security.

1.5 Having perfected title to a security, know the procedures necessary on its release, termination or sale.

2 *Be thoroughly conversant with life policies as security*

2.1 Assess the relative advantages and disadvantages of life policies as security and be aware of the different types of policy available.

2.2 Understand the essence of the life assurance contract.

2.3 Identify the parties required to sign the form of charge.

2.4 Understand in detail the procedures for perfecting a first and subsequent legal charge to ensure that a good title is obtained, and also the form of assignment in common bank usage and its terms.

2.5 Understand the procedures for perfecting an equitable charge both under hand and under seal and be aware of their benefits and shortcomings.

2.6 Appreciate how a life policy is valued for security purposes.

2.7 Assess the action to be taken on receipt of notice of a subsequent charge when lending on current account or loan account.

2.8 Outline the procedures for release of legal and equitable charges.

2.9 Outline the procedures for realisation of legal and equitable charges.

3 *Be thoroughly conversant with stocks and shares as security*

3.1 Assess the relative advantages and disadvantages of stocks and shares (quoted and unquoted) as security, and be aware of the different types of shares available.

3.2 Understand the relative practical advantages and disadvantages of legal and equitable charges, and the use of the bank's standard form of memorandum of deposit and its clauses.

3.3 Appreciate how stocks and shares are valued for security purposes.

3.4 Understand in detail the procedures for perfecting equitable and legal charges over all types of shares to ensure that the best possible title is obtained.

3.5 Understand in detail the procedures for perfecting as security an allotment letter, whether in fully or partly-paid form.

3.6 Distinguish between a bonus issue and a rights issue and assess their effect on the value of the security.

3.7 Outline the procedures for release and realisation of equitable and legal charges.

4 *Be thoroughly conversant with guarantees as security*

4.1 Assess the relative advantages and disadvantages of guarantees as security.

4.2 Identify: undue influence, fiduciary relationship and misrepresentation; be aware of the legal considerations and practical solutions.

4.3 Understand the legal position for claims of *non est factum*.

4.4 Understand the procedures for perfecting the guarantee and particularly the decision as to whether separate legal advice is required.

4.5 Appreciate the rights of the guarantor for information before and after completion of the guarantee and practical solutions to this problem.

4.6 Understand the standard clauses of a bank guarantee and how these affect the common law rights of the guarantor.

4.7 Define the procedure for requests to cancel the guarantee, whether given by the customer or the guarantor.

4.8 Define the procedure for determination of the guarantee and be aware of the various ways in which it may be determined.

4.9 Outline the action required on repayment of the debt by the debtor or the guarantor, or the co-surety.

4.10 Understand the additional practical and legal considerations when guarantees are given by companies or other bodies.

4.11 Assess the merits of unlimited guarantees as security.

5 *Understand the nature and procedures for taking land and buildings as security*

5.1 Assess the relative advantages and disadvantages of land as security.

5.2 Appreciate the different estates in land and the various methods of charging them as security.

5.3 Understand the clauses of a bank's legal and equitable charge forms.

5.4 Understand the procedures for perfecting a first and subsequent charge over unregistered land both freehold and leasehold.

5.5 Understand the procedures for perfecting a first and subsequent charge over registered land, both freehold and leasehold.

5.6 Appreciate the significance of the Matrimonial Homes Act 1983 and the cases of *Williams & Glyn's Bank Ltd* v *Boland* (1979) and *Williams & Glyn's Bank Ltd* v *Brown* (1979).

5.7 Outline the procedures for release on repayment and realisation on default for both legal and equitable charges.

5.8 Understand the method of perfecting sub-mortgage.

5.9 Assess the action to be taken on receipt of notice of a subsequent charge when lending on current account or loan account.

5.10 Appreciate the additional registrations which have to be made at Companies Registry when taking the security from companies.

6 *Be aware of solicitors' undertakings as security in relation to bridgeover facilities*

6.1 Appreciate the various standard undertakings agreed between the Committee of London Clearing Bankers and the Law Society and understand the benefits of using these forms.

6.2 Understand the disadvantages of not using the standard forms, in respect of solicitors' undertakings.

6.3 Appreciate the nature of the underlying transaction involved in solicitors' undertakings.

6.4 Understand the procedure for dealing with solicitors' undertakings.

7 *Thoroughly understand the use of company assets and debentures as security*

7.1 Assess the relative advantages and disadvantages of both fixed and floating charge debentures.

7.2 Understand the clauses of a bank's debenture form and the various charges it affords.

7.3 Appreciate the assets caught under a debenture and be aware of the problems of valuation and control of those assets.

7.4 Understand the procedures for perfecting a fixed and floating charge debenture.

7.5 Be able to identify which charges have to be registered at Companies Registry in accordance with sections 395 and 396 Companies Act 1985, as amended by section 93 Companies Act 1989.

7.6 Understand the remedies of the debenture holder and the procedure for cancellation of a charge registered at Companies Registry.

7.7 Understand priorities and postponement agreements with other secured lenders.

8 *Understand how book debts and assignment of contract moneys can be utilised as security*

8.1 Assess the relative advantages and disadvantages of charges over debts and contract moneys.

8.2 Understand the types of charge available and their valuation.

8.3 Understand the procedures for perfecting charges over book debts and contract moneys (including Milk Marketing Board contracts).

9 *Understand the nature of produce and merchandise as security*

9.1 Assess the relative advantages and disadvantages of taking produce and goods as security.

9.2 Understand the procedures for perfecting a charge over produce and goods, and their valuation – not forgetting any impact of 'Romalpa'.

9.3 Outline the procedure for realising and release of security ensuring adequate control over the produce or goods at all times.

The Examination Paper

The question paper is divided into three sections, from which candidates must answer five questions:

Section A: consists of a compulsory question which may be based on any part of the syllabus.

Section B: contains three questions of which two must be answered; questions will cover topics contained in Section I of the syllabus.

Section C: contains three questions of which two must be answered; questions will cover topics contained in Section II of the syllabus.

All questions carry 20 marks. Candidates must satisfy the examiner in Sections B and C as well as in the paper as a whole.

The questions will be based on practical banking situations, calling for a detailed account of steps to be taken and requiring adequate explanation why such steps are necessary. Candidates will be expected to support their answers by reference to any relevant statute or case law, and/or general principles governing good present-day banking practice in the UK.

In the examination, candidates will be allowed 15 minutes' reading time before the start of the three-hour period. During the reading time candidates may mark the question paper but may not write in the answer book.

Candidates may not use calculators (or mechanical or electronic aids of any kind) in this examination.

Advice for the Examination

The Branch Banking – Law and Practice examination looks at practical procedures and problems which occur in the branch situation. The questions set may be discursive, e.g. a discussion of possible different modes of action, or may merely require identification of the legal principles involved and how they are applied in practice. In many instances, the mnemonic 'PERKS' can provide a candidate with a structured framework with which to cover the relevant points.

'PERKS' can be defined as follows:

P = Principle

It is vital to read a question several times to establish what principle(s) are involved on the given facts. These principles must then be clearly stated in the answer so the examiner can see that you have understood the significance of the question. An example of a possible opening sentence to an answer could be 'the principle involved in this question concerns the bank's duty of secrecy'.

E = Elaborate

Explain the general rules relating to the principle(s) you have identified. These rules will normally be derived from statute or case law.

R = Relate

Tell the examiner how the facts in the question relate to the cases or statutes which you have already quoted.

K = Konclusion

You must give a conclusion. Sometimes the conclusion will be clear, but at other times you will need to give a qualified statement. An example of a qualified conclusion could be: 'If we assume that the endorsement is forged, then X cannot be a holder in due course, but if the endorsement on the cheque is genuine, then X fulfils all the criteria of a holder in due course.'

S = Success!

Work hard, keep up to date, and you should pass the exam.

Remember that the Chief Examiner prefers tabulated answers. 'PERKS' provides you with the framework to meet that criteria.

Use of cases and statutes for the exam

1   *How to quote cases*

    If a case is famous enough, or if one of the parties has a distinctive name, then that name is sufficient, for example *'Tournier case'* instead of *'Tournier* v *National Provincial and Union Bank of England* (1924)'. Dates of cases are not necessary; neither are the law report references.

    However, where a case is not as well known, or as distinctive, try to quote the names of all parties, e.g. *Higgins* v *Beauchamp*.

2   *How to quote Acts of Parliament*

    The full and correct title of the Act should be used, unless the title is particularly long. Thus the 'Law of Property (Miscellaneous Provisions) Act 1989' may be quoted as the 'Law of Property etc. Act 1989'.

    When an Act has been quoted once, it can be referred to by its initials if quoted again in the same question.

    You should quote the year of the Act, but a mark will not usually be lost if this is not done. The year is particularly important in cases such as the Companies Act, when it may be necessary to distinguish between the 1985 Act and the 1989 Act.

    Finally the letter 's' can be used as an abbreviation for section number.

Once you have been given the examination paper, it is advisable that you:

(a) Quickly read through it, looking for familiar words and phrases. This should enable you to identify several questions which cover the areas you have revised in detail.

(b) Read the questions slowly, deciding which ones to answer. Choose the questions carefully, ensuring you have interpreted the question correctly and that you have not read simply what you want to see there. Be clear about the topic the examiner has asked for.

(c) Having chosen the question, make sure you know what the examiner wants; this time, as you read through, underline the key words. Consider how you are going to answer the questions.

Remember that in this exam candidates will be allowed a 15-minute reading time before the start of the three-hour period. During the reading time candidates may mark the exam question paper but may not write in the answer book, hence you should write down the principles involved and the names of any relevant cases or statutes on the exam paper as soon as they come to mind.

(d) Choose the question you are going to answer first. Most students choose the one they find easiest, because this then gives them the confidence to answer others. Some students may prefer to do the easiest second as they have then had time to 'settle' into the exam while answering the first question and so can give their 'best' question their full attention, thus gaining the highest marks.

(e) Try to make your writing as legible as possible – it is important the examiner can read your answers. If your writing is poor and you cannot improve it, emphasise key words and phrases, perhaps printing them or writing them in block capitals. This is very important for cases and statutes.

(f) Remember the ABC of success for this examination: Accuracy, Brevity, Clarity.

UNIT 1

The Banker–Customer Relationship

Objectives

- Define the term 'bank'.
- Define the term 'customer'.
- Identify the relationships which exist between banker and customer.
- Detail the duties of a banker.
- Detail the procedure to be followed when closing a troublesome account which is in credit.
- Recognise when the bank's duty of secrecy can be ignored.
- Detail the duties of a customer.
- Appreciate the effect that the Limitations Act 1980 has on the banker–customer relationship.
- Outline the operation of the Banking Ombudsman scheme.

Student Activity 1

Write down your definition of a bank. Compare your definition with the information which follows.

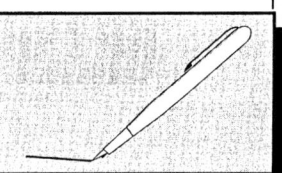

1.1 What is a Bank?

Two separate statutes and one case have considered this point. In chronological order they are:

(a) *The Bills of Exchange Act 1882*
    This defined the bank as 'a body of persons . . . who carry on the business of banking'.

(b) *United Dominions Trust* v *Kirkwood* (1966)
    This case defined a bank as an organisation which:

    (i)   accepted money from, and collected cheques for, customers;
    (ii)   honoured cheques or other withdrawal authorities given by customers;
    (iii) maintained current accounts or accounts of a similar nature;
    (iv)   had the reputation of being a bank within the financial community.

    Clearly on this basis many building societies and other similar financial services groups would apparently be classed as bankers. However, under the Banking Act 1987, they would fail to gain 'banking status'.

Note: Abbey National is no longer a building society: since it became a public limited company it has come under the Banking Act 1987 and is legally a bank.

(c) *The Banking Act 1987*

Today only an organisation which is recognised by the Bank of England as an authorised deposit taker under the 1987 Banking Act can use the description 'bank' in its title.

Thus, any organisation which is authorised to use the word 'bank' in its title under the 1987 Banking Act can be classed as a bank, and it would seem that any other financial services organisation which carries out what are generally considered to be banking activities could also be legally classed as a bank.

In practice, certain statutes have been designed to protect banks specifically, e.g. Cheques Act 1957. Thus it is apparent that it is necessary to know whether an organisation is a bank or not.

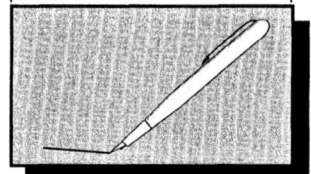

Student Activity 2

Write down your definition of a customer. Compare your definition with the information which follows.

1.2   What is a Customer?

There is no statutory definition of a 'customer'. In *Great Western Railway Co* v *London and County Banking Co* (1901) it was stated that some kind of account must exist for someone to be a customer of a banker.

However, in *Woods* v *Martins Bank Ltd* (1959) a bank gave investment advice to a non-account holder and the court held that, despite this fact, the bank still owed a similar responsibility as it would to a customer.

Therefore, it could be said that a person becomes a customer as soon as an account is opened or when a business relationship has been set up.

1.3   What Relationships Exist between Banker and Customer?

(a)   Debtor–creditor. This was confirmed in the case of *Foley* v *Hill* (1848).

(b)   Principal–agent, e.g. where a customer instructs a banker to buy or sell shares.

(c)   Bailor–bailee, e.g. when a customer keeps items in safe custody.

(d)   Trustee–beneficiary, e.g. when the bank's trust company acts as executor appointed under a will.

(e)   Mortgagor–mortgagee, e.g. when a customer mortgages property to a bank.

1.4 What are the Duties of a Banker?

The following duties were established in the case of *Joachimson* v *Swiss Bank Corporation* (1921):

(a) To receive a customer's cash and cheques for collection.

(b) To repay money on demand in accordance with the customer's written instructions.

(c) To give reasonable notice to a customer before closing a credit account (*Prosperity Ltd* v *Lloyds Bank Ltd* (1923)).

(d) To maintain secrecy regarding a customer's accounts and affairs.

(e) To advise a customer immediately forgery of the customer's signature is brought to the bank's attention.

(f) To provide a statement of account within a reasonable time, or to provide a balance of account on request.

1.5 What Constitutes 'Reasonable Notice' to a Customer Before Closing a Credit Account?

This has never been decided by the courts, and each situation therefore has to be examined on its merits. It is generally accepted that for the majority of private individuals, a month's notice would be ample time, but obviously a company customer could well require far in excess of a month, dependent upon the complexities of its financial affairs.

1.6 The Procedure to be Followed when a Bank Wishes to Close a Troublesome Account Which is in Credit

(a) Give written notice by registered or recorded delivery post to the customer, which will:

   (i)   State the last date on which credits/debits will be accepted by the bank, and the date of intended closure.
   (ii) Request return of unused cheques and plastic cards.
   (iii) Request the customer to make arrangements for the collection of the balance of the account.

(b) After the closure date, any cheque received for payment may be returned marked 'account closed'.

(c) Any credits received after closure of the account should be placed on a suspense account and the customer requested to call to collect the balance.

1.7 When Can the Banker's Duty of Secrecy be Ignored?

The case of *Tournier* v *National Provincial and Union Bank of England Ltd* (1924) identified occasions when disclosure of a customer's affairs is justified. They are as follows:

3

(a) By express or implied consent of the customer.
(b) Where there is a duty in the public interest.
(c) Where the interests of the bank require it.
(d) Under compulsion of law.

Details of some of the statutes under which compulsion of law would apply are given below.

(a) *Bankers' Books Evidence Act 1879*
A court order can be made to inspect and take copies of entries in a bank's books, provided that there are good grounds for this.

In *Barker* v *Wilson* (1980) microfilm was deemed to be admissible as a 'banker's book'. It was further stated that this term included any permanent record created by modern technology.

In *R.* v *Dadson* (1983) it was established that records not covered by this act, e.g. correspondence, must be produced where a bank is served with a subpoena or witness summons.

(b) *Police and Criminal Evidence Act 1984*
This is where a JP may make a PACE order on a bank to divulge a customer's affairs. (It is rare now for the police to seek an order under Bankers' Books Evidence Act 1879).

(c) *S.57 Finance Act 1976 referring to s.20 Taxes Management Act 1970*
The Inland Revenue is granted wide powers to obtain information from banks relating to any taxation liability.

(d) *S.17 Taxes Management Act 1970*
   (i) The Inland Revenue can obtain details of any stock registered in the name of the bank or its nominee company on behalf of a customer.
   (ii) Banks must complete returns to the Inland Revenue and disclose interest above a certain amount which has been credited to customers' accounts. This figure is regularly increased.

(e) *S.434 Companies Act 1985*
An order granted under this Act means that a bank must supply information relating to its company customer to a Department of Trade and Industry Inspector.

(f) *Financial Services Act (1986)*
The Trade and Industry Secretary can appoint inspectors to examine on oath any person able to supply information on suspected insider dealing. Witnesses can be compelled to produce any relevant documents.

(g) *Drug Trafficking Offences Act (1986)*
   (i) It is a criminal offence to hold, control or invest the proceeds of drug trafficking, or even to lend to a drug trafficker. However, it is not an offence or a breach of a bank's duty of secrecy if it discloses its knowledge or suspicions (s.24).
   (ii) A court may order a bank to allow access to its records by the authorities, who can retain them. This is known as a Production and Access Order. The bank must not advise the customer of this – to do so would be a criminal offence. A bank normally has seven days in which to comply with the order (s.27).

(iii) A court could grant a search warrant to enable the authorities access to bank premises to seize any documents or records which could assist their investigation (s.28).

(h) *Prevention of Terrorism Act (1989)*
Banks must disclose on suspicion the location of funds which might be used for possible offences under the Act.

1.8 What are the Duties of a Customer?

In the case of *Joachimson* v *Swiss Bank Corporation* (1921), it was established that a customer must:

(a) Seek out the banker if payment is required.

(b) Only issue cheques if there is a sufficient credit balance or unutilised overdraft.

(c) Pay charges as agreed, or as agreed as reasonable.

(d) Exercise reasonable care in drawing cheques, so that the bank will not be misled nor will fraud be easily facilitated. This duty only applies to normal precautions. It was established that a customer has no duty in the general course of business to prevent his or her employees forging cheques (*Tai Hing Cotton Mill Ltd* v *Liu Chong Hing Bank Ltd* (1986)).

Student Activity 3

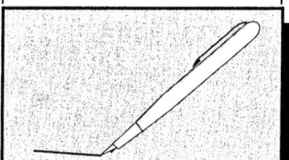

A code of practice which sets out good banking practice to be followed by banks, building societies and card issuers when dealing with personal customers was introduced in March 1992. (Full details are given in Appendix 1, pp. 267–279.) Examine how far cases mentioned earlier in this unit have been encapsulated in this code.

1.9 Statute of Limitations

The banker–customer relationship can be affected by the Limitations Act 1980. This states that legal action cannot be brought on a simple contract when more than six years has elapsed since the cause of action first arose. In the case of contracts made under seal, the time limit becomes 12 years.

In practice this means that any action to recover funds lent on overdraft becomes statute barred six years after demand for repayment has been made. This period can be extended where the customer has acknowledged the debt within the six years (s.6 Limitations Act 1980).

1.10 The Banking Ombudsman

Disagreements arise on occasions between banks and their customers. These are often resolved amicably. However, where this is not the case, resort to the courts may be necessary. An alternative to this step would be to use the Banking Ombudsman scheme which was set up in 1986 to act as an independent arbitrator.

The scheme is financed by 40 member banks plus some associate members who agree to abide by the Ombudsman's decisions. Funds are collected by the Board of the Ombudsman's Office, which also approves the election of the Ombudsman.

The Ombudsman is appointed by the Ombudsman Council, which consists of five lay assessors together with three representatives from the member banks. The aim of this Council is to ensure that the Ombudsman remains neutral in the matters which he investigates. It also provides details of his findings and annual report to the banks and consumers alike.

The Ombudsman scheme can be used by non-corporate customers and small companies whose turnover in the year prior to the complaint being made did not exceed £1m. Where a company is a member of a group of companies which have a combined annual turnover of more than £1m it will not be classed as a 'small company' within the Ombudsman scheme. It can be used on a wide range of areas within banking, provided that the amounts involved in the dispute do not exceed £100,000. All possible attempts should have been made to resolve the problem, both at branch and head office levels, before the Ombudsman is involved. If litigation has already commenced in the courts then the Ombudsman will decline to act.

Despite the recommendations of the report made by the Jack Committee (which investigated banking services, law and practice) the Ombudsman has no statutory powers. The Ombudsman also has little power concerning disputes over banks' investment services – these have to be referred either to the Securities and Investment Board or some other self-regulatory body. The Ombudsman also cannot deal with cases which involve the policies of banks pertaining to making commercial and lending decisions.

The Banking Ombudsman scheme gives bank customers an opportunity for redress without the inherent costs which would be involved if disputes were decided through the courts. The Ombudsman can make an award of up to £100,000, which may include payment not only for damages or loss, but also for any inconvenience caused to the claimant. As such, these are wider powers with regard to restitution than those enjoyed by the courts.

The Banking Ombudsman scheme is now being used widely by the public and it appears to help to identify areas within banking which perhaps need closer scrutiny by the banks themselves.

Summary

Now that you have read this unit, you should be able to:

☐ Define the term 'bank'.

☐ Define the term 'customer'.

☐ Identify the relationship which exists between banker and customer.

☐ Detail the duties of a banker.

☐ Detail the procedure to be followed when closing a troublesome account which is in credit.

☐ Recognise when the bank's duty of secrecy can be ignored.

☐ Detail the duties of a customer.

☐ Appreciate the effect that the Limitations Act 1980 has on the banker–customer relationship.

☐ Outline the operation of the Banking Ombudsman scheme.

If you can tick all the above boxes with confidence, you are ready to answer the questions that follow on pp. 8–10.

List of Cases

Barker v *Wilson* (1980)

Foley v *Hill* (1848)

Great Western Railway Co v *London and County Banking Co* (1901)

Joachimson v *Swiss Bank Corporation* (1921)

Prosperity Ltd v *Lloyds Bank Ltd* (1923)

R. v *Dadson* (1983)

Tai Hing Cotton Mill Ltd v *Liu Chong Hing Bank Ltd* (1986)

Tournier v *National Provincial and Union Bank of England Ltd* (1924)

United Dominions Trust v *Kirkwood* (1966)

Woods v *Martins Bank Ltd (1959)*

List of Statutes

Bankers' Books Evidence Act 1879

Banking Act 1987

Bills of Exchange Act 1882

Companies Act 1985

Drug Trafficking Offences Act 1986

Finance Act 1976

Financial Services Act 1986

Limitations Act 1980

Police and Criminal Evidence Act 1984

Prevention of Terrorism Act 1989

Taxes Management Act 1970

Self-assessment Questions

Short-answer questions

1 List five relationships which exist between banker and customer.

2 Which case in 1921 established the duties of banker and customer?

3 A member of your branch staff approaches you as manager and informs you that she witnessed one of your customers last night selling drugs at a disco.

Upon examining the records of the customer's account, you notice several large cash deposits and withdrawals which appear to be unusual when compared to the previous operation of the account. You therefore suspect that these transactions could be the result of illegally buying and selling drugs.

Can you divulge your suspicions to the authorities, or are you bound by the banker's duty of secrecy?

4 Which statute led to your answer in Q3?

5 Detective Constable Frank Charles, a customer of your branch, calls at your enquiries counter and asks to speak to you, as manager, urgently.

He advises you that he has just seen a 'local villain' pay in a large sum of money over the counter in your banking hall. He believes that it might be the proceeds from a series of recent burglaries.

From the description given by DC Charles you realise that the man to whom he refers is Chester Field, a customer who often pays in large amounts of money as he is an antiques dealer.

DC Charles asks to see a copy of Field's bank statement for the last three months so that he can ascertain whether any large deposits coincide with the recent burglaries.

Would you comply with this request?

6   What would you require in order to change your answer to Q5?

7   On 20 December 1991, you demanded repayment of £30,000 from your customer Frank Aqualugo. If your customer failed to repay and disappeared, when would this debt become statute barred?

8   Which statute led to your answer in Q7?

(Answers are given in Appendix 2, p. 283)

Multiple-choice questions

1   The bank wishes to close an unsatisfactory account which is in credit.

(a)   The bank can close the account immediately.

(b)   The bank must give its customer 'reasonable notice' before closing the account.

2   Which case supports your answer to Q1?

(a)   *Tai Hing Cotton Mill.*
(b)   *Woods* v *Martins Bank Ltd.*
(c)   *Prosperity Ltd* v *Lloyds Bank Ltd.*
(d)   *United Dominions Trust* v *Kirkwood.*

3   *Tournier* v *National Provincial and Union Bank of England Ltd* identified several occasions when a bank's duty of secrecy can be ignored. Which of the following did it identify?

(a)   By express consent of the customer.
(b)   By implied consent of the customer.
(c)   Where the interests of the bank require it.
(d)   Where there is a duty in the public interest.
(e)   Under compulsion of law.

4   Tick the correct statements about the Banking Ombudsman scheme which are given below:

(a)   The Ombudsman will not investigate a dispute where court action has already been taken.
(b)   The Ombudsman scheme can be used by all limited company customers.
(c)   The Ombudsman scheme can be used by non-corporate customers.
(d)   Disputes involving amounts in excess of £100,000 cannot be dealt with by the Banking Ombudsman.

(Answers are given in Appendix 2, p. 283)

Revision Questions

1   Dai Monde maintains high credit balances on his current and deposit accounts held at your branch. He also regularly places six-figure deposits with the Money Markets through your branch. He is a well-known, respected member of the local community and is a personal friend of yours.

You receive a telephone call from E. Ring Jewellers, an internationally known firm of diamond merchants who are based in Hatton Garden. They advise you that they have your customer, Dai Monde, on their premises and he wishes to buy merchandise from them amounting to £2,500. They tell you that Mr Monde wishes to pay by means of a personal cheque.

As the diamond merchants have never dealt with your customer before, they ask for your confirmation that the cheque will be paid upon presentation.

The balance of your customer's current account at present is £33,000 Cr.

What action would you take?

2   Mark Jukes opened an account with you nine months ago. The account has proved to be extremely troublesome over the last six months. You have had to dishonour several cheques due to lack of funds, despite repeated unheeded requests that Jukes should not issue cheques without sufficient cleared funds being available in his account. He has also issued a number of cheques and has then instructed the bank not to pay them.

You have, therefore, given Jukes 30 days' notice of closure of his account in writing. His account balance at that time was £37 Cr. Jukes has responded by writing to say that he intends to continue using his account even after the notice has expired. He adds that as he has not given instructions to the bank to close his account the bank has no right to close his account unilaterally.

What action can you take, if any, when the period of notice expires if Jukes continues to use his account?

(Answers are given in Appendix 2, pp. 283–84)

UNIT 2

Consumer Credit Act 1974

Objectives

- Recognise the circumstances under which the Consumer Credit Act 1974 (CCA) applies.
- Identify those entities which require a consumer credit licence.
- Appreciate the effect that connected lender liability can have on a bank.
- Recognise the circumstances under which canvassing is allowed.
- Detail information contained within regulated agreement documentation.
- Specify the different types of regulated agreement and the procedures involved with each.
- Detail documentation and procedures involved when direct security is given in connection with a regulated agreement.
- Appreciate the significance of details encapsulated in third party security documentation which has been given in connection with a regulated agreement.
- Identify the rights of borrowers and sureties under CCA.
- Specify the procedure regarding appropriation of payments in relation to regulated agreements.
- Detail the procedures to be followed concerning repayment of or recovery of a debt under CCA.
- Recognise the effect of CCA with regard to minors.

Introduction

The Consumer Credit Act 1974 became law as a result of the Crowther Report (Report of the Committee on Consumer Credit 1971), which felt that consumers needed statutory protection when entering credit agreements. It therefore seeks to protect non-corporate entities who receive up to £15,000 on credit.

2.1 Consumer Credit Licence

Credit reference agencies, lenders of money, debt counsellors, debt collectors, debt adjusters, credit brokers and providers of consumer hire must hold a consumer credit licence.

If a bank opens an account for any of the above it should see the appropriate licence. It should also see this again if it is asked to lend money, because if the trader is unlicensed any monies lent may be irrecoverable.

If a credit broker introduces a borrower to a bank, the bank must ensure that the broker is licensed, otherwise such lending to the introduced borrower will be irrecoverable unless the Director General of Fair Trading has given a special order. (The Director General has the power to revoke or suspend a licence.)

2.2 Connected Lender Liability

Connected lender liability can happen where an advance is made by way of overdraft, loan or credit card. This liability arises where a supplier of goods introduces its customer to the bank and the bank finances the underlying commercial contract. If, later, the customer has a claim against the supplier for breach of contract or misrepresentation, the customer will also have a right of action against the bank, which will be jointly and severally liable with the supplier. Obviously, the bank is entitled to be indemnified against loss by the supplier. Connected lender liability does not apply to items costing above £30,000, or £100 or less.

2.3 Canvassing

Canvassing is an oral attempt by a lender to persuade a potential borrower to enter into an agreement to borrow money from that lender. Under s.49(i) it is an offence to canvass away from 'trade premises' without a prior invitation.

Trade premises can be the bank's premises or the customer's business premises. With regard to private customers, a bank can only canvass away from its own premises if it has received a prior written invitation.

Sometimes, a banker may be embroiled in a discussion with a customer away from the bank's premises – e.g. the local golf club – which turns to financial matters. This is allowed, provided that the customer begins the discussion and the banker had not gone there with the intention of canvassing.

Telephone or written communication is allowed. Canvassing of overdrafts for existing customers is also allowed under s.49(3).

2.4 Banker's Opinions

Banks are not subject to the provisions of s.145(8) Consumer Credit Act 1974 when providing status enquiries. This means that a customer has no right to sight of or alteration to any opinion given by his bank. Bank correspondence relating to banker's opinions therefore state that the bank is neither a credit reference agency nor subject to the provisions of this section of the Act.

2.5 Regulated Agreement

A regulated agreement is one where credit up to and including £15,000 to a non-corporate borrower is granted.

Under s.74(1)(b) overdrafts are liable to the provision of simplified documentation to customers under CCA. Overdrafts which have not been agreed between a bank and its customer, and which do not revert to credit within 90 days, are also subject to this provision.

Regulated agreements will all mention the following four items:

(a) The amount of credit available.

(b) When repayments are due.

(c) The amount of each repayment.

(d) The rate of interest chargeable.

In addition to these, the following will normally be included:

(a) A heading to the agreement, e.g. 'Credit Agreement regulated by the Consumer Credit Act 1974'.

(b) The borrower's and lender's names and addresses.

(c) The annual percentage rate (APR).

(d) A description of the item or service which is the subject of the finance.

(e) The total charge for credit (TCC) with regard to fixed interest agreements only.

(f) The total amount repayable, capital interest and any other charges, applicable to fixed interest agreements only.

(g) Mention of any variable rates of interest or other charges which are used in calculating APR.

(h) Any security arrangements and requirements.

(i) Certain prescribed statutory notices which advise the borrower of his rights under the Act.

(j) In the event of default, any charges which will be applied.

2.6   Types of Regulated Agreements

There are a number of agreements referred to in the Act; bank branches will normally deal with four types.

(a) *A Non-Cancellable Agreement*
This will have been completed by all borrowers and the bank on the bank's premises. The borrowers will each receive a copy of the agreement and finance will be available immediately. Where an agreement is made secured by land it will be considered a non-cancellable agreement no matter where it was signed.

(b) *A Non-Cancellable Bridging Loan, or Loan for Purchase of Land*
In the case of bridging loans or loans for the purchase of land which are to be mortgaged to the bank as security, the agreement can be signed on or off bank premises and a signed copy must be given or sent to all borrowers. These agreements are non-cancellable.

(c) *Cancellable Agreements*
These normally arise where the agreement has not been signed by all the borrowers on the bank premises. This could happen where a bank has

received a written or telephone request from a customer for a loan and has sent the forms by post.

In such cases, the borrowers have the right to cancel under sections 67 and 69 of the Act. Also, under s.64, within seven days of the agreement being signed, the bank must advise the borrowers by post of his right to cancel. This advice will state that any cancellation must be in writing and be made within five days, commencing with the day following receipt of the advice. When this period has passed, the finance can be provided.

(d) *Land Agreements*

With regard to credit being provided, which is to be secured wholly or in part by a charge over land, specific rules apply.

Initially, the borrower will be given a period of not less than seven days in which to consider the agreement. No contact by the lender should be made during that time, unless the borrower requests advice.

The period will normally commence when the advance copy of the land agreement is sent to the potential borrower, marked 'Copy of Proposed Credit Agreement containing notice of your rights to withdraw. Do not sign or return this copy.'

At least seven days later, the regulated agreement form, which will have been signed by the bank, will be forwarded by post, to the borrower for signature, together with the borrower's copy, and completed copies of the security documents mentioned in it. A further consideration period of eight days then commences from the time that the documents were posted. If the borrower returns the documents, duly signed, before this period has expired, the consideration period has ended. In total, for land secured agreements, the consideration period extends to around 15 days. Once the process has been completed, the loan can be drawn down.

2.7 Modification of a Regulated Agreement

It is sometimes necessary to modify a regulated agreement – for example, when new security is required, or if a loan amount is increased. In such an event a modifying agreement or new agreement must be completed with the customer.

2.8 Direct Security for Regulated Agreements

Where direct security has been given by the borrower, it should be scheduled in the regulated agreement, a copy of which, together with a copy of the security form, should be given to the borrower. Most banks now ensure that their direct security forms refer to the security as being available for a liability under a regulated agreement.

2.9 Third-Party Security for Regulated Agreements

The Consumer Credit (Guarantees and Indemnities) Regulations 1983 required that any third-party security form covering a regulated agreement must include:

(a) a description of the regulated agreement secured;
(b) a statement of the rights of the third party;
(c) the names and addresses of all the security depositors.

It must also contain a box for the signature of the third party as indemnifier and, in addition, carry a warning that the third party should only sign if prepared to be legally bound.

Where security is to be taken from the third party in support of a guarantee liability, the guarantee must include details of this security.

Most banks have devised third-party guarantee and security forms to cover any regulated lending situation.

2.10 Negotiable Instruments

These are not allowed to be used as security for regulated agreement borrowing.

2.11 Rights of the Borrower and Surety

A borrower may request a statement of the amount due and repayments made on a fixed sum agreement. A fee is payable and the borrower can also receive additional copies of the regulated agreement and any security forms. The bank has 12 working days in which to comply with the request; if it should not do so, the agreement becomes unenforceable until the request has been met. If the bank has still not complied within a month, it is liable to penalties.

Concerning overdrafts on current accounts, regular bank statements should be sent giving details of all entries which have been passed through the account. The bank should also advise the borrower that details of interest calculations can be provided. Statements should be provided at not more than yearly intervals.

Each party to a joint account can receive a bank statement unless a party decides to waive that right.

Under s.107, upon payment of a fee, a third-party surety can obtain details of the total amount outstanding and the total amount paid by the debtor under the agreement, together with an analysis of these figures. In addition, the surety can obtain another copy of the executed agreement and any security document.

With regard to overdrafts, s.108 states that a third-party surety has to be given a signed statement detailing the state of the account, any amount currently due and amounts which will become due, together with the dates when they are payable, if no more drawings are made.

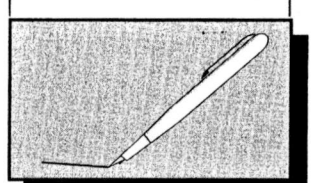

Student Activity 1

Obtain copies of your bank's regulated agreement forms relating to borrowing secured on land, other forms of security and guarantees. Compare details contained in these forms with the information included in this unit.

2.12 Appropriation of Payments with Regard to Regulated Agreements

A borrower can apply a payment to any regulated agreement where several exist.

Where the borrower does not do this, the bank can appropriate the amount.

If the borrower has both secured and unsecured agreements, the bank must place the sum first in reduction of the secured agreement liability.

Where several secured agreements exist, the bank must appropriate on a proportionate basis, unless instructed otherwise by the borrower.

2.13 Repayment before Due Date

Section 94 of the Act provides a borrower with the option of repaying a debt early if the borrower so wishes. The borrower will be advised of the total amount required and how it was calculated. Under s.95, for a structured loan, the borrower can receive a refund on the total interest charge which would have been made if the loan had run its full course.

2.14 Death of the Borrower

(a) The account must be 'stopped'.

(b) If the fixed amount outstanding is *fully secured*, early repayment cannot be demanded by the bank (where a date for repayment is provided in the agreement). The bank must wait for the date of repayment to arrive.

(c) If the fixed amount outstanding is *partially secured or unsecured*, the bank can only demand early repayment (where a date for repayment is provided in the agreement) after it has obtained a court order.

In cases (b) and (c) the executors/trustees may decide to repay the borrowing early in any case, in order to reduce interest charges.

(d) Where an overdraft exists on a current account, and providing that no agreement exists that the overdraft was available for a specific period, the bank can call in the debt immediately on the borrower's death.

2.15   Default of the Borrower

If a borrower commits a breach of a regulated agreement, the bank cannot immediately demand repayment or realise any security. It must first serve a pre-demand 'default notice' on the borrower and any depositor of collateral security.

This pre-demand default notice is issued in accordance with sections 87 and 88 and will provide the following information:

(a)   The nature of the breach of the agreement.

(b)   Whether this breach can be remedied; if so, how.

(c)   If the breach cannot be remedied, the date upon which demand will be made, and the amount involved. Where a breach is not corrected, the total lending will be called up after a specific period has elapsed, which must not be less than seven days.

2.16   Recovery of Debt due under a Regulated Agreement

Once the steps in 2.15 have been carried out, the bank can sue in the county court to recoup monies owing, or can obtain an order to enable it to realise any security held.

2.17   Minors

It is illegal to forward a circular to a minor inviting that person to borrow money, obtain services on credit or to apply for advice or information on borrowing or obtaining credit (s.50).

Conclusion

It can be seen from this unit that the Consumer Credit Act 1974 has had a major effect on documentation and procedures followed by banks when offering credit up to £15,000 to non-corporate entities.

Summary

Now that you have read this unit, you should be able to:

☐ Recognise the circumstances under which the Consumer Credit Act 1974 (CCA) applies.

☐ Identify those entities which require a consumer credit licence.

☐ Appreciate the effect that connected lender liability can have on a bank.

☐ Recognise the circumstances under which canvassing is allowed.

☐ Detail information contained within regulated agreement documentation.

☐ Specify the different types of regulated agreement and the procedures involved with each.

☐ Detail documentation and procedures involved when direct security is given in connection with a regulated agreement.

☐ Appreciate the significance of details encapsulated in third-party security documentation which has been given in connection with a regulated agreement.

☐ Identify the rights of borrowers and sureties under CCA.

☐ Specify the procedure regarding appropriation of payments in relation to regulated agreements.

☐ Detail the procedures to be followed concerning repayment of or recovery of a debt under CCA.

☐ Recognise the effect of CCA with regard to minors.

If you can tick all the above boxes with confidence, you are ready to answer the questions that follow.

Self-assessment Questions

Short-answer questions

1 What is the maximum amount covered by the Consumer Credit Act 1974?

2 Your personal customer, Manny Landers, calls at your branch today to open a business account entitled 'Manny Landers Debt Collecting Agency'. What specific document would you wish to see?

3 What is meant by 'canvassing', in connection with the CCA?

4   What section of the CCA states that it is an offence to canvass a debtor–creditor agreement away from trade premises without a prior invitation?

5   Mr and Mrs Smith call at your branch and sign an agreement to borrow £8,000 over three years on a personal loan. Is this a cancellable agreement?

6   What is the cancellation period on cancellable agreements?

7   A member of staff suggests that your branch should send personal credit literature to local schools for distribution to 16-year-old school leavers. What would be your response, and why?

(Answers are given in Appendix 2, pp. 284–85)

Multiple-choice questions

1   The Consumer Credit Act 1974 applies to:

(a)   Individuals.
(b)   Sole traders.
(c)   Partners.
(d)   Limited companies.

2   Connected lender liability does not apply to items costing:

(a)   Above £15,000 or below £100.
(b)   Above £20,000 or below £100.
(c)   Above £20,000 or £100 or less.
(d)   Above £30,000 or £100 or less.
(e)   Above £30,000 or below £100.

3   Regulated agreements will always mention:

(a)   The rate of interest chargeable.
(b)   When repayments are due.
(c)   The amount of each repayment.
(d)   The amount of credit available.

4   A regulated agreement which is secured by land is a:

(a)   cancellable agreement.
(b)   non-cancellable agreement.

5   Which of the following cannot be used as security for regulated agreement borrowing under the Consumer Credit Act?

(a)   A bill of exchange.
(b)   Midland Bank subordinated unsecured loan stock.
(c)   Rio Tinto Zinc bearer shares.
(d)   ICI ordinary shares.

(Answers are given in Appendix 2, p. 285)

Q

Revision questions

1   Joe King, a greengrocer, maintains a small business account with you. His account has proved troublesome during the last 12 months and you have had to return several cheques marked 'Refer to drawer'.

Joe King telephones you today to advise you that he has decided to change his suppliers and that the bank will be receiving a status enquiry from his new suppliers' bankers with regard to his being good for a contract of £2,000 per month. He says that he would like to see your reply before it is sent and adds that he believes that under the Consumer Credit Act 1974 he has a right to do this and have it altered if he so wishes.

What would be your response to your customer's request, and is he correct in his beliefs concerning the Consumer Credit Act 1974?

2   Peter Gill borrowed £2,000 from your branch on a personal loan which was to be repaid over three years by monthly transfers from his current account. Mr Gill is now unemployed and you have been unable to make the last two monthly transfers. The personal loan account balance is Dr £1,500 and the current account balance is Cr £1.25. You hold no security.

Your assistant suggests that you should make an immediate demand for repayment.

What would be your reaction to this suggestion, and what action would you take?

(Answers are given in Appendix 2, p. 285)

Past examination question

Mr and Mrs Boothman call at your branch and ask to borrow £12,000 to help to extend the dining room and kitchen of their matrimonial home, 14 Green Lane. The title to this property is registered land and the land certificate is held by West Country Building Society. The total cost of the work will be £15,000, and they agree to give you a second mortgage as security and to take the borrowing on a loan account, repayable over seven years.

Required

State how the Consumer Credit Act 1974 affects this loan and/or the security documentation and procedures.

[11 marks]
(Autumn 1989)

(Answers are given in Appendix 2, p. 286)

UNIT 3

Opening Bank Accounts and Operational Procedures

Objectives

- Appreciate the reasons why banks take references or similar precautions when opening bank accounts.
- Detail the procedures banks follow when opening bank accounts.
- Perceive the use of a power of attorney document, and its implications for the bank.
- Recognise the effect that death, bankruptcy or mental incapacity of the donee will have upon the power of attorney mandate.
- Identify when a power of attorney authority is determined.
- Appreciate the effects of, and operations relating to, the Enduring Powers of Attorney Act 1985.
- Recognise how the rule in *Clayton's* case affects bank accounts.
- Be able to detail what action a bank should take in the event of wrongful dishonour of a cheque or the crediting of an amount to a bank account in error.

Student Activity 1

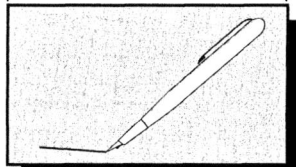

Find out whether your bank takes references when opening bank accounts. If not, what alternative precautions does your bank take?

Introduction

When banks open accounts for new customers, they follow certain procedures.

One of the major elements of such procedures for many years was the taking up of satisfactory references. The reasons for this, and also for the comparatively recent change in banking practice towards not taking up references, are given below.

3.1 References

When involved in legal proceedings, banks often have to prove that they have acted 'without negligence' in order to claim statutory protection.

In order to avoid this claim in the past, banks, when opening an account, have taken a reference for the would-be customer which has been followed up. If the referee has been unknown to the bank, a status enquiry has been made on the referee's bankers as to whether he or she was considered to be a fit person to introduce a new account holder.

Cases from which these practices originated were *Ladbroke* v *Todd* (1914) and *Hampstead Guardians* v *Barclays Bank Ltd* (1923).

In *Ladbroke* v *Todd* a bank was found guilty of conversion, having collected cheques for a new unknown customer without taking up a reference.

In *Hampstead Guardians* v *Barclays Bank Ltd* 'excellent' references were received from a stranger (whom it transpired was the customer himself). The bank was held to have been negligent by not having made adequate enquiries.

Nowadays, more and more banks are dispensing with references when opening accounts. Instead, having seen proof of identity, they tend to carry out searches on the voters roll and at credit bureaux. The reason for this seems to be that these banks are relying on the decision in *Marfani & Co Ltd* v *Midland Bank Ltd* (1968), where it was said that what enquiries should be made by a banker should depend upon current banking practice, and should change as that practice changes.

3.2 Other Steps Banks Take when Opening Bank Accounts

(a) Obtain the full name and address of the account holder. Also have a specimen signature card completed.

(b) In the case of accounts which are in other than a sole name, have a suitable mandate completed. This will give details such as how many signatures are required to activate instructions given to the bank. It will also establish the joint and several liability of account holders for any liability to the bank. This means that in the event of the bank seeking repayment of a debt it can take action against each account holder individually or against them jointly.

(c) Request the occupation of the account holder(s). In the case of *E B Savory & Co* v *Lloyds Bank Ltd* (1933) a dishonest clerk paid in stolen cheques to his wife's account. As the bank had not enquired as to her husband's occupation when his wife's account was opened, it was held to have been at fault. As a result of this, some banks ask for the occupation of all account holders.

However, some banks do not ask for any occupation details. This is because of the ruling in the case of *Orbit Mining and Trading Co Ltd* v *Westminster Bank Ltd* (1963), in which it was stated that a bank should not be expected to keep up to date regarding a customer's change of employment. These banks obviously feel that the risk to them in not obtaining such information is negligible.

(d) Issue a paying-in book, statement cover, cheque-book cover and, where applicable, a passbook.

(e) Note down the frequency for the dispatch of statements as required by the customer.

(f) Arrange for the issue of a cash dispenser card and credit card, if required.

(g) Cheque cards are not usually issued when an account is opened. The account normally has to operate satisfactorily for several months before a customer would be issued with one.

(h) In respect of interest-bearing accounts, the current rate of interest should be advised to the customer. In relation to current accounts, mention should be made concerning the bank's tariff for commission and interest charged.

(i) Order cheque-books, where applicable, but do not send them out to the customer until satisfactory references have been received and there is a cleared credit balance on the account.

(j) In the past, if a new customer, while opening an account, instructed the bank not to respond to any status enquiries, the bank would politely decline. This was because banking practice had always been to give replies to status enquiries and there was always the risk that such an instruction could be overlooked which could lead to a charge against the bank for breach of contract.

However, banks are currently reviewing their stance with regard to status enquiries. Lloyds Bank has already stated that it will no longer give bank references to third parties unless specifically requested to do so by customers and upon payment of a fee. Co-operative Bank has also stated that it will only provide bank references after obtaining its customer's consent. This is a controversial issue and other banks are considering their position.

Student Activity 2

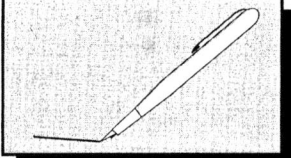

What is the policy of your bank with regard to replying to status enquiries? Does the Code of Banking Practice give any guidelines concerning this or any information to be given or procedures to be followed when a bank is dealing generally with a potential new customer? (See Appendix 1.)

3.3 Passbooks and Statements

It is part of the contract between banker and customer for statements of account to be forwarded at regular intervals to a customer, or for a passbook to be issued. Passbooks have largely been phased out by the banks, although Abbey National plc still widely issues passbooks despite its advent to bank status. This is largely due to its roots in the building society sector, where passbooks are still prevalent.

A customer is under no obligation to examine the entries made in a passbook – *Chatterton* v *London and County Bank* (1891). A similar ruling as regards statements has been confirmed in the cases of *Wealden Woodlands (Kent) Ltd* v *National Westminster Bank Ltd* (1983) and *Tai Hing Cotton Mill Ltd* v *Liu Chong Hing Bank Ltd* (1986).

It must be remembered that banks must comply with the Consumer Credit Act 1974 regarding the issue of statements when involved with regulated agreements for non-corporate customers. This means that statements should be provided on overdrawn current accounts at not more than 12 monthly intervals. With regard to joint accounts, all parties should be supplied with individual statements, unless they give written authority to waive that right.

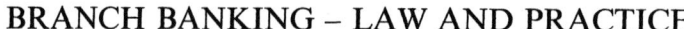

Student Activity 3

Obtain a copy of the mandate form which your bank uses when a third party is allowed to operate an account. Examine the clauses contained therein and consider their significance.

3.4 Powers of Attorney

A customer will sometimes require another person to operate their account, e.g. a customer may be working abroad for a short time and require someone to look after her affairs while she is away.

Thus, a power of attorney will be encapsulated in a written authority to the bank from the customer (donor) allowing another party (donee) to operate the customer's account without becoming a party to it.

This authority will normally be the bank's standard third-party mandate form. This is so that the bank will be protected should there be any abnormalities in the power of attorney, or if the customer disputes any transactions carried out by the attorney on the account.

3.4.1 What are the powers of the donee?

Under the Powers of Attorney Act 1971 the donee has all the powers that the donor has. However, generally, the donee cannot delegate his or her powers unless there is express provision for this.

3.4.2 What effect would the death, bankruptcy or mental incapacity of the donee have upon the power of attorney mandate?

When a bank has notice of the death or bankruptcy of the donee, and cheques are presented bearing the donee's signature, they may be paid. In the case of mental incapacity of a donee it would be wise for the bank to try and contact the donor concerning payment. If, however, contact could not be made with the donor, the cheque should be returned marked 'Agent's authority terminated.'

3.4.3 When will a power of attorney authority be determined?

A power of attorney authority can be determined by:

(a) The express revocation of the donor. This even applies when the power of attorney is said to be 'irrevocable'.

(b) The expiry of the period for which it was given.

24

(c)   The death or bankruptcy of the donor.

(d)   The mental incapacity of the donor. (However, note the effect of the Enduring Powers of Attorney Act 1985. See section 3.4.4.)

3.4.4   Enduring Powers of Attorney Act 1985

Under this Act an attorney (donee) can be appointed with the intention and power to carry on acting in the event of the donor's mental failure.

The donor must have been in full possession of his mental faculties at the time of the appointment. An enduring power of attorney can be fully operable prior to the mental incapacity of the donor taking place, provided that there is no restriction in the document. However, when the donor becomes mentally incapable of managing his affairs, or the attorney suspects this, the latter must register the power with the Court of Protection after giving notice of his intention to the donor and certain relatives specified in the Act.

During the interim period between the application to register the power and the order being made by the Court, the attorney has powers limited to maintaining the donor and people who the donor may be expected to provide for, e.g. the donor's family, and preventing loss to the donor's estate.

Thus a bank can allow the attorney to operate the donor's account pending registration of the power, provided that any disbursements meet the aforementioned criteria. Thus careful monitoring of the account will be required. If any cheques are presented which fall outside these criteria, they should be returned marked 'insufficient mandate'.

Once the power of attorney has been registered, it must be exhibited to the bank and the attorney can then use his or her powers to operate the donor's account.

3.5   The Effect of *Clayton's* case (1816) upon the Workings of a Bank Account

A customer who has two accounts which are overdrawn can stipulate which account is to be credited with any funds paid in. If the customer does not state which account is to be credited, the bank can allocate the funds to whichever account it wishes.

The rule established in *Clayton's* case (*Devaynes* v *Noble* (1816)) states that where a customer does not allocate a specific amount paid in to meet a particular payment to be paid out of the account, then the first sum paid in extinguishes the first sum paid out.

There are several problems for banks arising from the rule in *Clayton's* case.

3.5.1   Bank security forms

On accounts where there is a great deal of activity, application of the rule in *Clayton's* case would mean that old borrowing would be continually repaid and new borrowing created. Thus any security would only be available for lending which existed at the time the security was taken. Once sufficient credits had been received to repay the original borrowing, any new lending would be on an unsecured basis. Banks counteract this by including a 'continuing security' clause in their security forms. This means that the security is to cover all past, present and future borrowing, which overcomes the problem.

3.5.2 Death, bankruptcy, mental incapacity of one party to a joint account which is overdrawn

The normal banking practice is to stop the account. Failure to do this would mean that the liability of the deceased, bankrupt or mentally incapacitated party would be reduced by credits paid in and eventually extinguished.

3.5.3 Receipt of notice of subsequent mortgage

In *Deeley* v *Lloyds Bank Ltd* (1912), it was established that a bank must stop an overdrawn account upon receipt of notice of a subsequent mortgage over its security. Otherwise its charge may rank after that of the subsequent mortgagee if sufficient turnover has gone through the account.

3.5.4 Payment of wages when a company is subsequently placed into liquidation

The payment of wages can represent a preferential claim in the liquidation of a company, subject to certain conditions (detailed later in the course). However, high turnover on an account can mean that wages cheques are repaid by subsequent credits, applying the rule in *Clayton's* case, thus reducing the bank's preferential claim. This can be overcome by operating a separate wages account.

3.5.5 Is there any benefit from the rule in *Clayton's* case for banks?

The benefit of the rule in *Clayton's* case for banks can best be seen in relation to floating charges given over assets as security.

Under s.245 Insolvency Act 1986, a floating charge will be void if the company giving it goes into liquidation within 12 months of the giving of the security, unless it can be shown that it was solvent at the time. The floating charge will be good where it is given in consideration of new borrowing. Thus all debts created by cheques paid after the date of the charge will be secured and the remaining unsecured balance will gradually be repaid by credits paid in.

3.6 What Action can or will a Bank Take in Respect of Entries which have been Passed through an Account in Error?

3.6.1 Sums credited to an account in error

A bank cannot recover money credited to an account in error where the customer can show that by relying upon the accuracy of the entry and in good faith, he has altered his position. This was confirmed in the case of *Lloyds Bank Ltd* v *Brooks* (1950).

In *United Overseas Bank* v *Jiwani* (1976) it was held that a customer must prove all of the following criteria in order to be able to claim an amount credited in error:

(a) that the bank has misrepresented the state of the account;

(b) that the customer had been misled by this misrepresentation;

(c) that as a result, the customer had altered his or her position in such a way as to make it inequitable to have to repay the money.

3.6.2 Action to be taken if a cheque has been dishonoured due to a credit not being credited to the correct account

(a) Apologise to the customer.

(b) Contact the collecting banker and payee and explain the position by telephone, confirming it in writing.

(c) The bank should clearly admit fault and emphasise that the dishonour does not in any way reflect upon the creditworthiness of its customer.

(d) Refund any charges.

By doing this, in the event of the bank being sued by its customer for damages, any award made is likely to be reduced due to the action taken.

Summary

Now that you have read this unit, you should be able to:

☐ Appreciate the reasons why banks take references or similar precautions when opening bank accounts.

☐ Detail the procedures banks follow when opening bank accounts.

☐ Perceive the use of a power of attorney document, and its implications for the bank.

☐ Recognise the effect that death, bankruptcy or mental incapacity of the donee will have upon the power of attorney mandate.

☐ Identify when a power of attorney authority is determined.

☐ Appreciate the effects of, and operations relating to the Enduring Powers of Attorney Act 1985.

☐ Recognise how the rule in *Clayton's* case affects bank accounts.

☐ Detail what action a bank should take in the event of wrongful dishonour of a cheque or the crediting of an amount to a bank account in error.

If you can tick all the above boxes with confidence, you are ready to answer the questions that follow on pp. 28–30.

List of Cases

Chatterton v *London and County Bank* (1891)

Deeley v *Lloyds Bank Ltd* (1912)

Devaynes v *Noble* (1816)

Hampstead Guardians v *Barclays Bank Ltd* (1923)

Ladbroke v *Todd* (1914)

Lloyds Bank Ltd v *Brooks* (1950)

Marfani & Co Ltd v *Midland Bank Ltd* (1968)

Orbit Mining & Trading Co Ltd v *Westminster Bank Ltd* (1963)

E B Savory & Co v *Lloyds Bank Ltd* (1933)

Tai Hing Cotton Mill Ltd v *Liu Chong Hing Bank Ltd* (1986)

United Overseas Bank v *Jiwani* (1976)

Wealden Woodlands (Kent) Ltd v *National Westminster Bank Ltd* (1983)

List of Statutes

Consumer Credit Act 1974

Enduring Powers of Attorney Act 1985

Insolvency Act 1986

Powers of Attorney Act 1971

Self-assessment Questions

Short-answer questions

1   A power of attorney has been set up on an account and the donee dies. A cheque for £500 signed by the donee in that capacity is presented for payment the day after the bank has received notice of his death. The cheque is technically in order, no instructions have been received countermanding payment and there are sufficient funds on the account to meet the cheque. Can it be paid?

2   In what circumstances can a power of attorney authority be determined?

3   If a customer becomes mentally incapable and has previously set up an enduring power of attorney authority, when can the attorney act upon the account?

4   What does the rule in *Clayton's* case establish?

5   Which clause in a bank security form counteracts the effects of the rule in *Clayton's* case?

6   Can you state an occasion when the rule in *Clayton's* case can be of benefit to the bank?

(Answers are given in Appendix 2, pp. 286–87)

Multiple-choice questions

1   Many banks no longer take references when opening bank accounts. Instead, they carry out credit reference searches and take proof of identity. Which case decision are these banks relying upon?

(a)   *Ladbroke* v *Todd* (1914).
(b)   *Hampstead Guardians* v *Barclays Bank Ltd* (1923).
(c)   *Marfani & Co Ltd* v *Midland Bank Ltd* (1968).

2   Which case established that a bank need not keep up to date with a customer's changes of employment?

(a)   *Orbit Mining and Trading Co Ltd* v *Westminster Bank Ltd* (1963).
(b)   *E B Savory & Co* v *Lloyds Bank Ltd* (1933).
(c)   *Joachimson* v *Swiss Bank Corporation* (1921).

3   Which cases have confirmed that a customer need not examine his or her bank statement?

(a)   *Chatterton* v *London & County Bank* (1891).
(b)   *Wealden Woodlands (Kent) Ltd* v *National Westminster Bank Ltd* (1983).
(c)   *Tai Hing Cotton Mill Ltd* v *Liu Chong Hing Bank Ltd* (1986).

(Answers are given in Appendix 2, p. 287)

Past examination questions

1   Lady Good, whose current account always carries substantial credit balances, authorises you to accept direct debits for £250 per quarter from Mayfair Stores with effect from July 1981. Last November she wrote to you cancelling the authority but, when she received her quarterly statement in March 1984, she noticed that the January payment had been made and she wrote pointing this out to you.

Comment on the bank's position and state what steps may be available to rectify matters.

Give reasons for your answer.

[6 marks]
(April 1984)

2   Albert Black, an engineer, executed a power of attorney in favour of Tony White last March, when he went to Hong Kong on business. The power of attorney was expressed to be irrevocable for a period of 12 months. Black has

both a current and deposit account with you, and you hold a portfolio of shares and a locked tin box in safe custody on his behalf. The bank omitted to take the usual form of third-party mandate, but Mr White was given a specially prepared cheque book.

Recently there have been three developments, as follows. State with reasons, how you would have dealt with each of these successive developments.

(a) In July, Mr White asked you to supply a list of all items held in safe custody on Mr Black's behalf.

[6 marks]

(b) In August, in error you credited a remittance for Albert Black from Hong Kong to the account of Anthony Black, and subsequently dishonoured a cheque for £320 drawn by Tony White, as attorney for Albert Black, with the answer 'refer to drawer – please re-present'. This cheque was paid on its second presentation when the error came to light.

Mr White is now claiming compensation for damage to his credit.

[5 marks]

(c) Mr Black returned unexpectedly to the United Kingdom last week and wishes to operate his account again on his own.

[5 marks]
[Total – 16 marks]
(September 1982)

(Answers are given in Appendix 2, pp. 287–88)

UNIT 4

Types of Bank Accounts

Objectives

- Comprehend the effects of death and mental incapacity on sole and joint accounts.
- Recognise the effects that the death, mental incapacity or bankruptcy of a partner will have upon the partnership account.
- Identify the procedures to be followed upon the retirement of a partner or admission of a new partner.
- Appreciate the steps which must be taken upon the insolvency of a partnership.
- Recognise the method by which security for partnership borrowing is executed, and its effects.
- Identify the facets of a limited partnership.
- Recognise the special circumstances pertaining to the following accounts and account holders:

    minors
    solicitors
    estate agents
    insurance brokers
    liquidators
    executors and administrators
    trustees
    unincorporated associations, societies and clubs.

4.1 Sole Accounts

The procedure to be followed when opening a sole account was given in Unit 3.

4.2 Death of a Sole Account Holder

(a) Upon receipt of notice of death, the bank should stop the account and not allow any further payments from the account (s.75 Bills of Exchange Act 1882).

(b) Any credit balance on the account or items held in safe custody can only be released to the estate's executors or administrators after the production of probate or letters of administration. One exception to this is where the will is held in safe custody, as this obviously will be needed by the executors to obtain probate. The will can thus be released to executors if they are known to the bank, or if a satisfactory report is obtained from the solicitor acting for the executors.

(c) In the interim period between the bank receiving notice and the granting of probate and letters of administration, any credits received can either be placed in a suspense account or in the account itself. Credits which obviously cease upon the death of a customer, e.g. annuity, should be placed in a side account and the remitters advised. The executors or administrators of the deceased's estate should also be informed.

(d) Any matters which were in course prior to the customer's death, e.g. purchase of stocks and shares, can be completed.

(e) If the deceased's account was overdrawn at the time that the bank received notice of his death, the bank should claim in the deceased's estate for the full amount owing, plus accrued interest. It should also give details of any direct security held.

(f) Where the value of estates is small, i.e. less than £5,000 gross, the credit balance can be released to a near relative provided that:

(i) the relative has been identified;
(ii) the bank has had a satisfactory 'report' on the relative;
(iii) the bank has seen the death certificate (Administration of Estates (small payments) Amendment Act 1976 and the Increase of Limit Order 1984).

In such cases, sight of probate or letters of administration is not needed, although a bank will normally take an indemnity.

4.3 Joint Accounts

Joint accounts will comprise two or more account holders, e.g. husband and wife. As mentioned in Unit 3, the mandate taken will include a joint and several liability clause. It will also mention how many signatures will be required to activate instructions on the account, i.e. all to sign, either to sign, etc.

4.4 Death of a Joint Account Holder

The mandate held for joint accounts will give the bank a satisfactory discharge from the survivor on the death of a joint account holder.

(a) If a joint account is in credit, it can continue. This means that in the case of an account for a husband and wife, the surviving spouse will be able to continue to use the balance of the account without having to wait for probate to be obtained.

(b) If cheques are presented drawn on a joint account, signed by the deceased, they should be returned marked 'Drawer deceased', unless the surviving account holder is willing to authorise payment.

(c) If a joint account is overdrawn when notice of death of a party to a joint account is received, then that account should be stopped if the bank wishes to retain its claim against the deceased's estate. Otherwise the rule in *Clayton's* case (*Devaynes* v *Noble* (1816)) would mean that fresh credits would repay the earliest debits, thus reducing the bank's claim. This would mean that the bank would then only have a right to reclaim any drawings following receipt of notice of death from the survivor.

(d) If an overdrawn joint account is stopped to preserve the bank's claim, arrangements should be made with the survivor for a new account to be opened in the survivor's name.

(e) Where items are held in safe custody in joint names, banks will require a receipt from the survivor and also the executor or administrator of the deceased. This is because these items may not be jointly owned e.g. jewellery.

4.5 Mental Incapacity of a Sole or Joint Account Holder

If it is apparent that a sole or joint account customer is incapable, then the bank mandate should be cancelled and no further cheques paid until a receiver has been appointed by the Court of Protection and has presented his or her authority document to the bank. At this stage the receiver will take over the customer's assets. In the case of joint accounts the receiver will act in conjunction with the sane joint account holder. In exceptional circumstances, where a joint account is overdrawn and one party becomes mentally incapable, a bank may decide to release the mentally incapacitated customer's estate from liability and allow the account to be operated by the sane party, who would be liable for all future borrowing.

The receiver will probably open an account at the same branch as that of the mentally incapacitated customer. If the receiver is unknown to the bank, references should be taken before the account is opened.

A receiver has no power to borrow unless authorised to do so by the Court of Protection.

The receiver's authority ceases upon the death of the mentally incapacitated customer. The latter's affairs are then dealt with by the executors or administrators. The bank would normally obtain written authority from the receiver allowing the transfer of the balance of the receiver's account to the new executors' or administrators' account.

4.5.1 Operation of a mentally incapacitated customer's account without the appointment of a receiver

A bank is sometimes prepared to allow a close relative to operate a customer's account where the moneys are only to be used for 'necessaries' for the customer, such as food, lodgings and medication. This will normally only be agreed to where the relative is considered to be trustworthy and is prepared to provide the bank with a suitable indemnity.

In the case of *Davies, Banks and Co* v *Beavan* (1913) the bank agreed to allow the customer's son to operate his father's account when the latter became mentally incapable. Monies from the account were used to maintain the household. Upon the father's death his account was overdrawn and two of the four executors appointed under his will objected to the arrangement which had gone on before and refused to repay the bank.

The court held that as the payments out of the account were for 'necessaries', then by the doctrine of subrogation the bank should be reimbursed. However, the court dismissed the bank's claim for the repayment of the interest and commission due on the overdraft as these were not deemed to be 'necessities'.

In the case of *Scarth* v *National Provincial Bank Ltd* (1930) a customer became mentally incapacitated and the balance of his account was transferred into his wife's name after the bank had received a suitably completed indemnity from the wife and another member of the customer's family. These monies were used to meet Mr Scarth's debts. Mr Scarth subsequently recovered from his mental illness and sued the bank for recovery of the balance of his account. The court found for the bank, again stating that the bank could rely upon the doctrine of subrogation.

4.6 Partnership Accounts

4.6.1 Definition of a partnership

Under s.1 Partnership Act 1890, a partnership is stated to be 'the relationship which subsists between persons carrying on a business in common with a view to profit.'

A partnership is only allowed to have up to twenty partners for a normal business or, in the case of banking, up to ten. Some professions, e.g. accountants or solicitors, can have any number of partners.

A partnership can be formed orally, by conduct, or in writing. When a bank opens a partnership account it will normally require sight of a business letterhead which will show the trading name and the names of the partners. The bank mandate completed by the partners will include a clause whereby each partner accepts joint and several liability.

The bank will not wish to see any partnership deed, otherwise it will be bound by its clauses.

4.6.2 Borrowing

A general partner of a firm can normally bind the partnership in all matters relating to the partnership business. As regards to borrowing, a general partner in a trading partnership will normally have an implied power to borrow. However, this is not the case for a non-trading firm and a document signed by all the partners is desirable, expressing the amount required.

4.6.3 Partnership fraud

An important case relating to partnership fraud was *Baker* v *Barclays Bank Ltd* (1955), the details of which were as follows.

Jeffcott conducted a satisfactory account with Barclays Bank. He paid cheques payable to 'Modern Confections', into his account which had been endorsed in favour of Jeffcott by a person called Bainbridge. Jeffcott told the bank that this person was the sole proprietor and owed him money. He added that he was helping this business on the accounting side.

It later transpired that Modern Confections was, in fact, a partnership and that Bainbridge was defrauding his co-partner Baker.

Baker sued Barclays Bank for conversion. The bank set up its defence under s.82 Bills of Exchange Act 1882 (now encompassed in s.4 Cheques Act 1957), as it had collected the cheques in good faith and without negligence for a customer.

The court found against the bank, as it did not feel that enquiries had been made in sufficient depth by the collecting banker.

However, the important precedent set in this case was that as one of the partners had been guilty of fraud and partners shared profits equally, the defrauded partner was only entitled to half the value of the cheques collected.

If a partner transfers sums from the partnership account to his or her own account, the bank should not be put on enquiry unless it suspects fraud. However, a bank must not allow a partner to pay any cheques drawn payable to the partnership into a private account unless all partners expressly authorise it.

4.6.4 Death of a partner

A deceased partner's personal representatives are not liable for any debts incurred by the partnership after the partner's death.

If a partnership account is overdrawn upon the death of a partner and the bank wishes to preserve its rights against the deceased's estate, it should stop the account and lodge a claim in the estate. Failure to do this will mean that the rule in *Clayton's* case will apply and will result in the bank's claim being diminished or completely extinguished.

If the bank decides to stop the partnership account, any cheques presented for payment subsequently must be returned marked 'Partner Deceased'.

If the bank decides to allow the account to continue, cheques may be honoured, although it is often wise to obtain confirmation by the surviving partners that cheques signed by the deceased partner may be honoured.

If the partnership account is in credit the surviving partners can deal with the balance and may continue the business in order to wind it up.

It is often the case that the surviving partners will form a new partnership, in which case a new bank mandate must be completed.

4.6.5 Retirement of a partner

A partner who wishes to retire must give due notice of retirement in order to gain release from liability for partnership debts after he or she has retired.

When a partnership account is overdrawn at the time of retirement of a partner, the bank should stop the account to prevent the rule in *Clayton's* case operating against it if it wishes to preserve its rights against the retiring partner. The remaining partners should then open a new account.

A retiring partner can only be released from liability for partnership debts incurred prior to his or her retirement if the firms' creditors agree to accept the new partnership as the debtor in substitution.

4.6.6 Admission of a new partner to a firm

When a new partner joins a firm it is necessary to establish whether he or she will accept liabilities incurred by the partnership prior to the appointment, or not.

If he or she will not accept liability, the old partnership account may be stopped and a new account opened for the new partnership. Alternatively the bank may decide to allow the old partnership to continue, as the operation of the rule in *Clayton's* case will mean that any debt incurred by the old partnership will be repaid and any further borrowing will be monies drawn by the new firm, upon which the new partner will be liable.

4.6.7 Mental incapacity of a partner

The mental incapacity of a partner does not automatically dissolve a partnership, although another partner can apply to court for its dissolution.

If a bank wishes to preserve its rights against the estate of the mentally incapacitated partner when the partnership account is overdrawn it should stop the account, otherwise the rule in *Clayton's* case will operate.

4.6.8 Insolvency of a partnership

In accordance with the Insolvency Act 1986 and Insolvent Partnership Order 1986, when a winding-up order is made against the firm and a bankruptcy order against one or more of the partners, the firm's assets must be used initially to repay partnership debts and the private assets of each partner used to repay private debts. Any surplus remaining from the private assets will then be used to repay partnership debts.

A statement of affairs for both the firm and the individual partners must be drawn up.

A petitioning creditor can decide whether or not to petition for the bankruptcy of individual partners when seeking a winding-up order against a firm. If the petitioner only seeks the latter, the liquidator can still call upon the partners to contribute to any shortfall, should the partnership assets fail to meet the firm's liabilities completely.

When a bank learns of a winding-up order against a firm, all operations in the partnership account must be stopped. The partners' private accounts can continue, but where there is personal borrowing the bank may wish to call it in. Also if a partner's account is in credit, the bank may wish to appropriate the balance against its claim under the several liability clause in the bank's mandate for the partnership account.

Where a bank learns that a winding-up order has been made against the partnership and a bankruptcy order against one or more partners, all accounts must be stopped, whether in credit or overdrawn.

4.6.9 Bankruptcy of a partner

If a bankruptcy order is made against a partner and there is no winding-up order against the firm, then the partnership will be terminated unless the partnership articles allow otherwise. The remaining partners will have to account to the trustee in bankruptcy for the bankrupt partner's interest.

If the articles allow the partnership to continue, then the bankrupt partner will resign. If the firm's account is in credit then it may continue to operate, although any cheque drawn by the partner who is the subject of bankruptcy proceedings should not be paid without the authorisation of the other partners.

4.6.10 Security for a partnership

When giving a charge over partnership property, all partners should execute the bank's charge forms. A clause in the form will state that the security remains good despite any change in the constitution of the firm, such as the appointment of a new partner.

Where only one partner executes a legal mortgage over partnership property without authority, this may constitute an equitable charge, but difficulties are likely to arise with realisation, particularly if there is a partnership dispute.

4.6.11 Limited partnerships

These are governed by the Limited Partnerships Act 1907 and are fairly uncommon nowadays.

In such a partnership at least one of the partners must be a general partner and be liable for all the debts and liabilities of the firm. The remaining partners may have their liability limited to the extent of the capital which they have contributed.

Limited partners normally take no active part in the management of the firm, nor do they have the power to draw cheques.

The Limited Partnerships Act does not require the firm's name to show that it is a limited partnership. Therefore, if the information was not forthcoming a bank would have to enquire from the registrar of companies, where the limited partnerships will be registered.

The importance to the bank is that it may be relying on the standing of a partner who, it transpires, is a limited partner for a small amount.

4.7 Other Types of Account Holders

4.7.1 Minors

Contracts entered into by minors are subject to the Minors' Contracts Act 1987. Minors are not liable for contracts which they enter into unless they are for the purchase of necessaries. However, a minor can ratify an otherwise unenforceable contract on attaining the age of majority.

Under the Act, where a guarantee of a minor's debt is given by an adult, this guarantee is still valid, notwithstanding the minor's lack of capacity to contract.

Another important clause of the Act concerns the court's rights to order the return of property acquired by a minor under an unenforceable contract where it feels that it is just and equitable to do so. Thus contracts for loans and any underlying goods or property which represent the loans may be recoverable.

Other important points concerning minors are as follows:

(a) Provided an account holder has full contractual capacity, a minor can act as that person's agent on that account.

(b) A minor can be a director of a limited company, provided that its articles allow this.

(c) A minor cannot act as an executor or trustee.

(d) A minor cannot make a valid will unless he is on active service with the armed forces.

(e) A minor cannot give an enforceable guarantee, although, as stated earlier, he could ratify such a guarantee upon attaining the age of majority.

4.7.2 Solicitors' accounts

Under the Solicitors' Accounts Rules, solicitors must operate a clients' account in which to keep monies that they are handling for their clients. In addition to this, they will normally operate an office account for the daily accounting side of the practice. Withdrawals from a clients' account may only be authorised by a person who is either a solicitor with a current practising certificate, or who has been a fellow of the Institute of Legal Executives for three years. Licensed conveyancers can also authorise withdrawals from clients' accounts providing that they are dealing with conveyancing only. A clients' account should not become overdrawn, according to the Solicitors' Accounts Rules. Accordingly, banks should make strenuous enquiries were this to happen.

An important recent case concerning solicitors' accounts was *Lipkin Gorman* v *Karpnale* (1986). A partner in a firm of solicitors was known to be a compulsive gambler by the branch manager. Over a period of time the partner withdrew £323,000 from the clients' account to pay off gambling debts.

When the facts became known, the other partners in the firm of solicitors sued the bank for reimbursement, on the basis that the bank was a constructive trustee of the sums withdrawn. ('Constructive trustee' means the bank should have known that the funds were being used for fraudulent purposes.)

The court held that the bank was not liable, for the following reasons:

(a) Although the bank was aware of the gambling, it did not know about the purpose of the withdrawals.

(b) If the bank had divulged its knowledge of the gambling to other partners, it would have been a breach of its duty of secrecy towards the partner concerned.

(c) If the bank had refused to allow the withdrawals, it would have been in breach of its duty to honour the mandate if there are sufficient funds.

(d) Mere suspicion or unease is insufficient grounds to justify refusal to allow withdrawals which are in accordance with the mandate. The bank could be liable for wrongful dishonour if it refused to honour cheques on mere suspicion.

(e) The bank is not expected to be a private detective agency.

4.7.3 Estate agents' accounts

Similar to solicitors, estate agents must keep clients' monies in a separate clients' account.

4.7.4 Insurance brokers' accounts

Unless the broker is a member of Lloyd's, separate current or deposit accounts must be kept in which to keep monies relating to insurance transactions. These accounts are similar to solicitors' clients' accounts and will be styled 'insurance broking account'.

4.7.5 Liquidators' accounts

Only a licensed insolvency practitioner may act as a liquidator.

(a) *Compulsory winding up*
    The liquidator will be appointed by the court and is normally required to pay all monies into an insolvency services account at the Bank of England. However, if special permission is obtained from the Department of Trade and Industry, the liquidator may be able to open an account with a local bank. If this is the case, the bank will wish to see the court order appointing the liquidator, together with the authority from the Department of Trade prior to opening the account. The liquidator can usually borrow and charge company assets without court authority. However, where the liquidator wishes to carry on the business, authority from the court and the committee of inspection will be required for any borrowing and the provision of security.

(b) *Members' or creditors' voluntary winding up*

Unlike with a compulsory winding up, a liquidator does not have to maintain an account at the Bank of England and will operate an account with a local bank. The bank will wish to see a copy of the resolution appointing the liquidator. The liquidator may borrow and give security, although the authority of the liquidation committee will normally be obtained for this purpose.

'No, Mr McPhee, my memo said that we were to be the executors of Mr Jarvis!'

4.8 Executors and Administrators

An executor is appointed under a will. Executors are unable to deal with a deceased's estate until probate has been obtained, a prerequisite of which is the payment of any inheritance tax due.

An administrator is appointed when the deceased has not made a will or where an executor is unable or unwilling to act.

Where more than one executor/administrator is appointed, they will sign a bank mandate accepting joint and several liability for any borrowing. Executors/administrators are allowed to delegate and therefore the account can be operated on one or more signatures.

Where an executor/administrator dies, the remaining executor/administrator may continue to act. However, if the last surviving executor/administrator dies, his or her own executors can take over the executorship if they wish. If they do not, or if the executor has died intestate, interested parties can apply to the court for letters of administration.

There is no right of set-off between the credit balance in the name of an executor and a debit balance in the name of the deceased, or vice versa.

4.8.1 Borrowing by an executor/administrator

Unfortunately, the deceased's estate cannot be dealt with until probate or letters of administration are obtained, and these cannot be obtained until inheritance tax is paid. This will often necessitate the executor/administrator having to borrow on loan account for this purpose. The borrowing will normally be cleared from the sale of the deceased's assets in due course. In the interim period the executors/administrators will be personally liable for the debt. If the deceased owned a business but the will contained no express authority to continue that business, or if there was no will, then the personal representatives can only borrow for the purpose of winding it up or its sale in the short term.

If the personal representatives wish to borrow to carry on the business, the bank must first ensure that the creditors of the business have either already been paid off or have agreed that the bank's loan would take priority over their own rights for repayment.

The bank may require security for lending for this purpose. Assets owned by the personal representatives in their own right can be accepted without risk. However, the personal representatives do not have authority to charge the deceased's assets employed outside the business. Nevertheless, if the will allows, they can give a charge over assets used in the business.

4.8.2 Executors becoming trustees

After 12 months, an estate will normally have been wound up. If, however, an account is still open it would be pertinent to interview the personal representatives to see if they are now acting in the capacity of trustees. If this is the case, then a new mandate should be completed stipulating all trustees to sign, and the account should be restyled 'Trustees of . . . deceased'.

4.9 Trustees

A trustee is a person who deals with property for the benefit of persons, of whom he may himself be one.

The problem which bankers have to face is that they have to ensure that they do not become a party to any breach of trust as otherwise they could be liable for damages to the true beneficiaries.

In *Gray* v *Johnston* (1868), it was established that a bank would be guilty of a breach of trust if it were aware of the intent to misapply trust funds.

Therefore, if a bank receives funds from a trust account for the reduction of the personal borrowing of the trustee it could be guilty of a breach of trust.

4.9.1 Delegation

Usually, trustees are not allowed to delegate unless authorised to do so in the will or trust deed. However, the Trustee Act 1925 (as amended by the Powers of Attorney Act 1971) allows a trustee to delegate powers for up to 12 months under a power of attorney. Section 9 of the 1971 Act states that a trustee may delegate powers to any person or trust corporation except for a co-trustee, unless the latter is a trust corporation, e.g. a bank.

4.9.2 Borrowings

A trustee does not have an implied power to borrow. A bank would therefore examine the trust deed to see if specific borrowing powers existed. Where there is no power to borrow, sections 16 and 17 Trustee Act 1925 determine the ability of trustees to borrow on the security of the assets of the estate. Section 16 relates to borrowing for capital purposes and s.17 states that no purchaser or mortgagee, paying or advancing money on a sale or mortgage purporting to be made under any trust or power vested in trustees, need be concerned to see that the money is wanted or how it is used. This latter section is obviously of great benefit to the bank.

A trustee must not charge trust property to secure a borrowing on his or her own private account.

An important case relating to trustees is *Re Halletts Estate* (1880). This established that where a trustee's own money is mixed with trust money, it is presumed that the trustee's own money is drawn out first, in priority to the money held in trust. Thus the rule in *Clayton's* case does not apply.

4.9.3 Death

Upon the death of a trustee, the surviving trustees can continue to operate the account (s.18 Trustee Act 1925). They should, however, examine the trust deed to see if a replacement trustee should be appointed.

If the trustee account is overdrawn and the bank wishes to preserve the claim against the deceased's trustee's estate, it should stop the trust account.

Where all trustees have died and no replacements have been appointed, the personal representatives of the last trustee can take over until such time as a new trustee is appointed (s.18 Trustee Act 1925).

4.9.4 Bankruptcy

The bankruptcy of a trustee is not automatic grounds for resignation, and a bankrupt trustee can continue to act. However, an interested party can apply to the court for their removal and the appointment of a new trustee.

4.10 Unincorporated Associations, Societies and Clubs

Banks often open accounts for such bodies. These accounts can be opened in the name of the club or society, or can be styled in the name of the treasurer or secretary re the club, e.g. Phil Attlee re Sheffield Stamp Club. In this latter case, the individual is personally liable for any overdraft on the account. Banks must exercise care and must ensure that any cheques payable to an association or society are only accepted for the credit of the trust account. Transfers from the trust account to the trustee's private account should not be allowed without a satisfactory explanation, otherwise the bank could be guilty of conversion.

4.10.1 Mandate

Where the account is to be opened in the name of the club or society, a mandate should be taken, referring to the resolution passed by the club committee or members, and appointing the bank as the club's bankers. It will mention those officials who can operate the account, and who should, if possible, be termed in a general way, e.g. 'the treasurer and secretary for the time being', so that further resolutions will not be required by the bank every time club officials change. Specimen signatures will be supplied.

If a club account is to operate in credit, banks often do not require a copy of the club's rules. If a club is to borrow, the rules will be required. Occasionally, a club is incorporated and registered under the Companies Act. This type of club will be in the form of a limited company, often with the liability of shareholders limited by guarantee. The bank will obtain a copy of the memorandum and articles of association, a suitable minute governing the operation of the account and specimen signature of those authorised to sign. The word 'Limited' may be omitted, subject to the provisions of the Companies Acts, and the permission of the Department of Trade and Industry.

4.10.2 Borrowings

Unless a club or society is a limited company, it is not a separate legal entity and as such cannot be sued for the recovery of any debt which it may incur. In addition to this, the members of such a club or society will not be liable for any debts incurred upon the club's behalf by either the committee or the officers, unless they have personally agreed to be liable.

As regards the liability of officers, they can be liable for any borrowings sanctioned by the committee, acting within the club rules (if there are any). This was established in *Bradley Egg Farm Ltd* v *Clifford and Others* (1943).

Banks will normally lend, provided that they hold third-party security in the form of a guarantee including an indemnity clause whereby the signatories will assume primary liability.

Sometimes a club will have purchased property which is held in the names of trustees. If this property is offered as security, the bank should examine the club rules and the trust deed. It is important that all trustees should act and sign the form of charge and that the bank should ensure that there is no breach of trust. If in doubt, the bank should take legal advice.

4.10.3 Death of an officer

Where an authorised official dies, the death does not determine the bank's mandate to pay any cheque which the official might have signed, even though such a cheque may be presented for payment after the person's death. However, steps must be taken to appoint a new official and notice of appointment of this new official, together with a specimen signature, must be given to the bank forthwith.

Summary

Now that you have read this unit, you should be able to:

☐ Comprehend the effects of death and mental incapacity on sole and joint accounts.

☐ Recognise the effects that the death, mental incapacity or bankruptcy of a partner will have upon the partnership account.

☐ Identify the procedures to be followed upon the retirement of a partner or admission of a new partner.

☐ Appreciate the steps which must be taken upon the insolvency of a partnership.

☐ Recognise the method by which security for partnership borrowing is executed, and its effects.

☐ Identify the facets of a limited partnership.

☐ Recognise the special circumstances pertaining to the following accounts and account holders:
  minors
  solicitors
  estate agents
  insurance brokers
  liquidators
  executors and administrators
  trustees
  unincorporated associations, societies and clubs.

If you can tick all the above boxes with confidence, you are ready to answer the questions that follow on pp. 45–49.

List of Cases

Baker v *Barclays Bank Ltd* (1955)

Davies, Banks and Co. v *Beavan* (1913)

Bradley Egg Farm Ltd v *Clifford and Others* (1943)

Devaynes v *Noble* (1816)

Gray v *Johnston* (1868)

Re Halletts Estate (1880)

Lipkin Gorman v *Karpnale* (1986)

List of Statutes

Administration of Estates (Small Payments) Amendment Act 1976

Bills of Exchange Act 1882

Increase of Limit Order 1984

Insolvency Act 1986

Insolvent Partnership Order 1986

Limited Partnerships Act 1907

Minors' Contracts Act 1987

Partnership Act 1890

Powers of Attorney Act 1971

Trustee Act 1925

Self-assessment Questions

Short-answer questions

1   What action should a bank take when it receives notice of the death of a sole account holder?

2   George and Jane Parker hold a joint current account at your branch. There is a locked deed box lodged with you in safe custody in their joint names. Jane Parker calls to see you today with her son Norman and advises you that her husband has died. She brings with her the death certificate, a copy of her husband's will, together with a grant of probate naming Norman Parker as the executor of the deceased's estate. She wishes to withdraw the deed box from your branch.

Who will sign the receipt for the deed box?

3   Your customer, Jack Lill, has become mentally incapable and his nephew, Jimmy Booth, has been appointed as receiver by the Court of Protection.

Give two occasions when the receiver's authority could be revoked.

4   Define a partnership.

5   Carter, Collins and Cooper is a partnership of plumbers. On 7 October you are advised that Cooper has died. The balance of the account at that time is £5,700 Dr. The bank wishes to preserve its rights against the deceased's estate.

What actions should the bank take with regard to the partnership account?

6   Under the Minors' Contracts Act 1987, can a minor be liable on any contract which he enters into, and if so, what type of contract?

7   Lower Denby Travel Club has maintained a current account with you for several years. You have agreed to lend the club funds for the purchase of two minibuses against the security of a first mortgage over the club premises which are registered in the names of the club chairman and club secretary as trustees.

What preliminary steps should the bank take prior to taking security?

8   Lower Denby Travel Club cheques have to be signed by the club secretary and the club chairman. You learn today that the club chairman was killed in a motorway accident yesterday. There are several cheques drawn on Lower Denby Travel Club's account in today's clearing bearing the deceased chairman's signature in addition to the club secretary's signature. The cheques are technically in order and there are sufficient funds in the account.

Can the bank pay these cheques?

(Answers are given in Appendix 2, pp. 288–89)

Multiple-choice questions

1   Your customer, Fred Miles, has died. His son, James, calls at your branch and shows you his father's will in which he (James) is named as executor. He also has with him documents which will enable the credit balance on his father's account to be released to him by the bank.

Would these documents be:

(a)   Letters of administration?
(b)   Grant of probate?

2   A joint account, where the signing instructions are for either to sign, is in credit and one of the account holders dies. What action will the bank take concerning any cheques signed by the deceased which are presented for payment after the bank has received notification of death?

(a)   Pay the cheques.
(b)   Return the cheques, marked 'Drawer deceased'.
(c)   Pay the cheques if the surviving account holder authorises payment.

3   Davis, Evans and Jones is a small builders partnership. The account carries high credit balances. One of the partners, John Evans, dies and the bank agrees to allow the account to continue in order that it can be wound up. (The surviving partners are considering setting up a new partnership in just their own names.)

A cheque for £3,000 signed by the deceased partner in accordance with the mandate held is presented for payment after the bank had been notified of the partner's death.

Will the bank:

(a)   Return the cheque marked 'Partner deceased'?

(b) Pay the cheque, preferably having obtained the surviving partners' agreement first?

4   When a winding-up order is made against a partnership and a bankruptcy order is made against one or more partners, the firm's assets must be used to:

(a) Initially repay the partners' debts, with any residue going towards repayment of partnership debt.
(b) Initially repay the partnership debts, any residue going towards repayment of partners' private debts.

5   When a bank learns that a winding-up order has been served against a partnership and no bankruptcy order has been made against any partner, the bank may:

(a) Stop the partnership account alone.
(b) Stop the accounts of the partnership and all partners.
(c) Stop the partnership account and appropriate funds from the credit balance of a partner's account towards the repayment of any funds owed to the bank by the partnership.
(d) Stop the partnership account, but only if it has a debit balance.

6   Marks, Mills and Moore are opticians and trade as a partnership. As security, they offer the bank a charge over their retail shop, which is in the name of the partnership.

Who will have to execute the bank's charge form?

(a) Marks alone.
(b) Mills alone.
(c) Moore alone.
(d) Marks and Mills.
(e) Marks and Moore.
(f) Mills and Moore.
(g) All the partners.

7   Which of the following statements are correct?

(a) A minor can ratify a guarantee which he gave while he was a minor upon attaining the age of majority.
(b) A minor can never be a director of a limited company.
(c) A minor can act as an executor but not as a trustee.
(d) A minor cannot act as an executor but can act as a trustee.
(e) A minor cannot act as an executor or as a trustee.
(f) A minor can never make a valid will.

8   Which case established that where a trustee mixes trust money with his or her own, it is presumed that the trustee's money has been withdrawn first, in priority to the money held in trust?

(a) *Baker* v *Barclays Bank Ltd* (1955).
(b) *Gray* v *Johnston* (1868).
(c) *Re Halletts Estate* (1880).

9   One of the trustees on the account of Trustees of Neil Williams deceased has died. The trustee account has a credit balance.

Should the bank:

(a) Stop the account?

(b) Allow the account to continue and check the trust deed to ascertain whether a new trustee must be appointed?

(Answers are given in Appendix 2, p. 289)

Past examination questions

1   Bell, Book and Candle are a firm of estate agents banking at your branch. Mr Bell, the senior partner, aged 65, is due to retire on 31 December and a new partner, Mr Taper, will join the firm. Mr Book will then become the senior partner. Present account balances and securities held are as follows:

Balances:

Bell, Book and Candle	Cr	£34,210
Loan Account	Dr	£110,000
Clients' Account	Cr	£84,000
Trustees of N Light	Cr	£16,111

Security:

First legal mortgage over 112 High Street, given by Bell, Book and Candle (a firm): value £75,000;

Second legal mortgage over 17 Hazel Way, unregistered land by Mr Bell: value £40,000.

You are the Manager's Assistant, and one of your jobs is to prepare notes for the Manager's guidance before an interview.

Required

State what aspects you will include in your notes for the Manager's discussion with Messrs Bell, Book, Candle and Taper when they call today regarding banking arrangements for the firm after Mr Bell's retirement. Give reasons for your answer.

[16 marks]
(Autumn 1989)

2   Since June 1986 you have held the account for the executors of Charles Buck at your branch with a mandate authorising either Alice Carven or William Roberts to sign. Most of your dealings have been with William Roberts, but he now calls to tell you that he is being sent abroad to work for two years by his employer. He says that in future therefore all transactions on the account will be carried out by Alice Carven. He says that, as she will only need to issue cheques once a quarter (i.e. every three months) to the beneficiaries under the will, he assumes that there will be no difficulties; he says that in future he would like all correspondence to be sent to Alice Carven to handle.

Required

State how you would deal with this request, and what considerations you would have in mind.

[12 marks]
(Spring 1988)

(Answers are given in Appendix 2, pp. 289–90)

UNIT 5

Paying Banker

Objectives

- Identify reasons why cheques may be unpaid due to technical irregularities.
- Appreciate how the maxim of estoppel can be used by the paying bank as a defence when it has paid a cheque bearing a forged signature.
- Recognise the procedure to be followed when encashing an open cheque.
- Comprehend the problem which wrongful payment or dishonour of a cheque creates, and actions which should be taken in view of this.
- Identify statutory protections for the paying banker.
- Detail the procedure relating to the late return of cheques.
- Recognise the particular facets of cheque guarantee cards, bank drafts, banker's orders and direct debits.

Introduction

One of the main duties of a banker is to honour its customers' cheques. When it is carrying out this duty it is known as the *paying banker*.

Student Activity 1

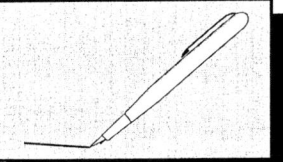

Look at the return cheques records in your branch and note the different reasons why cheques have been returned during the last month.

5.1 Technical Irregularities

(a) *Date*

If a cheque is dated in the future, it will be returned marked 'postdated' as it cannot be paid before that date.

Conversely, a cheque can become 'stale'. It is normal banking practice to allow six months to elapse before dishonouring a cheque with the reason 'Out of date'. Nevertheless, the drawer still remains liable on the cheque for six years from its date, but any endorser will be discharged if there is an unreasonable delay in the cheque being presented for payment.

At the beginning of a new year, banks are often faced with cheques which were apparently issued a year ago but have in fact been inadvertently dated with the previous year's date by their customers. Banks will normally pay these, providing that they are satisfied that it is a genuine mistake.

(b) *Payee*

If a cheque is not payable to bearer, it should bear the name of the payee. Sometimes cheques are payable to impersonal payees, e.g. cash, and in such circumstances banks will normally only cash such cheques for the drawer or the drawer's known agent.

Occasionally, banks have presented for payment cheques which have been altered from an 'order' cheque to a 'bearer' cheque, e.g. 'Pay John Jones or order' altered to 'Pay John Jones or bearer'. Banks should not pay such cheques unless the alteration has been signed by the drawer. However, in practice, some banks will pay these cheques where the alteration bears only the drawer's initials. Obviously, initials are easier to forge than signatures, but presumably these banks feel that the risk involved is minimal.

(c) *Amount*

Section 9(2) Bills of Exchange Act 1882 states that the amount payable is the amount in words. Banks, when handling cheques, normally take the amount in figures for accounting purposes through the clearing system. However, the paying banker will scrutinise the words and figures of the cheque prior to payment, to ensure that no discrepancy is apparent. If there is, it is usual for the bank to return the cheque marked 'Words and figures differ', unless the smaller amount has been claimed by the payee, in which case the bank may be prepared to pay the cheque.

One of the problems for the paying banker is where a cheque has been altered between the time when it was signed by the drawer and the time of presentation.

London Joint Stock Bank Ltd v *Macmillan and Arthur* (1918) confirmed that where additions or alterations to words and figures on a cheque were *non-apparent* and the bank paid that cheque, it was protected.

However, where there is an alteration which is *apparent* and has not been authenticated by the drawer of the cheque, the bank would be liable. In addition, s.64 Bills of Exchange Act 1882 states that where a cheque has been materially altered, all parties cease to be liable on it, except the party who altered it, or assented to or authorised the alteration, unless that party is an endorser subsequent to the alteration.

(d) *Crossings*

Crossed cheques, unlike 'open' cheques, should not be cashed except for the drawer or the drawer's known agent.

If a cheque is presented crossed by two banks it should only be paid if one of the banks is the agent of the other (s.79 Bills of Exchange Act 1882).

Where a person takes a crossed cheque bearing the words 'not negotiable', that person shall neither have nor be capable of giving a better title to the cheque than that which the person from whom it was taken had (s.81 Bills of Exchange Act 1882).

The Cheques Act 1992 has provided an additional s.81A to the Bills of Exchange Act which has given statutory recognition to the crossing 'Account [A/C] Payee', with or without the word 'only'. It confirmed that cheques bearing such a crossing were not transferable and were only valid between the drawer and the payee. If a bank pays such a cheque which has been endorsed to a third party, it is protected. (See Unit 5.3(c).)

(e) *Signature(s)* · ·

A bank will pay a cheque provided that it has been signed in accordance with the mandate held.

If a bank pays a cheque bearing a forged signature, it could face an action based on breach of mandate, conversion and negligence. (Section 24 Bills of Exchange Act 1882 states that a forged signature is 'wholly inoperative'.) Thus, if a bank is unsure as to the genuineness of a signature and is unable to obtain the drawer's confirmation, it should return the cheque marked 'signature differs'.

If a bank is sued for payment of a cheque bearing a forged signature, it may be able to use the maxim of estoppel as a defence. A customer could be stopped from denying the genuineness of his signature and thus taking action against the bank under the following circumstances:

(i) Where the customer has previously stated that the signature is genuine, and then retracts that statement (*Brown* v *Westminster Bank Ltd* (1964)).

(ii) Where the customer becomes aware that forged cheques are being presented on his or her account but fails to advise the bank (*Greenwood* v *Martins Bank Ltd* (1933)).

Another possible defence for the bank might be if it can show contributory negligence by the customer, but no law case has yet been decided on this issue in favour of a bank.

5.2 Dishonour of Cheques by Order of the Drawer

Banks have suffered losses by ignoring their customers' instructions to stop payment of cheques. The perils of such actions arise not only from having to reimburse the customer, but also because it will normally be too late to return the cheque unpaid. (Obviously, some of the loss can be offset by subrogation if goods have been purchased, as they can be sold.)

Another problem for a banker arises where other cheques may have been dishonoured as a result of the wrongful payment of a cheque, and this could result in damages being awarded against the bank.

An important case relating to wrongful payment was *Barclays Bank Ltd* v *W J Simms, Son and Cooke (Southern) Ltd and W Sowman* (1979). Here it was held that a person who paid money under a mistake of fact was entitled to recover it, although the claims might fail on three points:

(a) If the payer had intended that the payee should have the money whatever the circumstances, then the payer could not recover.

(b) If the payment was to discharge a debt owed to the payee by the payer or by a third party who was authorised to discharge the debt, the payer could not recover.

(c) If the payee's position had changed in good faith, recovery would not be possible.

In *Baines* v *National Provincial Bank Ltd* (1927), a customer tried to place a stop on a cheque which he had issued shortly before bank closing time the previous day, only to find that the cheque had been paid on the day of issue. It had been paid in at a sub-branch of the account-holding branch and had been paid in on the clerk's return to the main branch. The customer contended that in paying the cheque after its advertised closing time, the bank had not paid 'in the ordinary course of business'. The court held that 'a reasonable period' is needed after closing time for a bank to complete its work and found for the bank.

Instructions for stopping payment are often received by telephone. Confirmation in writing is required although, in practice, is seldom insisted upon. If a cheque is presented for payment prior to written confirmation being received, it should be returned marked 'Payment stopped, confirmation of countermand awaited'.

When stop instructions are received, the cheque number is an important detail. In *Westminster Bank Ltd* v *Hilton* (1926) it was held that a cheque number is unique to that cheque and if it was misquoted to the bank when payment was stopped, then that bank could not be liable when it paid that cheque.

5.3 Important Statute Law for the Paying Banker

(a) *Section 1 Cheques Act 1957*
Where a banker in good faith and in the ordinary course of business pays a cheque which is not endorsed or is irregularly endorsed, the banker does not, in doing so, incur any liability by reason only of the absence of, or irregularity in, endorsement, and is deemed to have paid it in due course.

(b) *Section 60 Bills of Exchange Act 1882*
This section states that where a bank pays a cheque in good faith and the ordinary course of business, it need not concern itself as to whether any endorsement is forged or unauthorised.

(c) *Section 80 Bills of Exchange Act 1882*
A paying banker is protected when a crossed cheque is paid in good faith, without negligence and in accordance with the crossing. Section 81A(2) adds that a paying banker will not be considered negligent, if paying a restrictively crossed cheque, merely for failing to be concerned with any purported endorsement of the cheque.

5.4 Procedures when a Cheque is Paid in at the Account-Holding Branch and the Payee asks whether it is Paid or not

In *Ringham* v *Hackett* (1980) it was held that in the above circumstances an answer as regards the cheque's fate could be given.

Many banks were unhappy with this decision, arguing that debit entries could already have been passed through the day's work relying upon the apparent credit balance, e.g. payment for the purchase of shares, and as such there was a great risk of loss for the bank.

Consequently, the Committee of London Clearing Bankers has advised banks not to give an immediate advice of fate. A payee who insists on a reply should be advised to instruct his or her own bank to telephone the drawee bank after the close of business, when an answer will be given. The only exception to this is if both payee and drawer of the cheque hold accounts with the same branch. In such circumstances, the Committee of London Clearing Bankers suggest that an immediate advice of the fate of the cheque should be given.

5.5 Wrongful Dishonour of a Cheque

If a cheque is wrongfully dishonoured a bank should do its utmost to remedy the situation. It should immediately contact the payee and presenting banker by telephone. It should explain that the fault lies with the bank and not with its customer in any way. This information should be confirmed in writing. Such action by the bank should reduce any damages awarded against the bank.

5.6 Late Returns Procedure

Any cheque paid into a collecting bank, other than the account-holding branch, will take a further two days before it is presented for payment to the paying bank. The paying bank should pay or dishonour the cheque on the day it is presented. If, however, it has inadvertently paid the cheque it can be returned on the day following presentation, providing that the reason is not due to a technical irregularity. Thus, if a 'stop' has been overlooked, or there are insufficient funds in the account, or the drawer has died, or a bankruptcy order has been served upon the drawer, or there is some similar reason, then a cheque can be returned 'late'. If, however, a cheque has been paid and the words and figures differed, this would be classed as a technical irregularity and would not be returned 'late'.

One additional duty which a paying banker must perform when using the late returns procedure is to telephone the collecting banker by 12 noon on the day following presentation to advise non-payment for all items over £500.

This amount is reviewed from time to time and students should therefore be aware of any changes to this figure which may occur.

5.7 Payment of an Open Cheque

Any cheque which does not bear a crossing is an open cheque. Such a cheque can be encashed at the account-holding branch by the payee. The branch will not require any means of identification from the payee unless there are suspicious circumstances, e.g. if the cheque is clearly made payable to a man and a woman presents the cheque for payment. The bank will, however, require to see that the cheque purports to be endorsed by the payee, following an agreement by the Committee of London Clearing Banks in 1957.

5.8 Bank Drafts

Bank drafts are dealt with in a similar manner to cheques, but because they are drawn by the bank as drawer they are considered to be almost as good as cash and are often issued for transactions where large sums of money are involved, e.g. house purchase.

The problem which arises for the bank occasionally is where a draft is subsequently lost or stolen. Banks do not like to refuse payment on their own paper as it might reflect adversely upon them. However, where a bank accepts a stop on a draft it will normally require an indemnity from its customer in case the original draft is presented for payment, particularly where a duplicate draft has been issued.

5.9 Banker's Orders

Banker's Orders are a means of making regular payments and are used by many account holders. They involve the customer giving written instructions to his bank to pay a certain sum to a beneficiary at specific times.

In respect of this, customers should take care to ensure that this authority is drawn up in such a way as not to facilitate fraud.

The main responsibility of the bank is to make payment on the due dates, providing that there are sufficient funds in the customer's account. If there are insufficient funds on the due date to meet a payment, there is no further obligation for the bank to its customer in respect of that particular instalment (*Whitehead* v *National Westminster Bank Ltd* (1982)).

A beneficiary cannot amend or cancel a customer's banking order instructions.

5.10 Direct Debits

Direct debits are similar to banker's orders, but are raised by the beneficiary, known as the originator.

All originators must execute an indemnity addressed to all the clearing banks and Scottish banks before being allowed to join the scheme. Under this indemnity, the originator agrees to indemnify them against actions arising from the use of the direct debit system.

Direct debits are often used where payments are for variable amounts. Where a bank receives a cancellation or amendments from its customer it should advise the originator. If, subsequently, the beneficiary originates an entry which the bank itself accepts by mistake, then it will be able to claim reimbursement under the indemnity which the originator gave when it entered the scheme.

Summary

Now that you have read this unit, you should be able to:

☐ Identify reasons why cheques may be unpaid due to technical irregularities.

☐ Appreciate how the maxim of estoppel can be used by a paying bank as a defence when it has paid a cheque bearing a forged signature.

☐ Recognise the procedure to be followed when encashing an open cheque.

☐ Comprehend the problem which wrongful payment or dishonour of a cheque creates, and actions which should taken in view of this.

☐ Define s.1 Cheques Act 1957 and s.60 Bills of Exchange Act 1882.

☐ Detail the procedure relating to the late return of cheques.

☐ Recognise the particular facets of cheque guarantee cards, bank drafts, banker's orders and direct debits.

If you can tick all the above boxes with confidence, you are ready to answer the questions that follow on pp. 58–60.

List of Cases

Baines v *National Provincial Bank Ltd* (1927)

Barclays Bank Ltd v *W J Simms, Son and Cooke (Southern) Ltd and W Sowman* (1979)

Brown v *Westminster Bank Ltd* (1964)

Greenwood v *Martins Bank Ltd* (1933)

London Joint Stock Bank Ltd v *Macmillan and Arthur* (1918)

Ringham v *Hackett* (1980)

Westminster Bank Ltd v *Hilton* (1926)

Whitehead v *National Westminster Bank Ltd* (1982)

List of Statutes

Bills of Exchange Act 1882

Cheques Act 1957

Cheques Act 1992

Self-assessment Questions

Short-answer questions

1 A stranger wishes to cash a crossed cheque at your bank counter drawn on your customer Keith Brown. The cheque is for £300 and is made payable to 'J Smith or bearer'. The cheque was originally an order cheque and has obviously been altered to read 'bearer', although there is no evidence of confirmation of this alteration. The stranger shows your cashier an envelope addressed to 'J Smith' as means of identification and tells her that he has nothing else with him with his name on. The balance of Keith Brown's account is £1,250 Cr. You know that Mr Brown left the UK yesterday for a safari holiday in Kenya.

What action would you take? Give reasons for your answer.

2 The drawer of a cheque cannot deny the genuineness of his signature where he has previously informed his bank that the signature on a cheque is genuine.

Which case confirms this statement?

3 If a customer becomes aware that cheques are being forged on his account and he does not advise his bank, he will be unable to deny the genuineness of his signature by the doctrine of estoppel.

Which case confirms this statement?

4 Edwin Rich, a valued customer, has been provided with a bank draft by your branch for £42,000 which he required for the purchase of an oil painting from a well-known London saleroom. You have just received a telephone call from Mr Rich advising you that he has lost the envelope containing the draft while imbibing at the local wine bar. He asks you to stop payment on the draft and to issue him with a duplicate.

What steps will you take, and why?

5 Martin Palmer pays £300 on the third day of each month by banker's order to Overtheodds Building Society. On 3 January you were unable to pay this banker's order as it would have created an unacceptable debit balance on Mr Palmer's account. On 4 January £5,000 cash was paid into Mr Palmer's account, which created a credit balance of £4,000. The building society's January payment was not made, despite this credit. Is the bank at fault in not making this payment?

Give reasons for your answer.

(Answers are given in Appendix 2, p. 291)

Multiple-choice questions

1 Today is 7 January 1992. In the clearing this morning there is a cheque for £200 drawn on your valued customer, Tony Briggs. There are sufficient

cleared funds to pay the cheque and the cheque is technically in order, except for the fact that it is dated 3 January 1991.

Which of the following actions would you take?

(a) Return the cheque marked 'Out of Date'.
(b) Pay the cheque.
(c) Ensure that the cheque has been issued from the chequebook which Mr Briggs is currently using, and if this is the case, pay the cheque.

2   Which of the following cases confirmed that any bank was protected which paid a cheque which bore a non-apparent alteration or addition?

(a) *Greenwood* v *Martins Bank Ltd* (1933).
(b) *Westminster Bank Ltd* v *Hilton* (1926).
(c) *London Joint Stock Bank Ltd* v *Macmillan and Arthur* (1918).
(d) *Baines* v *National Provincial Bank Ltd* (1927).

3   Which case held that a 'reasonable period' is needed after closing time for a bank to complete its work?

(a) *Baines* v *National Provincial Bank Ltd* (1927).
(b) *Westminster Bank Ltd* v *Hilton* (1926).
(c) *Whitehead* v *National Westminster Bank Ltd* (1982).

4   Which case established that a paying bank could not be held liable if it paid a cheque, where the customer had given instructions not to pay, if the customer had quoted the incorrect cheque number?

(a) *Ringham* v *Hackett* (1980).
(b) *Brown* v *Westminster Bank Ltd* (1964).
(c) *Whitehead* v *National Westminster Bank Ltd* (1982).
(d) *Westminster Bank Ltd* v *Hilton* (1926).

5   A payee of a cheque, who pays that cheque in at the branch upon which the cheque was drawn, is entitled to an answer if he or she should ask for the fate of that cheque. Which case established this?

(a) *Barclays Bank Ltd* v *W J Simms, Son and Cooke (Southern) Ltd and W Sowman* (1979).
(b) *Ringham* v *Hackett* (1980).
(c) *Greenwood* v *Martins Bank Ltd* (1933).

(Answers are given in Appendix 2, p. 291)

Revision question

Gwen Williams has maintained a satisfactory account at your branch for several years. At 11 o'clock this morning you see her at the enquiries counter. She shows you a print-out of a temporary statement of her account which she has just obtained from a machine in your banking hall. She explains that last week she wrote you a letter instructing the bank not to pay a cheque for £2,500 payable to Maguire and Jones, and that according to the print-out it had been debited to her account yesterday. She demands to know the reason for this and insists that the bank refunds £2,500 to her bank account immediately. You are aware that the bank received the instructions

mentioned several days ago. The cheque concerned came through the clearing system yesterday.

What action would you take?

(Answer is given in Appendix 2, pp. 291–92)

UNIT 6

Collecting Banker

Objectives

- Identify the criteria which must be satisfied in order that a collecting banker can obtain statutory protection when accused of conversion.
- Recognise protections, other than those which are statutory, which are available to the collecting banker.
- Appreciate how a collecting banker can become a holder for value or a holder in due course.

Introduction

When a bank accepts cheques for the credit of a customer's account, it is said to be acting in the role of *collecting banker.*

Problems arise for the collecting bank when it collects a cheque for a customer who is not the true owner and thereby leaves itself liable to a charge of conversion. There are a number of protections which the collecting banker will seek in such circumstances.

6.1 What Statutory Protection does a Collecting Banker have when Sued for Conversion?

Statutory protection is provided for the collecting banker by s.4 Cheques Act 1957. This protects the collecting banker when a cheque is collected:

(a) in good faith;
(b) for a customer;
(c) without negligence.

This section also extends to 'analogous instruments' such as bank drafts and dividend and interest warrants. However, it does not apply to postal orders, although a bank may be protected by s.21 Post Office Act 1953.

6.2 What Problems have Collecting Bankers Encountered in Meeting the Criteria laid down in s.4 Cheques Act 1957?

The collecting banker can normally satisfy the requirements of acting in good faith and collecting a cheque for a customer. (Good faith is defined in the

Bills of Exchange Act 1882 as something done honestly, whether negligently or not.)

The problem usually concerns collecting a cheque without negligence. There are three general areas where collecting bankers fail the 'without negligence' test:

(a) When account opening procedures are not completed properly.

(b) Where inadequate or no enquiries are made when a fiduciary relationship exists between the customer and the drawer or the customer and the payee.

(c) Where inadequate or no enquiries are made when there are suspicious or unusual circumstances.

6.3 Relevant Cases and Statutes Relating to Negligence

6.3.1 When account opening procedures are not completed properly

Until the 1980s, it was normal banking practice to obtain references from new customers and to follow these up. Failure to do this led to banks being guilty of negligence in several cases, including *Ladbroke* v *Todd* (1914) (failure to take references) and *Hampstead Guardians* v *Barclays Bank* (1923) (failure to follow up references).

To a great extent, the taking of references has been superseded by obtaining some means of identification and carrying out a search at a credit reference agency. This change has largely been due to banks relying upon the acceptance in the *Marfani and Co Ltd* v *Midland Bank Ltd* (1968) case that current practice carried out by careful bankers was unlikely to be construed as negligent.

Another important case is *E B Savory and Company* v *Lloyds Bank Ltd* (1932), where two clerks dishonestly misappropriated bearer cheques payable to third parties drawn on their employer's accounts. They paid these in at city offices of Lloyds Bank for the credit of accounts held at country branches, one of which was the account of the wife of one of the clerks. It was held that the bank was negligent by not obtaining the name of the customer's employer. Also, even though details of the cheques were not written on the credit slip, the bank had all the necessary information which could have been passed on to the account-holding branch and would have helped to prevent the fraud. As regards the account of the wife of one of the clerks, it was held that the bank should have noted down her husband's occupation and also the employer's name when the account was opened.

As a result of this case, banks now note down details of third-party cheques, normally on the bank giro credit, when paid in for the credit of other branches' accounts and pass them on. Alternatively, they send both the credit and the cheques direct. However, most banks have dispensed with enquiring as to the employment of the customer's spouse in recent years. It should also be noted that banks are not expected to keep abreast of a customer's changes of employment. This was confirmed in the case of *Orbit Mining and Trading Co Ltd* v *Westminster Bank* (1962).

6.3.2 Where inadequate or no enquiry is made when a fiduciary relationship exists between the customer and the drawer, or the customer and the payee

In *Foxton* v *Manchester and Liverpool District Banking Co.* (1881), it was established that where an executor drew a cheque upon the estate's account payable to himself, a bank must make suitable enquiries and receive adequate answers before collecting the cheque, otherwise it would have acted negligently.

In *Morison* v *London County and Westminster Bank Ltd* (1914), it was held that where an agent is allowed to draw cheques on a principal's account and such cheques are then collected by a bank for the credit of that agent's account, then that bank could be liable for conversion if it failed to make suitable enquiries or receive no satisfactory answers.

The case of *Marquess of Bute* v *Barclays Bank Ltd* (1955) highlighted the need for the collecting bank to make enquiries and receive suitable answers when cheques made payable to a person in the capacity of agent were collected for the private account of that person.

Midland Bank Ltd v *Reckitt and Others* (1933) identified that a collecting bank must be vigilant and be put on enquiry when cheques are drawn by an agent on the principal's account payable to the agent and are paid in for the credit of the agent's personal account.

In *A L Underwood Ltd* v *Bank of Liverpool and Martins Ltd* (1924) the managing director of A L Underwood Ltd paid cheques into his personal account which were made payable to the company and had been endorsed. This happened over several years without the bank making any enquiries. The bank was therefore held to have acted negligently. Partly as a result of this case, banks will rarely accept cheques, payable to companies, being collected for other accounts. This standpoint was further enhanced in the case of *London and Montrose Shipbuilding and Repairing Co Ltd* v *Barclays Bank Ltd* (1926), where it was stated that a bank must make enquiries when a cheque payable to one company is collected for the credit of the account of another company. However, banks will allow this practice where companies are members of the same group of companies, providing that they receive suitable authorities and indemnities from the companies concerned.

As regards cheques payable to partnerships, these should not be collected for other accounts unless extensive enquiries and undoubted answers have been made (*Baker* v *Barclays Bank* (1955)). In practice, it is very rare for such cheques to be collected for other accounts.

Student Activity 1

Ascertain what your bank's rules are concerning the collection of cheques payable to a partnership for other than the account of the named payee.

6.3.3 Where inadequate or no enquiries are made when suspicious or unusual circumstances exist

Often, these suspicious or unusual circumstances are a one-off situation and each has to be evaluated on its merits.

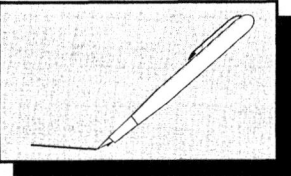

One such occasion would be where cheques are collected for the account of someone, where the amounts are far in excess of those which would be expected, given the position in life which that person held (*Nu-Stilo Footwear Ltd* v *Lloyds Bank Ltd* (1956)).

Another occasion would be where the past running of the account should have placed a bank upon enquiry when collecting cheques for the credit of that account (particularly third-party cheques). In *Motor Traders Guarantee Corporation Ltd* v *Midland Bank Ltd* (1937) it was held that, although a cashier had queried the transaction, the bank was negligent due to not having researched the past history of the account. An interesting side issue here was that the cashier had breached the internal rules of the bank by not referring the third-party collection to the branch manager. However, it was held that such action did not in itself mean that the bank had been negligent.

To emphasise the fact that each situation should be evaluated on its merits, it is worth looking at the case of *Penmount Estates Limited* v *National Provincial Bank Limited* (1945). Here, a solicitor paid cheques into his clients' account which were made payable to a company and had been endorsed over to him. When the bank enquired as to the circumstances regarding the cheques, the solicitor untruthfully replied that part of the cheques were in payment for legal fees which the company had incurred and that he would be paying over the residue to his company client by means of a cheque drawn on the clients' account. The court held that the bank had been correct in accepting this explanation, as it was in keeping with the practice followed by solicitors.

As mentioned in Unit 5.1(d) the Cheques Act 1992 has legalised the crossing 'account payee'. Cheques bearing such a crossing are valid between the named payee and drawer only. Therefore, any bank collecting a cheque which has an 'account payee' crossing for other than the named payee, risks a claim for conversion and is unlikely to be able to say that it acted without negligence. Banks are therefore refusing to accept such cheques for the credit of accounts other than the named payee. One exception to this would be where the named payee and the holder of the account to which the cheque is being credited are one and the same, e.g. where a cheque is made payable to a woman in her maiden name and she has subsequently changed her name through marriage.

6.4 Other Protections against Conversion for the Collecting Banker

(a) *Contributory negligence*

When the true owner has by his or her own actions contributed to the fraud, the damages payable by the collecting banker will be reduced to the extent of such contribution – s.1, Law Reform (Contributory Negligence) Act 1945, upheld by the Banking Act 1987.

If the collecting banker can rely upon s.4 Cheques Act 1957, it will not be necessary to rely upon the doctrine of contributory negligence. However, if s.4 does not apply, then the doctrine of contributory negligence may reduce the damages levied. In *Lumsden and Co* v *London*

Trustee Savings Bank (1971) the plaintiffs' damages were reduced by 10% because their own carelessness had contributed to the fraud.

(b) *Ex Turpi Causa Non Oritur Actio*

This may be translated as 'out of an immoral situation an action does not arise'. In *Thackwell* v *Barclays* (1986), the collecting bank could not rely on s.4 Cheques Act 1957, but the 'true owner's' claim arose indirectly out of a criminal act. Hence the court refused to allow a claim against the bank to succeed.

(c) Where a collecting banker can set himself up as a holder for value or a holder in due course.

6.5 What is a Holder for Value/Holder in Due Course?

6.5.1 Holder for value

A holder for value is the holder of a bill for which value has at some time been given: s.27(2) Bills of Exchange Act 1882. A holder for value:

(a) can sue on the bill in his own name;

(b) can enforce payment against any party who became a party to the bill *before* the last giving of value;

(c) cannot obtain a better title to the bill than the person from whom it was transferred. Thus if there were a prior defect in the title, then the holder for value will take the instrument subject to this defect. If there is no defect, the same rights as the transferor are acquired and the holder for value would thus be able to exercise full rights of recovery.

6.5.2 Holder in due course

Section 29(1) Bills of Exchange Act 1882:

A holder in due course is a holder who has taken a bill, complete and regular on the face of it, under the following conditions, viz:

(i) That he became the holder of it before it was overdue, and without notice that it had been previously dishonoured, if such was the fact:

(ii) That he took the bill in good faith and for value, and that at the time the bill was negotiated to him he had no notice of any defect in the title of the person who negotiated it.

(Note to students: memorise this definition.)

Points to notice

(a) There must be no prior forgery on the instrument, e.g. forged endorsement.

(b) There can be no holder in due course where an instrument is crossed 'not negotiable', 'not transferable', 'account payee' or drawn or endorsed 'Pay A Brown only'.

(c) A payee cannot be a holder in due course: *R E Jones* v *Waring and Gillow* (1926). By definition, a bill is issued to a payee; it is not negotiated to him.

Privileges

A holder in due course can:

(a) Sue on the bill in his own name.

(b) Enforce payment against all parties liable on the bill.

(c) Hold it free from any defect of title of prior parties.

(d) Pass on a good title to the bill.

6.6 When is a Collecting Banker Considered to have Given Value within the Meaning Contained in the Definitions of a Holder for Value or a Holder in Due Course?

(a) *Paying cheques against uncleared effects following an express or implied agreement with the customer*

Westminster Bank v *Zang* (1965) confirmed that there must be an agreement for a customer to draw against uncleared effects in order for value to be said to have been given. Most banks state in either their cheque-books or paying-in books that they reserve the right to refuse payment against uncleared effects. Thus, in such circumstances, any agreement must be 'express'.

(b) *Accepting a cheque in specific reduction of an overdraft or loan*

'Specific' in this context means 'permanent' and the relevant case is *M'Lean* v *Clydesdale Banking Co* (1883). Here it was held that a bank had not given value by merely crediting a cheque to an overdrawn account in the ordinary course of business. Hence, to have given value, the bank must have specifically accepted the cheque in reduction of an overdraft or loan – for example, by having threatened legal action and then having called off the action because the customer paid in a cheque to the account.

(c) *When a bank cashes a cheque drawn on another bank for the holder prior to sending that cheque to the drawee bank for payment*

This would normally occur where a customer did not wish to pay the cheque into the account in the normal way and the bank agreed to the request to cash it.

(d) *When a bank is said to have a lien over a cheque*

Section 27(3) Bills of Exchange Act 1882 establishes that 'where the holder of a bill has a lien on it, arising either from contract or by implication of law, he is deemed to be a holder for value to the extent of the sum for which he has a lien.'

Thus, under this statute, if a banker collects a cheque, for a customer's account, which is subsequently dishonoured and this creates or adds to an overdrawn position on that account, then, provided that the cheque is retained, the banker will be a holder for value by way of lien up to the value of the cheque or the extent of the overdraft, whichever is the lower. This was confirmed in *Barclays Bank Ltd* v *Astley Industrial Trust Ltd* (1970).

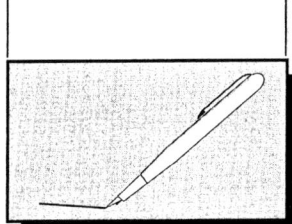

Student Activity 2

Student Activity 2

What action (if any) does your bank take to emphasise the fact that it has given value (e.g. debiting the cheque to a suspense account)?

6.7 What other Points should be Considered when Looking at a Collecting Bank's Position as a Holder for Value, or Holder in Due Course?

Westminster Bank v *Zang* (1965) held that a collecting bank must retain possession of a dishonoured cheque, otherwise it will lose its rights against the drawer.

Section 2 Cheques Act 1957 protects the collecting banker's position as a holder for value or holder in due course, even when a cheque lacks an endorsement. It states the following:

> A banker who gives value for, or has a lien on, a cheque payable to order, which the holder delivers to him for collection without endorsing it, has such (if any) rights as he would have had if, upon delivery, the holder had endorsed in blank.

The effect of this was seen in the case of *Barclays Bank Ltd* v *Harding* (1962). A substantial cheque made payable to the company customer's trading name was paid in (unendorsed) to the company account. In reliance of this, the bank paid several cheques issued by the company. Unfortunately, the drawer of the substantial cheque countermanded payment. The court held that the bank's position as a holder in due course was not flawed, due to the lack of endorsement on the cheque (s.2 Cheques Act 1957).

Finally, it must be remembered that, in order to be a holder in due course, a holder must give full value on a cheque. If only partial value has been given, then the holder of the cheque can only be a holder for value.

6.8 Rules Governing a Bank when it is Acting as Both Collecting and Paying Banker

It sometimes occurs that a bank will hold both the account of the drawer of a cheque and also the account into which the cheque is to be paid. In such circumstances, if the bank was accused of conversion, it would have to show that it satisfied both statutory protections for collecting and paying banker alike. This was confirmed in *Carpenters Company* v *British Mutual Banking Co Ltd* (1938).

Summary

Now that you have read this unit, you should be able to:

☐ Identify the criteria which must be satisfied in order that a collecting banker can obtain statutory protection when accused of conversion.

☐ Recognise protections, other than statutory, which are available to the collecting banker.

☐ Appreciate how a collecting banker can become a holder for value or a holder in due course.

If you can tick all the above boxes with confidence, you are ready to answer the questions which follow on pp. 69–71.

List of Cases

Baker v *Barclays Bank* (1955)

Barclays Bank Ltd v *Astley Industrial Trust Ltd* (1970)

Barclays Bank Ltd v *Harding* (1962)

Carpenters' Company v *British Mutual Banking Co Ltd* (1938)

Foxton v *Manchester and Liverpool District Banking Co* (1881)

Hampstead Guardians v *Barclays Bank* (1923)

R E Jones v *Waring and Gillow* (1926)

Ladbroke v *Todd* (1914)

London and Montrose Shipbuilding and Repairing Co Ltd v *Barclays Bank Ltd* (1926)

Lumsden and Co v *London Trustee Savings Bank* (1971)

Marfani and Co Ltd v *Midland Bank Ltd* (1968)

Marquess of Bute v *Barclays Bank Ltd* (1955)

Midland Bank Ltd v *Reckitt and Others* (1933)

M'Lean v *Clydesdale Banking Co* (1883)

Morison v *London County and Westminster Bank Ltd* (1914)

Motor Traders Guarantee Corporation Ltd v *Midland Bank Ltd* (1937)

Nu-Stilo Footwear Ltd v *Lloyds Bank Ltd* (1956)

Orbit Mining and Trading Co Ltd v *Westminster Bank* (1962)

Penmount Estates Limited v *National Provincial Bank Limited* (1945)

E B Savory and Company v *Lloyds Bank Ltd* (1932)

Thackwell v *Barclays* (1986)

A L Underwood Ltd v *Bank of Liverpool and Martins Ltd* (1924)

Westminster Bank v *Zang* (1965)

List of Statutes

Banking Act 1987

Bills of Exchange Act 1882

Cheques Act 1957

Law Reform (Contributory Negligence) Act (1945)

Post Office Act 1953

Self-assessment Questions

Short-answer questions

1   Which case held that a bank was negligent when it did not obtain details of its customer's employer when it opened an account?

2   Which case established that a bank could be held to be negligent if it did not obtain details of the occupation and the employer of a customer's spouse?

3   Which case stated that a bank was under no obligation to keep up to date with its customers' changes of employment?

4   Under what circumstances might a collecting banker accept a cheque which is payable to one company for the credit of another company?

5   Define a holder in due course.

6   Why can the payee of a cheque not be a holder in due course?

(Answers are given in Appendix 2, p. 292)

Multiple-choice questions

1   What is the major statutory protection for the collecting banker?

(a)   S.1 Cheques Act 1957.
(b)   S.4 Cheques Act 1957.

2   In order to gain the protection given in Q1, a banker must collect a cheque:

(a)   In good faith.
(b)   For a customer.
(c)   In the ordinary course of business.
(d)   Without negligence.

3   Which case established that cheques payable to partnerships should not be collected for the account of other than the named payee unless suitable enquiries have been made and satisfactory answers received?

(a) *Ladbroke v Todd* (1914).
(b) *Morison v London County and Westminster Bank Ltd* (1914).
(c) *London and Montrose Shipbuilding and Repairing Co Ltd v Barclays Bank Ltd* (1926).
(d) *Baker v Barclays Bank* (1955).

4   The doctrine of contributory negligence was confirmed in which case:

(a) *Nu-Stilo Footwear Ltd v Lloyds Bank Ltd* (1956).
(b) *Lumsden Co v London Trustee Savings Bank* (1971).
(c) *Penmount Estates Limited v National Provincial Bank Limited* (1945).

5   Which section of the Bills of Exchange Act 1882 refers to a holder for value?

(a) S.24.
(b) S.27.
(c) S.29.
(d) S.60.

6   Which section of the Bills of Exchange Act 1882 refers to a holder in due course?

(a) S.24.
(b) S.27.
(c) S.29.
(d) S.60.

7   Which case confirmed that a payee cannot be a holder in due course?

(a) *R E Jones v Waring and Gillow* (1926).
(b) *Thackwell v Barclays* (1986).
(c) *Barclays Bank Ltd v Harding* (1962).

8   In order to retain its rights against the drawer of a cheque as a holder in due course or a holder for value, a collecting banker must retain possession of that cheque. Which case confirmed this?

(a) *Barclays Bank Ltd v Harding* (1962).
(b) *Marfani and Co Ltd v Midland Bank Ltd* (1968).
(c) *Westminster Bank v Zang* (1965).

9   If a bank has acted as both paying and collecting banker, it must satisfy both statutory protections in order to defeat an allegation of conversion. Which case established this?

(a) *M'Lean v Clydesdale Banking Co* (1883).
(b) *Westminster Bank v Zang* (1965).
(c) *Carpenters' Company v British Mutual Banking Co Ltd* (1938).

10 Which case confirmed that there must be an agreement for a customer to draw against uncleared effects in order for value to be said to have been given by a collecting banker?

(a) *R E Jones* v *Waring and Gillow* (1926).
(b) *M'Lean* v *Clydesdale Banking Co* (1883).
(c) *Westminster Bank* v *Zang* (1965).

(Answers are given in Appendix 2, pp. 292–93)

Past examination questions

1 Alan Carter, the manager of a local grocery supermarket, has been known to you for some four years as he calls at the bank each day to pay in shop takings for the account of Neighbourhood Groceries plc, an account at your City branch. You have occasionally helped Mr Carter with his personal banking requirements, such as supplying traveller's cheques against payment in cash, and selling him National Savings Certificates. He has, however, always been adamant that he will not open an account with you or any other bank which, as he puts it, 'charges for looking after his own money'. Some weeks ago, as a favour, and in the hope that one day he would open an account, you encashed a cheque for £400 drawn on Beta Bank by Robert Flint in favour of A Carter.

You have now had a letter from a firm of solicitors acting for Mr Alec Carter claiming that they have ascertained that you cleared a cheque for £400 to which their client was entitled. They say that this cheque was stolen from him by his brother Alan. They further inform you that Alan Carter has disappeared, and seek reimbursement in view of the conversion which you facilitated.

Required:

(a) Comment on the bank's position, with reasons.

[14 marks]

(b) State the points you would cover in your reply to the solicitor's letter.

[3 marks]

(Autumn 1984)

2 Brian Speed, a second-hand car dealer, paid a cheque for £420 into his account last week and, since he had been known to you for some years, your assistant manager allowed him to draw out £450 in cash, although the balance of his account before these transactions was only £50 credit.

Today the cheque for £420 has been returned marked 'Payment countermanded by order of drawer'.

What action would you take to protect the bank as fully as possible in these circumstances?

[8 marks]
(Autumn 1983)

(Answers are given in Appendix 2, pp. 293–94)

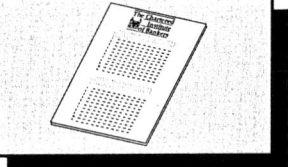

UNIT 7

Payment Cards and Other Money Transmission Services

Objectives

- Appreciate the differences between various types of payment card.
- Recognise the liabilities which card issuers and card holders attract in the event of loss or misuse of a card.
- Identify the effects which the Consumer Credit Act has on payment cards.
- Illustrate how the credit transfer system operates.
- Recognise how problems surrounding the direct debit system can be solved.
- Explain the operation of CHAPS.
- Define truncation and explain the legal problems regarding its introduction.

Introduction

With the emergence of modern information technology, various money transmission mechanisms have evolved to improve the efficiency of the banks in transferring money from point A to point B. There is also an increasing trend to reduce the amount of paper used in the banking system by means of computerised methods.

This unit principally looks at these various recent developments.

7.1 What is a Payment Card?

The term 'payment card' refers to any form of plastic card which can be used to withdraw cash or to pay for goods or services.

7.2 What Types of Payment Card are There?

There are many types of payment cards, with new forms being marketed continuously.

The most common examples of payment cards are given below.

7.2.1 Charge cards

Charge cards are generally used for the purchase of goods and services, although some cards also permit cash withdrawals to be made. An annual fee is charged and card holders have to repay the full amount outstanding upon receipt of a monthly statement.

Well-known examples of charge cards are those issued by American Express and Diners Club.

7.2.2 Credit cards

Credit cards can be used to buy goods or services on credit, or for cash advances. Card holders will normally receive monthly statements and can pay off the balance either in full or in monthly instalments, subject to a minimum repayment amount. An annual fee for credit cards is now becoming the norm, although there are still some card issuers who make no annual charge. Where card holders repay in monthly instalments, interest is charged on the outstanding balance.

7.2.3 Budget cards

Budget cards are similar to credit cards. However, budget card customers agree to pay a fixed monthly amount into their card account.

7.2.4 Store cards

Store cards parallel credit cards but can only be used in the outlets of the companies which issue them, e.g. Marks and Spencer.

7.2.5 Debit cards

Debit cards are seen as the eventual replacement for cheques. They can be used for payment for goods and services at point of sale, as well as to obtain cash. As with cheques, all transactions will be debited subsequently to the customer's account, without any delay in payment.

7.2.6 Cheque guarantee cards

Cheque guarantee cards utilised in association with cheques assure payment up to the amount stated on the card, providing that they are used within the terms and conditions of the issue of the cards concerned.

7.2.7 Eurocheque cards

Eurocheque cards are a particular kind of cheque guarantee card which, when accompanied by eurocheques, can be used to pay for services or goods or to withdraw cash. They are used mainly in the UK and other European countries.

7.2.8 Cash cards

Cash cards have evolved as a direct result of modern technology. Each holder of a cash card is issued with a confidential personal identification number (PIN). By using the PIN, card holders can obtain cash from automated teller machines (ATM) which may be situated in the outside wall of the bank or in the banking hall. It is envisaged that special terminals will be sited at retail outlets so that payment for goods or services can be authorised by use of the cash card together with the PIN. This is known as EFTPOS (electronic funds transfer point of sale).

One payment card can have several functions. For example, a card may act as a credit card, cheque guarantee card, cash card and debit card. Where a card has a number of functions, the card issuer will advise the customer. Under the Code of Banking Practice, the customer can request not to be issued with a PIN by the card issuer, where there is no wish to use those functions which are operated by a PIN.

7.3 Payment Cards and the Code of Banking Practice

During the last 20 years the issue of payment cards has increased rapidly. Unfortunately, organised crime has recognised the opportunities which these cards offer and this has led to a criminal trade in stolen cards, which has caused the banks huge losses. It has also led to disputes between customers and banks over 'phantom' withdrawals. Many of these have been referred to the Banking Ombudsman. It is largely due to this that a specific section of the Code of Banking Practice has been devoted to payment cards.

Student Activity 1

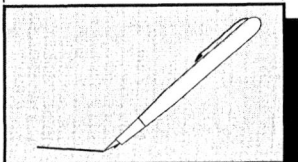

Examine the Code of Banking Practice in Appendix 1 and refer to the section on cards. How far do your bank's internal rules vary from the guidelines laid down there?

7.4 Issue of Cards and their Terms and Conditions of Use

Cards will only be issued initially to customers who make a written request. Their issue will depend upon the customer satisfying the card issuer as regards identity and financial standing.

Written details of the terms and conditions of a card service will be provided by the card issuer. Any amendment to these terms and conditions will be advised to the card holder and reasonable notice will be given before such amendments will come into force. The method by which these amendments will be notified to the card holder will be made known by the card issuer.

Card issuers will provide card holders with statements. They will advise their customers of the frequency of these statements and also how long it will normally take for a transaction to appear on their account.

As mentioned earlier, banks (and their customers) are faced with the risk of loss through fraud and thefts of cards. Card issuers therefore take certain security precautions.

At the outset, card issuers will forward PINs separately from the cards to which they pertain. They will advise card holders:

(a) not to allow other people to use their cards and PINs;

(b) to ensure that they keep their PINs secret and to take all reasonable precautions to keep their cards safe;

(c) to never write their PINs on the cards nor keep a note of them with the cards;

(d) not to write down their PINs without disguising them.

7.5 What Should a Customer do if he Loses his Card?

Card holders can take out insurance with certain organisations which will cover them against loss due to card-related fraud above a certain amount, which is usually £50. By making one telephone call to this organisation, the latter will notify all card issuers.

However, many card holders do not have such insurance. They should therefore advise card issuers in the event of the following circumstances:

(a) loss or theft of a card;
(b) where another person knows their PIN;
(c) where an unknown transaction appears on their account.

This can be done by telephone. Card issuers may also request written confirmation.

7.6 Who is Liable for Losses Incurred due to the Misuse or Loss of a Card?

Liability will depend upon the surrounding circumstances. Card issuers will be liable for the full losses:

(a) where the card has not been received by the customer and is misused;

(b) for unauthorised transactions where the customer has advised the card issuer of the theft or loss of a card, or that a third party may know the PIN;

(c) where there are faults in machines or systems used which cause losses to the customer, unless such faults were obvious or advised by a message or notice on display.

Losses to card issuers are limited to the total amounts wrongly charged to the customer's account plus any interest relating to those transactions.

Customers will be liable for unauthorised transactions up to a maximum of £50 where a card has been misused or a third party knows the PIN and prior to the card issuer receiving notification of the problems relating to the card or PIN.

If customers have acted fraudulently they will be held liable for all losses. Where they have been guilty of gross negligence they *may* be liable for all losses.

Where a dispute arises over a transaction between the card issuer and the customer the burden of proof, with regard to gross negligence, fraud or the receipt of a card by a customer, lies with the card issuer. In such circumstances, card issuers will expect the co-operation of their customers with their enquiries.

7.7 What Action Should a Customer Take in the Event of Having a Complaint?

All card issuers have their own procedures when dealing with complaints. These procedures will be advised to the customer and also what additional steps can be taken should the customer feel that the complaint has not been treated satisfactorily by the card issuer. This may involve use of the Banking Ombudsman Scheme or some similar entity.

7.8 Payment Cards and the Consumer Credit Act 1974

Under CCA 1974 s.14(1), certain cards are classed as credit tokens. Section 14(1) defines a credit token as:

> a card, check, voucher, coupon, stamp, form, booklet, or other document or thing given to an individual by a person carrying on a consumer credit business who undertakes:
>
> (a) that on the production of it, he will supply cash, goods and services on credit; or
>
> (b) that where, on production of it to a third party, the third party supplies cash, goods and services, he will pay the third party for them, in return for payment to him by the individual.

Thus, credit cards and charge cards are credit tokens. However, cheque guarantee cards are not credit tokens because settlement is by payment of cheques and not payment of goods (s.14(1)(b)). Similarly, cash cards are not credit tokens, as withdrawals are debited immediately. Nor are debit cards credit tokens, as payments are either debited immediately or within three days. Cash cards and debit cards are exempted from regulation under s.89 Banking Act 1987.

7.9 Connected Lender Liability and Credit Cards

Section 75 CCA states that connected lender liability can apply when someone wishes to purchase goods from a certain supplier, and requires credit. If the supplier introduces the customer to the provider of the loan, then the provider of the loan can become jointly and severally liable with the supplier for any defects in the goods.

If the goods are the subject of misrepresentation or breach of contract, the borrower can take action against both the supplier of the goods and the lender. If the lender has to recompense the borrower, then the lender can take action against the supplier to recoup the loss.

The above provisions only apply to items which cost no more than £30,000 and not less than £101.

Connected lender liability extends to the provision of credit by overdraft, loan or credit card. In recent years, examples of connected lender liability have been seen where customers have used their credit cards to purchase overseas holidays. When the travel companies have entered liquidation, the credit card customer has been able to claim reimbursement from the credit card companies.

7.10 The Liquidation of a Credit Card Company

In Re *Charge Card Services* (1988) it was held that in the liquidation of a credit card company:

(a) The retailer has no claim whatsoever against the purchaser of goods (card holder), even though the relevant vouchers given by the card holder have been dishonoured by the credit card company (or by its liquidator). Payment by credit card is unconditional, i.e. the retailer has no recourse against the card holder.

(b) The retailer is an unsecured creditor (unless some security is held, which is most unlikely) in the liquidation of the credit card company. The retailer must submit a proof to the liquidator in the usual way (Insolvency Act 1986).

(c) The liquidator of the credit card will take over all rights of the credit card company against card holders. Thus card holders are liable to pay their agreed instalments on outstanding amounts to the liquidator of the credit card company. (Note the position in (d) below when the credit card company has borrowed and has itself given security.)

(d) If the credit card company has given any security to a bank or other organisation, that security can be enforced by the lender in the usual way. In *Charge Card Services,* a factoring company had made an advance to the credit card company against a charge over the book debts (i.e. amounts due from card holders to the credit card company). The factoring company was entitled to all sums received from the card holders.

7.11 Transfer of Funds by Means of a Credit Transfer/ Bank Giro Credit

A credit transfer involves the transfer of funds, initiated by the payer, within the same bank or between two banks.

When the transfer is within the same bank, the payer provides written details of the account to be credited, and either hands over cash or an authority to debit his or her own bank account. The bank will put the transfer into effect during the course of the day's work, and the payee's account will be credited that day.

When the transfer takes place between different banks, the clearing system is used. The timescale for crediting the payee's account is as follows:

Day one

The payer provides written details of the payee's account, together with an authority to debit his or her own account (or cash). At the end of the day the credit transfer slip is sent to the clearing house.

Day two

Each bank agrees the credit totals at the clearing house.

Day three

The banks complete final settlement and the payee's account is credited.

7.12 Completion of Payment for Credit Transfer

7.12.1 Where the accounts are at the same bank and the clearing system is not used

In *Gibson* v *Minet* (1791) it was held that payment was complete and irrevocable as soon as both the payer's and payee's accounts had been debited/credited.

In *Momm and Ors* v *Barclays Bank International Ltd* (1976) it was held that payment was complete when the bank had decided to accept the instructions to credit the payee's account and had set the computer processes in motion. It is immaterial whether the payee has been advised of the transfer.

In the *Momm* case the bank transferred funds from one account to another at the same branch in accordance with the payer's instructions. Next morning it was discovered that the payer's account had become overdrawn as a result of the transfer. The bank then reversed the entries to recredit the payer's account.

Once the facts came to light, it was held that the reversal was invalid, because the mistake lay between the bank and the payer and not between the bank and the payee.

Similar reasoning applied in *Chambers* v *Miller* (1862) when a bank cashed a cheque on presentation, but immediately afterwards discovered that the drawer, its customer, had no funds. The recipient had not left the bank and still had the money. It was held that payment was irrevocable and that innocent third parties should not suffer for a mistake made between the bank and its own customer.

7.12.2 When the clearing system is used

There is no specific case which has decided when payment is irrevocable, but it is considered that when the clearing house is used, payment is completed when the net amount to be paid by one bank to another is agreed between them. Prior to that time, the collecting bank can return wrongly delivered forms, and the paying bank can request the return of wrongly delivered forms.

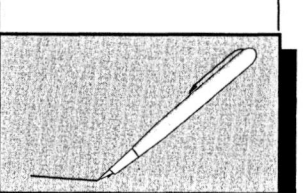

Student Activity 2

Write down your thoughts as to why it is important to establish the time when payment is completed for a credit transfer.

7.13 Defects in Payee's Title for Credit Transfers

Once the time for completion of payment has passed, the transaction cannot be reversed. If the payer wishes to obtain reimbursement of the transfer, for whatever reason, he will have to take action via the courts if payment has been completed.

Prior to completion of payment, the transaction itself may be reversed.

7.13.1   Forged or unauthorised instruction from the payer

In accordance with s.24 of the Bills of Exchange Act, and in accordance with the *Tai Hing* case, the payer's bank has no authority to debit a payer whose signature on the authority to debit the account has been forged or is unauthorised. An example of an unauthorised signature would occur when the payer had provided a mandate for the bank to accept the authority of an agent to make credit transfers up to a specified limit. If the limit has been exceeded, the agent's instruction would be unauthorised. (Note: the above would be reversed if the bank could establish estoppel.)

The paying bank must reimburse its customer in the case of forged or unauthorised instructions and can then claim from the forger/unauthorised agent in deceit or for breach of warranty (*Orr* v *Union Bank of Scotland* (1854)). If the payment, despite being unauthorised, was in respect of genuine obligations of the customer, there would be a defence under *B Liggett (Liverpool) Ltd* v *Barclays Bank Ltd* (1928).

In *National Westminster Bank* v *Barclays Bank International* (1975) it was held that, provided the collecting bank did not know about the fraud, the payer or the payer's bank could recover from the collecting bank only such amounts as had not been paid out to the payee or on the payee's instructions. If all else fails, the bank can claim from the payee (*Barclays* v *W J Simms Son and Cooke (Southern) Ltd and W Sowman* (1979).

7.13.2   Credit transfer made by mistake of fact

This could arise in two situations:

(a)   The payer may sign a credit transfer form by mistake, believing it to be an entirely different document. In such cases the payer could plead *non est factum,* in other words that he or she was completely mistaken as to the nature of the transaction.

In *Saunders* v *Anglia Building Society* (1970) it was held that in the absence of misrepresentation, literate persons of sound mind who sign documents which they broadly understand are bound by such contracts. The case of *Lloyds Bank* v *Waterhouse* (1990), however, laid down the principle that if an illiterate person is misled by the explanation of the other party, then the transaction is voidable.

(b) The payer may have made the transfer in the belief that he or she was under an obligation to pay, when this was not in fact the case.

Examples of payment by mistake of fact are seen in:

(i) *Kelly* v *Solari* (1841), where the payer wrongly believed that he was under an obligation to make a payment, or at least would not have paid if he had known the true situation.

(ii) *Cundy* v *Lindsay* (1878), where there was a case of mistaken identity.

Student Activity 3

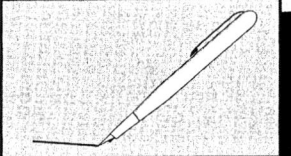

Imagine that you are a payer who has initiated a credit transfer under mistake of fact.

Note down who you believe you could sue for recovery of the money.

7.13.3 Position of payer's bank, collecting bank and payee when a credit transfer has been made under mistake of fact

(a) *Payer's bank*
This bank cannot be liable unless it knew or ought to have known of the mistake. The bank is simply carrying out its customer's mandate.

(b) *The collecting bank*
It is considered that s.4(1) and (2) of the Cheques Act 1957 would probably apply in connection with credit tranfers. Thus if the collecting bank acts for a customer, in good faith and without negligence, there will be no liability to the payer. (See also *National Westminster Bank* v *Barclays Bank International* (1975).)

(c) *The payer*
The payer could claim from the payee (*Barclays* v *W J Simms and Cooke (Southern) Ltd and W Sowman* (1979).

7.14 Operation of Direct Debits

In Unit 5 we looked briefly at direct debits. This section provides more information concerning their operation, and revises other aspects.

The payer completes an authority instructing the bank to allow the payer's account to be debited in connection with payments originated by the payee.

Only a limited class of payees may originate direct debits, usually major limited companies or public authorities. As a condition of being allowed to join the system, a payee must complete a general indemnity in favour of all the London and Scottish clearing banks. This promises to reimburse these banks against all claims, actions or damages which might arise because of any direct debit which may have been initiated by that payee.

A general understanding of the operation of the direct debit system is necessary so that the legal implications can be understood. Some payees use a computerised system linked to BACS (Bankers Automated Clearing System), whilst others use paper-based systems.

(a) *BACS system*

The payee, or the payee's bankers acting on their behalf, deliver to BACS, a computer-based list of all the names, bank account details and amounts due from the payers. BACS then arranges for the individual payers' bank accounts to be debited and for the payee's bank account to be credited with the total amalgamated amount for the day. The debits and credits are passed through the respective bank accounts on the same day.

(b) *Paper-based systems*

The payee sends a direct debit voucher containing details of the debt, including the payer's and the payee's bank account details, to the London head office of the payer's bank. Arrangements are then made for the respective accounts to be debited and credited two working days later. The practical effect is that the debit and credit will take effect on the same day.

It should be noted that the payer's bank may refuse to accept a direct debit if there are insufficient funds or if the payer has revoked his authority to pay.

In such cases the payer's bank claims reimbursement from the payee's bank through the mechanics of the clearing process, and ultimately the payee's account will be debited back.

The payer's bank must give a reason for dishonour of the direct debits; the typical answers to be seen are:

(i)   'Refer to payer' (i.e. lack of funds);
(ii) 'No mandate' (i.e. no authority held to pay);
(iii) 'Payer deceased' (i.e. equivalent to drawer deceased with a cheque);
(iv) 'Mandate cancelled' (i.e. the payer has 'stopped payment').

7.15 Completion of Payment for Direct Debits

The payer's bank may dishonour a direct debit on the day of presentation. In addition, a 'late returns' process has been agreed by the banks for any items debited inadvertently to the payer's account, similar to the one operated for cheques.

It follows that payment will be completed on the day the respective bank accounts are debited and credited, unless the payer's bank dishonours the debit. Hence, as between the payee and payer, payment will be irrevocable at close of business on the day the direct debit has been presented at the payer's bank. The only exception will arise if there is scope for the 'late returns' process to be used.

7.16 Defects in the Payee's Title for Direct Debits

7.16.1 Where the payer's signature has been forged or where the signature on the direct debit authority is unauthorised

The payer will have the right to claim immediate reimbursement from his or her bank, and the payer's bank will have a right of action against the forger for deceit or breach of warranty. However, the major practical difference is that the payer's bank will be able to claim reimbursement from the payee because of the general indemnity which the payee will have signed. A claim under the indemnity will be a much quicker and simpler process to enforce than would an action for deceit or breach of warranty which was taken via the courts.

7.16.2 Where payment has been made under mistake of fact

The principles are similar to those already described for credit transfers. The main difference is that if either the payer's bank or the payee's bank had to refund to the payer, these banks could automatically claim reimbursement from the payee under the terms of the general indemnity.

7.17 CHAPS (Clearing House Automated Payments System)

The main features of CHAPS are as follows:

(a) The system can be used for transfers of sterling between different UK bank accounts. The minimum amount of a single transfer is £1,000.

(b) The transfer will normally be effected in a single day, but the bank's authority will state that there are various cut-off times after which payment can be effected only on the next working day.

(c) The branch receives a customer's instructions to transfer money to the beneficiary.

(d) The customer's account is debited and a message is transmitted to the bank's gateway.

(e) The message is then passed via the British Telecom switching service (PSS) to the gateway of the beneficiary's bank.

(f) The funds are immediately credited to the beneficiary's account and are treated as cleared.

7.18 Completion of CHAPS Payment

Once the payment message has passed through the remitting bank's gateway, the bank is committed to that payment and the payer cannot 'stop' the transaction.

7.19 Defect in Payee's Title

7.19.1 Can a recipient bank refund a CHAPS payment at the request of the paying bank?

The recipient bank must not do so unless the beneficiary authorises a refund. This applies irrespective of whether the beneficiary had been advised of the payment (*Momm and Ors v Barclays Bank International* (1976)).

It also applies even if the payee's account has not been credited, as the payee has an accrued right to payment (*Royal Products Limited v Midland Bank Limited* (1981)). One rare exception to this would be if the following two conditions were satisfied:

(a) the paying bank had made an 'input error', thus transferring a wrong amount, or crediting the wrong beneficiary;

(b) the beneficiary had not been advised.

In this exceptional case, a refund could be made, relying on the principles in *National Westminster Bank v Barclays Bank International* (1975).

If the beneficiary had been advised, the recipient bank could ask for authority to refund. In the absence of such authority, the paying bank would have to sue to obtain reimbursement.

The principles would be as in the case of *Barclays v W J Simms Son and Cooke (Southern) Ltd and W Sowman* (1979) which enabled a bank which had paid a stopped cheque in error to obtain reimbursement from the payee, so long as the payee had not altered his or her financial position in the belief that the cheque had been honoured. If the funds had not been withdrawn from the payee's account, the paying bank could claim reimbursement from the recipient bank. If the funds had been withdrawn, no claim could be made (*National Westminster Bank v Barclays Bank International* (1975)).

7.19.2 What is the position of the payer's bank if there is a defect in the payer's instruction?

(a) *Forgery of payer's signature*

The position is likely to be the same as that for a drawee bank when the drawer's signature is forged. The payer's bank must refund the transfer, even if the payer had been careless and had left the CHAPS authorities lying around unsupervised (*Tai Hing Cotton Mills v Liu Chong Hing Bank and others* (1985)).

(b) *Unauthorised amendment*

The case of *London Joint Stock Bank v Macmillan and Arthur* (1918) established that a customer must draw cheques so as not to facilitate fraud. The same applies to CHAPS instructions. Therefore, the payer's bank is likely to be protected if the signature is genuine, but there had been an unauthorised amendment which was not apparent. This presumes that the customer's carelessness in completing the authority had facilitated the non-apparent alteration.

(c) *Instruction not signed as per mandate*

The bank is protected if the transfers are to meet genuine partnership/company liabilities (*B Liggett (Liverpool) Ltd* v *Barclays Bank Ltd* (1928)).

In other cases, the bank will have to refund (*Catlin* v *Cyprus Finance Corporation (London) Ltd* (1983)).

7.19.3 Position of CHAPS transfers under bank cash management systems

Most banks offer systems to major corporates whereby authorised officials of the corporate can initiate CHAPS transfers by use of desktop computers located in the office of the corporate. Whilst the systems vary, CHAPS transfers will usually be initiated by the corporate's bank, provided the correct pass-code is used.

It is easy to imagine how a dishonest employee of the corporate could ascertain the code-word and initiate fraudulent CHAPS transfers. Banks try and incorporate a clause in the agreement for the system which will make the customer responsible for all fraudulent CHAPS transfers initiated in this way; the clause must not contravene the Unfair Contract Terms Act 1977. However, competitive pressures mean that sometimes a bank will accept an agreement without such a clause, in which case the legal position for fraudulently initiated transfers is unclear.

7.20 What is meant by 'Truncation'?

Truncation is the method by which cheques, when paid into a bank for collection, physically proceed no further through the banking system. The details from the cheques are transmitted by means of special terminals to the banks concerned so that accounts can be debited and credited accordingly. Truncation is already in operation in several countries and has reduced substantially the costs incurred in collecting cheques.

7.20.1 What are the legal problems with truncation?

As cheques are not physically presented for payment when the truncation system is used, it would appear that s.45 Bills of Exchange Act 1882 is being breached.

Section 45 of the act states that a cheque must 'be duly presented for payment' and 'be presented at the proper place'. It must also be remembered that banks do not normally pay cheques, unless they are physically presented for payment. Thus, it must be considered dubious as to whether a bank can debit its customer's account when it has only received details of what is stated to be on a cheque.

It can therefore be seen that there is a need for new legislation to clarify the situation regarding truncation. This was recommended in the Jack Report on banking services in 1989. Until such legislation has appeared on the statute books, banks should only operate the truncation system with their customers' express agreement.

Summary

Now that you have read this unit, you should be able to:

☐ Appreciate the differences between various types of payment card.

☐ Recognise the liabilities which card issuers and card holders attract in the event of loss or misuse of a card.

☐ Identify the effects which the Consumer Credit Act has on payment cards.

☐ Illustrate how the credit transfer system operates.

☐ Recognise how problems surrounding the direct debit system can be solved.

☐ Explain the operation of CHAPS.

☐ Define truncation and explain the legal problems regarding its introduction.

If you can tick all the above boxes with confidence, you are ready to answer the questions which follow on pp. 87–89.

List of Cases

Barclays v *W J Simms, Son and Cooke (Southern) Ltd and W Sowman* (1979)

Catlin v *Cyprus Finance Corporation (London) Ltd* (1983)

Chambers v *Miller* (1862)

Cundy v *Lindsay* (1878)

Gibson v *Minet* (1791)

Kelly v *Solari* (1841)

B Liggett (Liverpool) Ltd v *Barclays Bank Ltd* (1928)

Lloyds Bank v *Waterhouse* (1990)

London Joint Stock Bank v *Macmillan and Arthur* (1918)

Momm and Ors v *Barclays Bank International* (1976)

National Westminster Bank v *Barclays Bank International* (1975)

Orr v *Union Bank of Scotland* (1854)

Re Charge Card Services (1988)

Royal Products Limited v *Midland Bank Limited* (1981)

Saunders v *Anglia Building Society* (1970)

Tai Hing Cotton Mills v *Liu Chong Hing Bank and Others* (1985)

List of Statutes

Bills of Exchange Act 1882

Cheques Act 1957

Consumer Credit Act 1974

Self-assessment Questions

Short-answer questions

1   Define the term 'payment card'.

2   What is meant by 'PIN'?

3   If there is a dispute which cannot be satisfactorily concluded between a bank and its customer over 'phantom' withdrawals using a cash card from the customer's account, to whom can the matter be referred?

4   Under what circumstances should a card holder contact a card issuer with regard to the use (or possible misuse) of a card?

5   Connected lender liability extends to credit cards. What are the merits of this for a card holder?

6   How long does it take for a credit transfer paid in at one bank to be credited to the account held at another bank?

7   What is CHAPS?

8   What is truncation?

(Answers are given in Appendix 2, p. 294)

Multiple-choice questions

1   Which type of card is subject to an annual fee and requires the full amount outstanding to be repaid in one instalment?

(a)   Credit card.
(b)   Debit card.
(c)   Charge card.

2   Card issuers will provide card holders with which of the following instructions concerning their PINs?

(a)   To allow third parties to use their cards and PINs.
(b)   To make all reasonable efforts to keep their PINs secret and their cards safe.
(c)   To keep their PINs and cards together.
(d)   Not to write down their PINs without disguising them.
(e)   Not to write down their PINs.

3   When a card is lost, stolen or misused the card issuer will be liable for the full losses under which of the following circumstances?

(a)   Where the card has not been received by the customer and is misused.
(b)   Whenever the card has been received by the customer and is misused.
(c)   For all unauthorised transactions.
(d)   For unauthorised transactions where the customer has advised the card issuer of possible misuse.
(e)   Where there is a machine or system breakdown which was not apparent to the customer.

4   Under CCA 1974, which of the following cards are considered to be credit tokens?

(a)   Credit cards.
(b)   Debit cards.
(c)   Cash cards.
(d)   Cheque guarantee cards.
(e)   Charge cards.

5   Funds were transferred from one account to another within the same branch. The following day it was discovered that the transfer had caused the payer's account to become overdrawn. The payee had not been advised of the transfer. Can the bank reverse the entries without the payee's agreement?

(a)   Yes
(b)   No

6   Which case confirms the answer in Q5?

(a)   *Gibson* v *Minet* (1791).
(b)   *Lloyds Bank* v *Waterhouse* (1990).
(c)   *Momm and Ors* v *Barclays Bank International* (1976).
(d)   *National Westminster Bank* v *Barclays Bank International* (1975).

(Answers are given in Appendix 2, p. 295)

Past examination question

You are the Manager of North Bank and have today received a telephone call from Mary West regarding a cash dispenser withdrawal of £60 debited to her account on 1 May. She cannot recall making any such withdrawal and, as she still has the cash dispenser card in her possession, she assumes that there must have been a mistake on the bank's part. She requests that the sum of £60 be recredited to her account.

Required:

State how you would react to Mary's request. Give reasons for your answer.

[5 marks]
(Spring 1991)

(Answer is given in Appendix 2, p. 295)

UNIT 8

Mock Examination

Answer all questions. Time allowed three hours plus 15 minutes' reading time.

1 Twelve months ago you opened a joint deposit account for Patricia Bradly and Peter Smith. The bank's usual form of mandate was signed, incorporating joint and several liability and instructions that withdrawals should only be allowed against the signatures of both parties. The account was opened with a transfer from Patricia Bradly's current account which was already maintained at your branch, and subsequently the only transactions have been credits, in the form of cash, received over the counter.

Miss Bradly explained, when the joint account was opened, that Mr Smith was her fiancé and that the deposit account was a 'savings' account to assist them to set up home when they married. You took no further reference on Mr Smith at that time.

Miss Bradly has now called to see you, and says that her engagement was broken off three months ago, that Peter Smith has now married somebody else, and she has lost contact with him. She says that all the funds in the joint account have been provided by herself, and she asks you to transfer the balance of £1,050 to her current account to enable her to issue a cheque to a travel agent, as she is taking a long holiday abroad to recover from her experience.

(a) How would you deal with her request? Give reasons for your answer.

[13 marks]

(b) Would your approach be different, if, when the account had been opened, you had omitted to take a mandate?

[4 marks]

(c) Would your approach be different if all the entries in the deposit account had been by way of internal transfer from Miss Bradly's current account?

[3 marks]
[Total 20 marks]
(Spring 1980)

2 (a) Mollie New has maintained a current account at your branch for several years. Unfortunately, you have to monitor her account closely due to her tendency to overdraw her account without arrangement. She has been advised that she must maintain her account in credit in future, otherwise her cheques will be returned unpaid.

Today's date is 11 January 1991. Your clerk refers Mollie New's current account to you and provides you with the following information:

Balance at close of business 10 January 1991 – Dr £75

The cheques which caused this debit balance were as follows:

Cheque number	Payee	Dated	Amount £
100278	B Raines	3 January 1990	35
100478	J Munro	7 May 1990	55
400110	P Knowles	3 January 1990	20
400111	N Price	4 January 1991	15
400112	C McCann	4 January 1991	40

(None of these cheques bear a cheque card number on the reverse.)

State which of the above cheques you would not pay, what reasons you would give on the cheques for non-payment, and what considerations you would have borne in mind in reaching your decision(s).

[10 marks]

(b) Ian Forest has operated a current account with you for many years. He calls to see you today and provides you with a list of cheques drawn on his account over the last two years.

He advises you that these cheques were not issued by him and therefore must bear a forged signature. Your clerk locates the most recent cheques, which were issued over two months ago. The signatures on them are very similar to Mr Forest's signature.

Mr Forest tells you that the person who has forged his signature is his wife, who died six weeks ago. He adds that he had known for some time that his wife had been forging cheques, but as he knew that 'a forged signature is no signature', he had not thought that the bank would pay them. He continues by saying that as he had not looked at a bank statement for years but had left them unopened in a box he had not been aware of the situation until now, when he had opened one of them. Having seen what had happened he had added up the amounts concerned and he reckoned that the bank had paid forged cheques totalling £7,678. He therefore asks you to arrange for this amount to be refunded to him as it was obviously the bank's error which had caused this problem.

What would be your response to this? Give reasons for your answer.

[10 marks]
[Total 20 marks]

3 (a) Mr Silver, a valued customer, calls to say that he is going abroad for three months, and that he wishes his son, John, to be able to operate his accounts should the need arise, whilst he is away. Mr Silver is a widower, and he says that John will continue to board at his local public school in his absence. Whilst John is unknown to you, you are aware that he is aged 15. How would you deal with Mr Silver's request? Give reasons for your answer.

[8 marks]

(b) George and Mary Ruskin have a joint account at your branch, operating under the bank's usual mandate form, incorporating joint and several liability, and authorising you to pay cheques on the signature of either. Recently Mary Ruskin drew a cheque for £960 in favour of a local furrier, but before it was presented you received a visit from George Ruskin who countermanded payment. He said that he was not going to allow his wife to buy a fur coat out of his earnings when other items were needed for the family. You duly returned the cheque with the answer 'payment stopped' when it was presented three days ago.

Today, Mary Ruskin calls to see you, in some distress. She says that there are disagreements over money, but that the funds in the account have all been provided by her and the cheque must be paid on re-presentation. The balance on the account is £1,908 credit.

How would you deal with this situation? Give reasons for your answer.

[12 marks]

[Total 20 marks]

(Spring 1981)

4 Avast plc issued a CHAPS payment instruction to its bank, Friendly Bank, to pay Duff Ltd £100,000. The instruction was transmitted from Avast plc's computer terminal to Friendly Bank's computer terminal in accordance with agreed arrangements between them. Friendly Bank immediately sent the necessary CHAPS payment instruction to Chum Bank for Duff Ltd's account.

One hour later Mr Block, Treasurer of Avast plc, telephoned Friendly Bank to say he had just discovered the payment instruction had been fraudulently given by a former accounts clerk who had been an authorised giver of CHAPS payment instructions for Avast plc until being transferred the week before to another department. Mr Block demanded that the payment instruction be revoked and that Avast plc's account should not be debited.

On contacting Chum Bank the same day, Friendly Bank learned that a petition for the winding up of Duff Ltd had just been served and Chum Bank felt unable to reverse the payment, even though it had not yet credited Duff Ltd's account.

(a) Can Avast plc insist on Mr Block's demands (i) for Friendly Bank to revoke the payment instruction and (ii) for Avast plc's account not to be debited?

[10 marks]

(b) Is Chum Bank obliged to credit Duff Ltd's account? (Assume that Duff Ltd's rights and obligations are the same whether or not a winding up order is made. Do NOT discuss the law of winding up.)

[10 marks]

[Total 20 marks]

(Law Relating to Banking Services – Spring 1991)

5   On 12 December 1989 a customer of your branch, Helen Barker, called in to say that her husband, Alan Barker, had just been admitted as a patient to a private local mental hospital for treatment. (Enquiries were made and this information was confirmed to be correct.) On that day the balance of Helen Barker's account was £1,117 credit and that of Alan Barker's account was £982 credit. Also Helen and Alan Barker had a joint deposit account, balance £3,000 credit.

Upon her request, the balance in Alan Barker's current account and the balance in the joint deposit account were transferred to a new account in Helen Barker's name, styled 'Helen Barker No.2. Account', which she said she would use to pay the hospital bills for her husband and to settle household accounts outstanding.

You were appointed Manager of the branch in March this year, following your predecessor's retirement, and today (14 May 1990) Alan Barker calls in, introduces himself and says that, although he has been ill, he is now fully fit again. He asks you to supply him with a new cheque book for his account and is astounded to learn that his account has been closed; you tell him of the transfer and also of the transfer of the joint account balance. Alan Barker reacts by saying that he intends to see his solicitors who, he adds, are now handling his divorce. He claims that the bank should not have dealt with the balance of the accounts as it did.

Required

Comment on the bank's position with reference to the actions it took at the time when Mr Barker was admitted to hospital. State how you will deal with the present situation. Give reasons for your answer.

[20 marks]

(Spring 1990)

(Answers are given in Appendix 2, pp. 295–99)

UNIT 9

Safe Custody; Purchase and Sale of Investments; Indemnities and Counter-indemnities

Objectives

- Recognise the procedures to be followed by banks regarding items held in safe custody.
- Ascertain the extent to which banks can give investment advice.
- Identify the procedures to be followed when buying or selling investments.
- Recognise the types of indemnity which a bank may be asked to give.
- Identify the benefits which a counter-indemnity provides for a bank.
- Identify those occasions when a bank may require an indemnity to be completed in its favour.

9.1 Safe Custody

Banks offer the service of keeping customers' property in safe custody. In such circumstances the customer is known as the *bailor* and the bank is known as the *bailee*. The bank only has a duty to its customer and therefore will only accept instructions from its customer as regards items held in safe custody, even if these items are in the name of a third party and that third party wishes to withdraw them, e.g. life policy.

Sometimes, a bailor will provide a third party with written authority to have access to safe custody items. In such circumstances, a bank official should be present when the items are examined and should ensure that no items are removed without the bailor's explicit instructions.

Upon the death of a sole bailor, probate must be produced before safe custody items can be released. The one exception to this is if the deceased's will is held in safe custody. This will be released to the executors (once they have been satisfactorily identified), as otherwise they will be unable to obtain probate. Sometimes you will receive requests for the removal of certain items for probate valuation purposes, e.g. stamp collections, paintings, jewellery. This cannot be allowed and any valuations for probate purposes should be carried out on the bank's premises, in the presence of at least one bank official. Obviously, once probate has been granted the executors can withdraw such items from the bank.

When items are lodged and held in joint names and one of these parties dies, the items do not automatically become the property of the surviving party. While items which are registered in joint names, e.g. deeds, can be safely released to the surviving party, the release of fine art, locked boxes or sealed envelopes may prove to be problematic. It is therefore common practice to take a receipt from both the survivor and the executor/administrator of the deceased's estate in order to obtain a good discharge.

If a bank receives notice of the beginning of bankruptcy proceedings against a bailor, no items held in safe custody should be released.

In the event that a bankruptcy order is made against one party to a joint account, items held in safe custody will require the authority of the other parties to the account, together with the authority of the trustee in bankruptcy.

As regards partnership property held in safe custody, where one partner is the subject of a bankruptcy order, the remaining partners can normally give a good discharge to the bank. Where there are any doubts concerning the ownership of the partnership property, reference should be made to the trustee in bankruptcy to see if the matter can be clarified. If this is not possible, reference should be made to the bank's legal department.

In the case of a receiver appointed by the Court of Protection when a customer has become mentally incapacitated, a bank must check the powers of the receiver as any order must cover the delivery of safe custody items. If it does not, the receiver will have to apply to the court for another order.

9.1.1 Night safe service

A particular type of safe custody concerns customers being able to deposit money for overnight safe keeping in a bank's night safe. The procedure involves the customer being issued with a wallet in which the cash will be placed and a key to that wallet. The customer will also be given a key to the night safe which is normally accessed through the outside wall of the bank. The customer will complete an agreement which will create a safe custody contract between the customer and the bank, with the customer undertaking to be responsible for any loss which should occur.

Any wallets deposited in the night safe will be removed by two bank officers the morning of the following business day, and they will be entered in a register. The customer or customer's named agent will collect the wallet, signing the bank's form as a receipt; the bank should ensure that the signature agrees with the specimen held. The customer can then either take the wallet away or pay the contents into an account.

There are other wallets available, to which the bank has a key in addition to the customer. This enables the bank to open the wallet when it is taken out of the night safe and to check the contents against the credit slip which would accompany the cash and cheques. They could then be credited to the customer's account. This process will normally be carried out in the presence of two bank officers. As with the aforementioned wallets, the customer or customer's named agent would call for the wallet and give the bank a receipt.

The night safe service is most often used by retail shop customers.

9.2 Investment Advice, Purchase and Sale

9.2.1 Investment advice

Investment advice comes in various packages. Most banks have an investment management service, which basically will look after a customer's investment requirements, tailoring a customer's portfolio to their individual needs. It will be particularly appealing to people who cannot devote sufficient time to deal with their investments, or who do not have the necessary expertise. The service allows customers to give the bank complete control of the investment portfolio without having to refer back to them should the bank wish to buy or sell certain investments. If a customer wishes to maintain some control over the portfolio this can also be accommodated. The bank, in these circumstances, would confer with the customer before any alteration in the constituents of the portfolio took place. The banks charge a fee for this service which will either be based upon the amount of work involved or alternatively the value of the investments. The service will normally be restricted to customers who have a minimum of £25,000 to invest.

Obviously, some customers will either not wish to avail themselves of a bank's investment management service or they may have smaller amounts to invest. If a bank is approached for advice in such circumstances, it will refer the customer to a stockbroker. Obviously, the stockbroker will require all pertinent details, e.g. the amount to be invested, individual requirements from investments, the tax position of customer, before giving any recommendation. Some banks have their own stockbroking arm.

Bank managers will not normally give particular investment advice. This is because should such advice prove to be negligent, then the bank could be held to be liable. Even if the person requiring the advice is a non-customer, the bank still owes a duty of care (*Woods* v *Martins Bank* (1958)).

9.2.2 Procedure to be followed when banks buy or sell investments for customers

(a) *Stocks and shares*

Banks will normally take a written instruction for the purchase or sale of stocks and shares.

This instruction will specify the following:

(i) The full name and type of stock to be purchased/sold, e.g. XYZ plc 50p ordinary shares.

(ii) The amount to be purchased/invested or sold, e.g. invest £1,000 in XYZ plc 50p ordinary shares; purchase 1,000 XYZ plc 50p ordinary shares.

(iii) Whether the purchase/sale is to be completed within a certain limit or whether it is to be completed 'at best'.

(iv) In respect of purchases, the name of the person in whose name the shares are to be registered should be given, and the customer should sign the instruction.

(v) In respect of sales, all registered holders of the stock to be sold must sign the instruction and also a Talisman transfer form where required for registered stock and gilts on the Bank of England register.

Whether buying or selling, the customer should indicate which account is to be debited or credited with the transaction. In respect of purchases, the customer should give instructions as to which account any dividends should be credited to. In respect of sales, the vendor should deposit the relevant share certificate with the bank for onward submission to the stockbroker.

When accepting instructions to buy shares, a bank must ensure that the customer has adequate funds to pay for the shares when called for. If there are any doubts, some banks insist that these funds be placed in a suspense account at the time that the deal is made. (Students should note that the stock exchange works on fortnightly account periods, with settlement being concluded ten days after the expiry of each period.)

(b) *Miscellaneous investments*
Some banks carry stocks of Premium Savings Bonds and National Savings Certificates, and will deal with the purchase and sale of these, charging a commission fee for this service. They will also deal with the purchase and sale of gilts on the Bank of England register or the National Savings Stock Register. These transactions regarding gilts are normally carried out by stockbrokers.

9.3 Indemnities/Counter-Indemnities

9.3.1 What is an indemnity?

An example of an indemnity is where a bank accepts primary liability in respect of a customer's obligations to a third party.

9.3.2 When will a bank be called upon to issue an indemnity?

This can happen in a wide variety of circumstances, some of which are mentioned below.

(a) *Bonds*
Industrial contractors will often be asked by customers such as local authorities or, if transacting business abroad, foreign governments, to provide bank indemnities, known as bonds, in respect of various facets of an agreed contract. Some examples of these are advance payment bonds, tender bonds, performance bonds and warranty bonds. If the contractor fails to meet contractual obligations, then the client can look to the bank for compensation under such a bond.

(b) *Lost bills of lading*
When goods are sent by sea, the documents of title to the goods will normally be represented by bills of lading. These will be issued to the exporter who, having endorsed them in blank, will forward them either directly or indirectly (where the banking system is used) to the importer. In order to obtain the goods the importer must produce a bill of lading. If such bills of lading have been lost in transit then the importer has obvious problems. These can be alleviated if the importer's bank is willing to issue an indemnity in favour of the shipping company, which

would cover the release of the goods without production of a bill of lading.

(c) *Lost share certificates*

Shareholders often mislay/lose share certificates and then require a duplicate. Registrars will only comply with such a request where a shareholder is able to obtain an indemnity from a respectable financial institution in favour of the registrar.

Student Activity 1

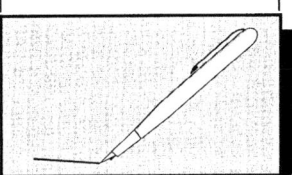

Check your branch records and identify the reasons why your bank has given indemnities recently.

9.3.3 If a claim is made against the bank under an indemnity, who will it look to for recompense?

When a bank agrees to give an indemnity it will only do so if it considers its customer good for that amount. It will also take a counter-indemnity from the customer which will stipulate that should the bank receive a claim under the indemnity then it can immediately debit its customer's account. Additional clauses will also give the bank an immediate right of set-off between accounts and a lien over items which are held by the bank, including those held in safe custody. It must be remembered that indemnities can be conditional (upon proof of loss being provided) or unconditional (where a bank would have to pay up immediately, without any reason needing to be given).

9.3.4 What procedure should a bank follow if called upon to issue an indemnity?

(a) Examine the indemnity to ascertain the maximum liability and whether it is conditional or unconditional.

(b) Ensure that the customer is considered good for the liability.

(c) Ascertain whether additional security will be required in support of the counter-indemnity.

(d) Have the indemnity signed on behalf of the bank by Head Office or Regional Office.

(e) Contact the customer to call at branch to sign the counter-indemnity (normally supplied by Head Office or Regional Office). These counter-indemnities may be either specific or general. In the case of limited companies, ensure that they are allowed under their constitution to give counter-indemnities.

(f) Once the counter-indemnity has been signed, the indemnity can be given to the customer or forwarded to the beneficiary.

(g) Any charge for the giving of the indemnity will now be debited to the customer's account.

9.3.5　When might a bank ask for an indemnity to be issued in its favour?

The most likely circumstance would be in the event of one of its customers dying and the deceased's estate being valued at under £5,000. In accordance with the Administration of Estates (Small Payments) Amendment Act 1976 and the Increase of Limit Order 1984, banks are authorised to release amounts, where the estate is valued at less than £5,000, to the next of kin without the production of letters of administration or grant of probate. In such cases, the bank will need to see a copy of the death certificate and will have to identify the next of kin. The next of kin will also have to complete an indemnity before any monies can be released. This will state that this person will obtain a grant of probate or letters of administration if asked to do so by the bank. In addition, it will contain an undertaking from the next of kin to pay over any sum in respect of a subsequent claim which the bank may receive pertaining to the balance of the deceased's account and also to reimburse any costs incurred by the bank.

Another instance when a bank may request an indemnity to be completed would be if it was requested to issue a duplicate bank draft. This again would protect the bank if, for example, a holder in due course presented the original bank draft for payment. In such circumstances, the bank would be able to make an immediate claim against its customer.

Student Activity 2

Have any of your branch's customers given an indemnity in your bank's favour recently? If so, what were the circumstances?

Summary

Now that you have read this unit, you should be able to:

☐ Recognise the procedures to be followed by banks regarding items held in safe custody.

☐ Ascertain the extent to which banks can give investment advice.

☐ Identify the procedures to be followed when buying or selling investments.

☐ Recognise the types of indemnity which a bank may be asked to give.

☐ Identify the benefits which a counter-indemnity provides for a bank.

☐ Identify those occasions when a bank may require an indemnity to be completed in its favour.

If you can tick all the above boxes with confidence, you are ready to answer the questions which follow on pp. 101–03.

List of Cases

Woods v *Martins Bank* (1958)

List of Statutes

Administration of Estates (Small Payments) Amendment Act 1976

Increase of Limit Order 1984

Self-assessment Questions

Short-answer questions

1   George Apple, a customer of your branch, deposits an unsealed envelope in safe custody with you which is marked 'share certificates in the name of James Pear.'

Several months later, a stranger who identifies himself as James Pear and shows you his passport asks for this envelope to be given to him as he has arranged to sell them through his stockbroker. Would you comply with his request?

2   Where items are lodged in joint names in safe custody and one party dies, who will normally complete the form of receipt before the bank releases them?

3   Your customer, Ian McFee, advises you that he has been left £10,000 in his aunt's will. He has no investment knowledge and does not want to be bothered with dealing with his legacy's investment but would prefer to be guided by 'experts'. Given this information, do you think that Mr McFee could benefit from your bank's investment management service?

(Answers are given in Appendix 2, p. 299)

Multiple-choice questions

1   Which of the following could be released from safe custody to an executor of a deceased customer prior to the grant of probate or issue of letters of administration, assuming that the executor could produce proof of identity?

(a)   A life policy taken out on the life of the deceased.
(b)   A will of the deceased.
(c)   A locked deed-box.
(d)   A coin collection.

2   If a customer uses a bank's night safe service, what banker–customer relationship is established initially?

(a)   Bailor–bailee.
(b)   Debtor–creditor.
(c)   Mortgagor–mortgagee.

3 A bank owes a duty of care to a non-customer if it gives investment advice. This was confirmed in which case?

(a) *Ladbroke* v *Todd* (1914).
(b) *Prosperity* v *Lloyds Bank* (1923).
(c) *Joachimson* v *Swiss Bank Corporation* (1921).
(d) *Woods* v *Martins Bank* (1958).

4 Under which of the following circumstances would a bank require an indemnity, rather than a counter-indemnity?

(a) Where it issues a duplicate bank draft.
(b) Where bills of lading are missing.
(c) Where it releases the balance of a deceased customer's account to an executor/administrator without production of a grant of probate/letters of administration, because the value of the deceased's estate is less than £5,000.

(Answers are given in Appendix 2, p. 299)

Past examination questions

1 Your customer, Norman Dorrington, left a locked tin box at your branch for safe custody last year. He is a director of a local engineering company which banks with you, and his personal secretary frequently visits the bank on company business. Last month, Mr Dorrington asked his secretary, when in the bank, to list the contents of the box and he sent a letter to the bank authorising her to have access to it.

Mr Dorrington has now called at the bank to examine his box and in some concern he says to you, the manager, that a valuable gold bracelet is missing and that his secretary must have removed it. He says that his secretary resigned three weeks ago, and that he is no longer in touch with her. Mr Dorrington claims that the bank has quite obviously been negligent and that it is accordingly liable for restitution and damages.

Required:

State your views on Mr Dorrington's claim and the aspects which you would consider in dealing with it.

[10 marks]

(Autumn 1988)

2 You have at your branch the account of William Cowper. Today, with credit balances of £196 on his current account and £4,250 on his high interest cheque account, you receive a visit from his daughter, Mrs Browning. She tells you that her father died last week in hospital.

Mrs Browning informs you that there is no will and that she is the sole surviving relative, her mother having died several years earlier. Also, since her father's only assets are the deposits at your branch, she has been advised by a solicitor that she need not take out letters of administration. She therefore asks you to transfer the balances of her late father's account to her own account, which you establish is maintained at a local branch of your bank.

SAFE CUSTODY; PURCHASE AND SALE OF INVESTMENTS

Required:

State, with reasons, how you would react to this approach and, if you are prepared to release the funds, the steps you would take to ensure the bank is fully protected.

[10 marks]

(Autumn 1991)

(Answers are given in Appendix 2, pp. 300–01)

UNIT 10

Set Off; Garnishees; Mareva Injunctions; Writs of Sequestration

Objectives

- Define set off.
- Recognise those conditions which must exist for set off to apply.
- Ascertain the difference in procedures for a garnishee summons and a garnishee order.
- Differentiate between garnishees, Mareva injunctions and writs of sequestration.

10.1 Set Off

Set off is where a debtor or that person's creditor wishes to ascertain the net position which exists between them. For example, if Perry owes Wood £10,000 and then Wood buys an antique table from Perry for £2,000, Wood could set off the two amounts, arriving at a net sum of £8,000, rather than paying in cash for the table separately.

10.1.1 Conditions which must exist for set off to take place (confirmed in *Garnett* v *McKewan* (1872))

The sums must be

(a) Certain and clearly ascertained.

(b) Due between the same parties.

(c) Due in the same right, e.g. where a customer has a number of private accounts and no element of trust is indicated on any of them.

10.1.2 Situations where automatic set off applies

An automatic right of set off exists in the following circumstances:

(a) Notice of death of a customer.

(b) Notice of mental incapacity of a customer.

(c) Notice of a bankruptcy order against a customer.

(d) Liquidation of a company customer beginning. This was confirmed in *National Westminster Bank Ltd* v *Halesowen Presswork and Assemblies Ltd* (1972).

10.1.3 Loan accounts and set off

Except where automatic set off applies, a bank cannot set off a loan account and a credit balance on current account unless repayments are not up to date (*Bradford Old Bank Ltd* v *Sutcliffe* (1918)).

10.1.4 Important cases

(a) *Barclays Bank Ltd* v *Quistclose Investments Ltd* (1968)

The company owed money to Barclays Bank. It had insufficient funds to pay its dividend, so it borrowed funds for this purpose from another bank and placed them on a separate account with Barclays Bank. The company was put into liquidation before the dividend could be paid. Barclays were aware of the purpose of the dividend account, but sought to set off this credit balance against the company's borrowing. It was held that where a loan has been made for a specific purpose, and this purpose fails, the money will be held on resulting trust for the lender and will not form part of the assets of the company. This presumes that the person or bank holding the funds is aware of the trust.

(b) *Re Unit 2 Windows Ltd* (1985)

Where there is no guidance to the contrary, a credit balance must be set off pro rata against preferential and non-preferential claims. (To avoid this occurring, a completed letter of set off would clarify the situation and would place the bank in a strong position.)

(c) *Garnett* v *McKewan* (1872)

This case established that accounts at different branches could be set off. This was confirmed in *Barclays Bank Ltd* v *Okenarhe* (1966).

(d) *Buckingham and Co* v *London and Midland Bank Ltd* (1895)

A loan had been granted to a customer against the security of a mortgage over the customer's house. The loan account repayments were kept up to date but, upon reviewing the security held, the branch manager felt that the lending was at risk. He therefore appropriated the credit balance on current account in reduction of the loan account and closed the current account, advising his customer accordingly. The customer advised the bank that there were cheques outstanding but the bank dishonoured them. The customer sued the bank and the court held that 'reasonable notice' should have been given prior to action being taken, and awarded damages for wrongful dishonour.

(e) *Re K* (1990)

This case confirmed that a bank can exercise its right of set off where a restraining order under s.8 of the Drug Trafficking Offences Act 1986 has been issued. The court did, however, state that it would be prudent for a bank to apply for a variation to the restraint order, prior to setting off accounts subject to the order.

(f) *Re Norman Holding Co Ltd* (1990)

In the event of the liquidation of a limited company, a creditor must set off any monies owing to the company when proving in the liquidation for an unsecured debt. However, where that creditor has a secured debt, the principles of set off need not be applied against that debt unless the creditor also wishes to prove for that debt in the liquidation.

10.2 Garnishee Orders and Summonses

Garnishment is whereby a judgment creditor can take control of funds held by a third party who owes these funds to the judgment debtor. Thus, if Smith (the judgment creditor) obtains judgment against Jones (the judgment debtor) he can apply for a garnishee which can be served on the bankers of Jones in order to recover the debt from the balances on his bank account.

Garnishees can be granted in the county court or the High Court. In the county court they are known as *garnishee summonses*, and in the High Court as *garnishee orders*.

If a garnishee summons is served on a bank, then all monies attached thereto can be paid to the court immediately. However, garnishee orders are different from garnishee summonses, in that there are two separate stages to them.

The first stage, garnishee order *nisi,* is a holding measure whereby debts due to a judgment debtor by a garnishee (the bank) are frozen pending further court proceedings. When these proceedings have been heard it is only then that the garnishee will become a garnishee order absolute, unless proceedings are dismissed, in which case the funds will become unfrozen.

Upon a garnishee order becoming absolute, funds can be paid over to the court by the bank, but not before that event.

Garnishee orders or summonses can be served upon both the head office and the branch of the bank concerned and will only affect those funds which were due or accruing due at the time that the garnishee was served. Obviously some short time may elapse before the head office and branch liaise with each other, particularly where a branch has not been specifically named in a garnishee served on a bank's head office. In such cases, the courts will normally allow a reasonable time for research and liaison to take place.

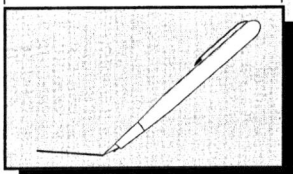

Student Activity 1

Examine your bank's internal rules regarding the procedure to be followed upon receipt of a garnishee order or summons. Compare this procedure with the following sections.

10.2.1 Procedure upon receipt of a garnishee for a limited amount

When an account is overdrawn, no funds are attached under the garnishee and the account can therefore continue as before. The bank will, however, contact its customer to discover the circumstances surrounding the judgment.

Where an account is in credit and the order is for a limited amount, the amount stated in the garnishee or the balance of the account, whichever is the smaller, should be placed in a suspense account. These funds will normally be cleared monies unless the customer has expressed or implied (by practice) permission to draw against uncleared effects, in which case uncleared monies will also be attached. This was confirmed in *Fern v Bishop Burns* (1980), *Jones and Co* v *Coventry* (1909), *A L Underwood Limited* v *Barclays Bank*

(1924). Where these funds are attached by a garnishee summons, they should be forwarded via the bank's solicitors to the court.

Where they are attached by a garnishee order *nisi*, the bank's solicitors will be instructed to attend the hearing for the garnishee order absolute after which, if the order absolute is granted, the funds will be forwarded to the court again via the bank's solicitors.

Any cheques received in the branch at the time that the garnishee is served should be returned marked 'Funds attached by garnishee order' or 'Refer to drawer', unless the fate of the cheque has already been communicated as 'paid' to interested parties. Where cheques bear cheque card numbers it is likely that they have been 'constructively paid', although there is no case law to support this at present.

10.2.2   Procedure upon receipt of a garnishee for an unlimited amount

When a bank receives an unlimited garnishee order or summons, the customer's cleared credit balance must be frozen, even when this exceeds the judgment debt stated in the document. Such action will normally necessitate a new account being opened for the customer. The customer, as usual, will be informed of the receipt of the garnishee and will be asked for an update of the situation.

10.2.3   Accounts and proceeds which are affected by receipt of a garnishee order or summons

In *Hirschorn* v *Evans* (1938) it was established that any balance held in joint names will not be attached where the garnishee summons or order is in the name of only one judgment debtor.

Where the order or summons is in two names, then not only will accounts designated in the joint names be attached, but also accounts in the judgment debtors' sole names.

Trust accounts, e.g. A Smith re Master R Smith, and accounts such as clients' accounts for estate agents and solicitors, will initially be attached (*Plunkett* v *Barclays Bank* (1936)), although once the court is satisfied as to the trust element of the funds they will normally be released.

Choice Investments Ltd v *Jeromnimon; Midland Bank Garnishee* (1980), confirmed that cleared balances held on foreign currency accounts were attachable. Upon receipt of an order or summons, the bank will calculate what the sterling equivalent of the foreign currency is and will advise the court accordingly. The bank will not be held responsible for any adverse exchange rate movement between the time of this advice and the garnishee order becoming absolute.

Any cleared funds in the bank's hands at the time of the garnishee are attached, even if they have not been placed to the credit of the account. This includes bank giro credits paid into another branch of the bank.

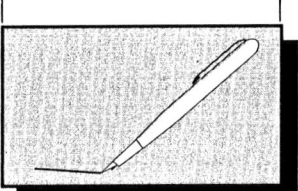

Student Activity 2

Check the procedure which your bank follows upon receipt of a Mareva injunction. Compare this procedure with the section which follows.

10.3 Mareva Injunctions

Mareva injunctions prevent persons, against whom court proceedings have been taken, from moving their assets around prior to the court hearing and decision.

Upon receipt of notice of an injunction, which will be issued by the High Court, the bank should freeze the account named and should not allow any dissipation of assets, including those held in safe custody. Such assets should remain frozen until a further court order is received releasing the assets. It must be remembered that both cleared and uncleared balances on an account are frozen by the injunction, even if the customer is not allowed to draw against uncleared effects.

Any cheques which are returned must be marked 'Refer to drawer–injunction served'. The bank can still honour cheques supported by a cheque card and any transactions which involve the bank's guarantee, e.g. letters of credit, share purchases, and were entered into prior to receipt of the injunction.

Before making any payment to the Court, the bank can set off all contingent liabilities, including guarantees given by the customer in respect of borrowings by other customers of the bank, against the credit balance.

Mareva injunctions are a continuing area of legal change and students should monitor any recent changes.

'Perkins, I don't think you quite understood when I said that we would have to freeze Mr Sherman's assets?'

10.4 Writ of Sequestration

The most celebrated writ of sequestration in recent years was the one served on the National Union of Mineworkers during the strike in the mid-1980s.

A writ of sequestration is a court order appointing usually an accountant or lawyer as sequestrator. This sequestrator can seize and control the assets of a party.

This can obviously affect banks. Upon hearing of a writ being issued against a customer, a bank should freeze that customer's account up to any limit mentioned, and such an order will also affect any items held in safe custody or as security.

The bank will need to work closely with the sequestrator, and disclosure of its customer's affairs is not considered to be a breach of the banker's duty of secrecy.

The bank can release funds from the account and assets to the sequestrator, against the sequestrator's receipt.

Occasionally, the customer is allowed to carry out certain transactions. In such circumstances when a bank has a number of cheques presented for payment and it is not sure whether these cheques are permissible, it can either refer the matter to the sequestrator or return the cheques marked 'Writ of sequestration obtained. Written confirmation of sequestration commissioners required'.

Summary

Now that you have read this unit, you should be able to:

- [ ] Define set off.

- [ ] Recognise those conditions which must exist for set off to apply.

- [ ] Ascertain the difference in procedures for a garnishee summons and a garnishee order.

- [ ] Differentiate between garnishees, Mareva injunctions and writs of sequestration.

If you can tick all the above boxes with confidence, you are ready to answer the questions which follow on pp. 111–14.

List of Cases

Barclays Bank Ltd v *Okenarhe* (1966)

Barclays Bank Ltd v *Quistclose Investments Ltd* (1968)

Bradford Old Bank Ltd v *Sutcliffe* (1918)

Buckingham and Co v *London and Midland Bank Ltd* (1895)

Choice Investments Ltd v *Jeromnimon; Midland Bank Garnishee* (1980)

Fern v *Bishop Burns* (1980)

Garnett v *McKewan* (1872)

Hirschorn v *Evans* (1938)

Jones and Co v *Coventry* (1909)

National Westminster Bank Ltd v *Halesowen Presswork and Assemblies Ltd* (1972)

Plunkett v *Barclays Bank* (1936)

Re K (1990)

Re Norman Holding Co Ltd (1990)

Re Unit 2 Windows Ltd (1985)

A L Underwood Limited v *Barclays Bank* (1924)

List of Statutes

Drug Trafficking Offences Act 1986

Self-assessment Questions

Short-answer questions

1 What conditions must exist for set off to take place?

2 Which case confirmed that a bank has an automatic right of set off when a company customer entered liquidation?

3 Which type of garnishee is granted by the county court?

4 If a garnishee summons is served on a bank, when should any monies attached be paid to the court?

5 A garnishee order/summons can be served upon both the head office of the bank concerned and at the branch where the judgment debtor's account is believed to be held. Why should a judgment creditor bother to have a garnishee served on a bank's head office?

6 Which case confirmed that cleared balances on a foreign currency account were attachable if a garnishee was served upon a bank?

7 What is the purpose of a Mareva injunction?

8 If a writ of sequestration is served on a bank's customer, the bank can only release funds held on the customer's account to whom?

(Answers are given in Appendix 2, p. 301)

Multiple-choice questions

1 In which of the following circumstances does an automatic right of set off apply?

(a) Notice of death of a customer.
(b) Notice of mental incapacity of a customer.
(c) Notice of bankruptcy of a customer.

2 Which case confirmed that, except in the case of an automatic right of set off, a bank cannot set off a loan account and a credit balance on a current account unless repayments are not up to date?

(a) *Garnett* v *McKewan* (1872).
(b) *Re K* (1990).
(c) *Bradford Old Bank Ltd* v *Sutcliffe* (1918).

3 Which case established that, where there was no agreement to the contrary, a credit balance must be set off pro rata against preferential and non-preferential debts?

(a) *Barclays Bank Ltd* v *Okenarhe* (1966).
(b) *Re Unit 2 Windows Ltd* (1985).
(c) *Re K* (1990).

4 Which case confirmed that a bank can exercise its right of set off where a restraining order under the Drug Trafficking Offences Act 1986 has been issued?

(a) *Buckingham and Co* v *London and Midland Bank Ltd* (1895).
(b) *Re K* (1990).
(c) *Re Norman Holding Co Ltd* (1990).

5 A garnishee will normally attach cleared monies. It will only attach uncleared effects if the customer has expressed or implied permission to draw against them. Which case confirmed this?

(a) *Fern* v *Bishop Burns* (1980).
(b) *Jones and Co* v *Coventry* (1909).
(c) *A L Underwood Limited* v *Barclays Bank* (1924).

6 A garnishee summons in the name of Alan Bream has been served on your branch. All the accounts with which Alan Bream is associated have cleared credit balances. The garnishee is limited to £5,000. Which of the following accounts would be attached?

(a) A and Mrs J Bream current account Cr £150.
(b) A Bream current account Cr £200.
(c) A Bream trading as Freewater Supplies Cr £2,500.
(d) Angling Trippers Cr £1,000 (partners: A Bream, B Carp and C Dace).

7 A Mareva injunction freezes which of the following?

(a) Cleared balances only.
(b) Uncleared balances only.
(c) Cleared and uncleared balances.

(d) Cleared and uncleared balances, but only for the latter when a customer has been given express or implied consent to draw against uncleared effects.

8 Where a writ of sequestration has been served upon a bank's customer, but that customer has been given leave to carry out certain transactions by the court or sequestrator, and the bank has several cheques presented for payment but it is unsure which cheques relate to the allowable transactions, it could:

(a) Refer the cheques to the sequestrator and act upon his instructions?
(b) Pay all the cheques without reference to the sequestrator?
(c) Return the cheques marked 'Writ of sequestration obtained. Written confirmation of sequestration commissioners required.'?

(Answers are given in Appendix 2, p. 301)

Past examination questions

1 Your customer, Kitchens Limited, has current account borrowing facilities of £40,000 against the security of deeds worth £70,000. The directors call to say that the company is experiencing trading difficulties but that they have taken steps to correct matters and hope to survive. They say that in case their efforts should not succeed, and in case the company is forced into liquidation, they wish to ensure that moneys paid to them by customers as deposits on orders for fitted kitchens should be capable of being returned to the customer. They say that they wish to open a deposit account in the name of the company for this purpose, and that they will make transfers to the company's current account as and when orders are fulfilled.

Required

State the reasons for the directors' request. Explain how you would deal with their wishes, giving reasons for your answer.

[17 marks]

(Spring 1988)

2 Robert Pearson and his wife, Thelma Pearson, are estate agents and your branch holds their business and private accounts.

As at the close of business last night, the balances of these accounts were:

Pearsons – (Robert Pearson and Thelma Pearson so trading)
Current account

Ledger balance	Cr £718.42
Cleared balance	Cr £718.42

Pearsons – (Robert Pearson and Thelma Pearson so trading)
Clients' account
Current account:

Ledger balance	Cr £6,488.66
Cleared balance	Cr £3,216.84

Robert Pearson and Thelma Pearson
Current account:

Ledger balance	Cr £411.11
Cleared balance	Dr £206.11

Robert Pearson No.1 Account
Current account:

Ledger balance	Cr £1,210.15
Cleared balance	Cr £1,210.15

Robert Pearson No.2 Account
Current account:

Ledger balance	Dr £800.72
Cleared balance	Dr £800.72

Thelma Pearson
Current account:

Ledger balance	Dr £48.98
Cleared balance	Dr £48.98

Robert and Thelma Pearson
Dollar deposit account:

Ledger balance	Cr $1,500
Cleared balance	Cr $1,500

Thelma Pearson re Kim Pearson
Deposit account:

Ledger balance	Cr £129.19
Cleared balance	Cr £129.19

At 9.30am this morning your branch was served with an unlimited garnishee order. This named Alan Cole and Sons as judgment creditors for £9,711.72 and costs. The judgment debtors are named as Robert Pearson and Thelma Pearson.

Required

State what action you would take in respect of each account. Give reasons for your answer.

[17 marks]

(Autumn 1990)

(Answers are given in Appendix 2, pp. 302–03)

UNIT 11

Limited Companies

Objectives

- Differentiate between private and public limited companies.
- Recognise the effect which the Companies Act 1989 has had on bank procedures when dealing with company customers.
- Be able to follow the procedure for opening a company account.
- Recognise the procedure to be followed when there is a dispute between directors.
- Identify the exceptions to the rules that companies cannot give financial assistance for the purchase of their own shares or to directors and connected persons.
- Recognise the procedures to be followed where directors are interested parties in the giving of company security.

11.1 Limited Companies

11.1.1 Definition

Limited companies are considered in law as separate legal entities from their members (*Salomon* v *Salomon & Co Ltd* (1897)). Although there are some companies which are limited by guarantee, and a few statutory companies which have been created by Acts of Parliament, the most common companies are public and private companies. Their constitution and operations are in the main governed by the Companies Act 1985 as amended by the Companies Act 1989.

11.1.2 What is a public limited company?

The Companies Act 1985 defines a public limited company as one which:

(a) is limited by shares;

(b) is identified as a public company in its memorandum of association;

(c) has a minimum of two shareholders;

(d) ends its name with 'Plc' or 'Public Ltd Co', or the Welsh equivalent if its registered office is in Wales;

(e) has a minimum authorised and issued share capital of £50,000;

(f) has been correctly registered or re-registered as a public limited company.

11.1.3 What is a private limited company?

Any company which does not meet the above criteria is a private limited company (s.1(4) Companies Act 1985).

11.1.4 What are the differences between a private and a public limited company?

A private company:

(a) cannot offer its shares or debentures to the public, whereas a public company can;

(b) is not subject to the £50,000 minimum capital rule. It need only have a minimum issued share capital of £2;

(c) will have the word 'Limited' or 'Ltd' after its name;

(d) need have only one director, provided that person is not also the company secretary. A public company must have a minimum of two directors;

(e) can restrict the transfer of its shares in its articles. A public company cannot restrict the transferability of its shares;

(f) can have one member.

11.2 What are a Company's Memorandum and Articles of Association?

A limited company is set up by following a certain procedure as laid down in the Companies Act 1985. The initial step is to draw up the company's memorandum and articles of association.

11.2.1 Memorandum of association

This is a statement of the powers and constitution of the company. It contains six major clauses:

(a) A statement quoting the full name of the company.

(b) Details of the domicile of the company's registered office, i.e. whether it is in England, Wales or Scotland.

(c) A clause itemising the powers and the objects of the company.

(d) A statement that the liability of the members is limited to the amount unpaid on the shares. Thus the shareholder only has personal liability with partly paid shares.

(e) A statement of the maximum amount of share capital that the company can currently issue (its authorised capital).

(f) The association clause which gives details of the original shareholders.

11.2.2 Articles of association

These cover the following matters:

(a) The powers of the directors.
(b) The issue and transfer of shares.
(c) The rights of shareholders.
(d) The conduct of meetings.
(e) The appointment of directors.
(f) The retirement of directors.
(g) The disqualification and removal of directors.
(h) The accounts of the company.
(i) The winding up of the company.

Instead of drawing up their own articles, many companies adopt the model articles encompassed in the Companies Act which was law when they were incorporated.

11.3 How is a Limited Company Set Up?

As stated previously, a company is set up by following a procedure as laid down in the Companies Act 1985.

(a) The memorandum of association and the articles of association must be drawn up.

(b) These will be filed with the registrar of companies, who will ensure that they meet the criteria laid down in the Companies Act. The company also has to file details of the first directors and secretary of the company, in addition to a statutory declaration issued by the company's solicitor that all the legal requirements have been met.

(c) The registrar will then issue a certificate of incorporation, provided that everything is in order. Upon receipt of this certificate a private company can begin trading. However, for a public company, a director or secretary must make a statutory declaration that the £50,000 minimum share capital has been raised.

(d) The registrar will then issue a trading certificate to the public limited company. Upon receipt of this the public limited company may commence trading.

11.3.1 If a limited company begins to trade prior to receiving its certificate of incorporation, is a transaction carried out at that time binding on the company?

As it did not legally exist at that time, the company cannot be held liable on any transactions. However, under s.35 Companies Act 1985, the directors of the company would be personally liable for such transactions.

11.3.2 What is the position if a public limited company commences trading after receipt of its certificate of incorporation, but before receipt of its trading certificate?

Any transactions entered into under the above circumstances would not be void. If the company failed to meet its obligation within 21 days of being asked to do so in writing, then the directors become personally liable for any losses suffered by the other party to the transaction.

11.4 The Companies Act 1989 and *Ultra Vires*

The memorandum of association contains the objectives and powers of the company, and the articles of association detail the powers of the directors. If the company or the directors acted outside the limitations of these powers they would be said to be acting *ultra vires,* i.e. beyond their powers. Before the 1989 Companies Act became law, such *ultra vires* acts could have been void.

The 1989 Companies Act has provided a new section 3A for the 1985 Companies Act which enables a company to adopt an objects clause which states that its object is 'to carry on business as a general commercial company'. This basically gives companies freedom to do anything which contributes to the running of the business. This therefore removes the problems with *ultra vires* acts for companies which have adopted this objects clause.

11.4.1 The Companies Act 1989 and the memorandum and articles of association

The 1989 Companies Act has substituted a new section 35 in the 1985 Companies Act. The important extracts from this section are as follows:

Section 35 (1)

> The validity of an act done by a company shall not be called into question on the ground of lack of capacity by reason of anything in the company's memorandum.

Section 35 (a) (1)

> In favour of a person dealing with a company in good faith, the power of the board of directors to find the company, or authorise others to do so, shall be deemed to be free of any limitation under the company's constitution.

Section 35 (b) (1)

> A party to a transaction with a company is not bound to enquire as to whether it is permitted by the company's memorandum or as to any limitation on the powers of the board of directors to bind the company or authorise others to do so.

These clauses are of particular interest to banks when they are lending to companies and taking security. They basically mean that a bank need not examine a company's memorandum and articles of association when lending to a company, as such lending (and any security given in support of that lending) will be valid providing that there is commercial justification and that there are no statutory prohibitions e.g. ss.151–8 Companies Act 1985 (see later).

Prior to these clauses becoming law, banks used to ask for a copy of the memorandum and articles of association of a company when that company opened an account. Banks can now dispense with this request.

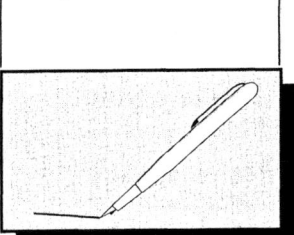

Student Activity 1

Check whether your bank still requires companies to produce their memorandum and articles of association when they open their accounts, or at other times.

11.5 Opening a Company Account

(a) Carry out normal reference procedures on the company and its directors, unless they are already known to the bank.

(b) Obtain sight of the company's certificate of incorporation. The name, number and date of incorporation should be noted in the bank's records. If the company is a public limited company then the bank should also see the company's trading certificate.

(c) If the company is to be newly incorporated then the bank can open an account for the company prior to incorporation. However, only credits for the purchase of the new shares can be credited to the account, and no disbursements can be allowed until incorporation formalities have been completed.

(d) The bank will arrange for the company to pass a resolution appointing the bank as its bankers, and also for completion of the standard bank mandate form. This will contain details of authorised signatories on the account and will contain an undertaking by the company to advise the bank of any changes in directors and authorised signatories. It will also contain an undertaking to supply the bank with a copy of the annual accounts each year.

(e) Take an authority from the company to divulge information to its auditors.

(f) Agree commission and interest rates to be applied to the account.

(g) Order cheque and paying-in books.

(h) Fix frequency of statements.

11.6 Groups of Companies

It often occurs that companies form trading groups for commercial benefits. This will sometimes result in a structure whereby there will be a parent company, also known as a holding company, and several subsidiary companies.

Section 36 Companies Act 1985 as amended by Companies Act 1989 states that a company will be a subsidiary company of a holding company if:

(a) the latter holds the majority of the voting rights in the former; or

(b) the latter is a member of the former and in addition has the right by voting control to remove or appoint a majority of its board of directors; or

(c) the latter is a member of the former and controls a majority of the voting rights, pursuant to an agreement with other members or shareholders; or

(d) it is a subsidiary of a company which is itself a subsidiary of the other company.

Banks recognise the existence of groups of companies, and this will include special group charging procedures and taking inter-company security such as cross-guarantees.

When a company gives security there must exist commercial justification for it being given. This was established in the case of *Charterbridge Corporation Ltd* v *Lloyds Bank Ltd* (1969). Commercial justification is where some benefit accrues to the company concerned. This could arise out of some trading relationship, as with groups of companies, or could be as a result of the company's commercial interest.

As mentioned above, one of the main types of security offered by company groups are cross-guarantees, i.e. where each member company of the group guarantees the liabilities of other member companies of the group. Sometimes, however, companies are either unwilling or unable to give guarantees, and instead offer a letter of comfort. A letter of comfort is basically a promise to be liable for another's debts. The problem from a bank's point of view is that they are often considered to be only moral promises and not legally binding, as was the situation in *Kleinwort Benson Ltd* v *Malaysia Mining Corporation Berhad* (1988). Thus, banks must ensure when accepting a letter of comfort that it depicts an intention to create a legal obligation, and that consideration is evident, e.g. the granting of a loan. This was confirmed in *Chemco Leasing S.p.A* v *Rediffusion Ltd* (1987).

11.7 Collecting Cheques for Limited Company Accounts

As with private individuals, banks have to take care when collecting cheques for limited company accounts. Failure to do so can render banks liable for conversion. It seems at times that banks lose sight of the fact that limited companies are separate legal entities, and this can often cause problems.

It is very unusual for a bank to collect cheques which are payable to one limited company for the account of another limited company, even where the cheque has been properly endorsed. One occasion when this might happen is when a cheque payable to a subsidiary company in a group of companies is presented for collection for credit to another member company of the same group. In such an instance the bank should make reasonable enquiries and receive acceptable answers before agreeing to the collection (*London and Montrose Shipbuilding and Repairing Co Ltd* v *Barclays Bank Ltd* (1926). If such occurrences are likely to happen in the future, the bank should arrange with the companies concerned for them to pass an appropriate board resolution.

11.8 Disputes between Directors

Where the bank receives notice of a dispute between two directors of a company, who are the only directors of the company, and the bank holds a mandate for 'either to sign', then the bank must take action. This will normally involve advising the company and directors that in future the bank will only accept instructions which carry both directors' signatures.

With larger companies the bank will normally advise the company that even though it is aware of a dispute between directors, it will continue to rely on its existing mandate until it receives a copy of a board of directors' resolution indicating that it is to be amended.

Until this amendment has been received, as a constructive trustee of the company, the bank will scrutinise cheques which are presented for payment to ensure that they appear to be settlement for real trade debts. Where there are no doubts concerning the payment being for true company debts, the bank should request written confirmation from the company's auditors or accountants. If this is not forthcoming then the bank would be within its rights as a constructive trustee to refuse to pay the cheque for the reason 'no authority to pay'.

The bank would normally try to get the parties in dispute to visit the bank so that some effort could be made to rectify the situation. Obviously if the dispute cannot be resolved then this could affect the running of the company and reference to the courts may be needed to try to reach some agreement. If no agreement can be reached ultimately then it may result in the company ceasing to operate.

11.9 Does a Director incur Personal Liability when Signing a Company Cheque in that Capacity, if he does not indicate this?

Bondina Ltd v *Rollaway Shower Blinds Ltd* (1986) confirmed that it was no longer essential for a signatory on a company cheque to indicate his or her agency capacity where the company's name is correctly shown. Where the company's name is incorrectly shown, the signatory attracts personal liability. Should an action against a signatory be successful, it is highly likely that a counterclaim for negligence against the bank would receive a favourable hearing. Banks should therefore ensure that the printing on cheque-books is correct before sending them to the customers.

11.9.1 What effect will the death of a director have on the running of a company account?

Normally, the death of a company director has a minimal effect on the operation of the company's bank account. As a director is acting in the capacity of agent when signing cheques on the company's behalf, these cheques can still be paid after receipt of notice of the director's death by the bank. The bank will normally refer to its mandate to discover whether any further action need be taken with regard to the future operation of the account, and will contact the company if this is the case.

Difficulties may arise in respect of private limited companies where, for example, there may only be two directors, who also own all the shares in a company, and one dies. Usually a clause in the company's articles of association will contain instructions concerning the appointment of a new director; if this is not the case, referral to the courts by the surviving director would be required.

In the event of both directors dying, their personal representatives would have to apply to the courts for them to be appointed as shareholders and for the appointment of new directors. Until this situation has been resolved, the bank would allow payments for company debts to be made by the personal representatives; if the latter were unknown to the bank then satisfactory status reports would be sought.

11.10   The Giving of Financial Assistance by Companies

This comes under two headings: financial assistance to enable the purchase of its own shares, and financial assistance to directors and connected persons.

11.10.1   Assistance to purchase own shares

Sections 151–8, Companies Act 1985, generally prohibits the provision of financial assistance by a company, either directly or indirectly or by gift, to enable an individual to purchase its own shares. Direct assistance is by way of money or loan, indirect assistance by way of guaranteeing or giving security against the borrowing of the individual – s.152 Companies Act 1985. A company cannot give financial assistance in the purchase of its own shares where such assistance is given before or at the time of the acquisition – s.151, Companies Act 1985.

A company cannot give financial assistance to reduce or discharge a liability undertaken by a third party for the purchase of the company's shares – s.152(2), Companies Act 1985. Thus, care needs to be exercised by a bank, especially in a takeover where the bidder suggests that when they have acquired the company, the company will declare a dividend or give some form of security shortly afterwards to reduce or repay or secure any borrowing by the bidder. A dividend declared lawfully, i.e. the usual interim or final dividend declared by a company, is not affected.

There are various exceptions laid down in ss.151–8 that enable companies to give financial assistance under certain circumstances. Under s.153(1), which relates solely to public limited companies, financial assistance for share purchase is valid where 'the company's purpose in giving the assistance is not solely to assist share purchase, or where assistance is part of some larger purpose of the company'; the assistance must also be given 'in good faith in the best interests of the company'.

The definition of 'larger purpose' is somewhat vague, and in *Brady and Another* v *Brady and Another* (1988), the House of Lords decided that a narrow concept must be given to this definition. However, this narrow concept has not been specifically defined, and is not enshrined in the Companies Act 1989.

An example of a large purpose could be if a company made a takeover bid for another company. The target company (the one being bid for) could agree to guarantee a loan to the bidder in order to enable the bidder to purchase the target's shares. If the agreement to guarantee the loan were just a 'gentleman's agreement' (albeit in writing), then the financial assistance would be a criminal offence. However, if the target company were part of a group of companies, and if the group would benefit from the bidder becoming part of the group, then the guarantee from the group would be valid as it would benefit the 'larger purpose' of the group – s.153(1) Companies Act 1985.

There are certain occasions where financial assistance to purchase the company's shares is valid. These are laid down in s.153, Companies Act 1985 as follows:

(a) When lending money is the company's ordinary business. Thus a bank can lend its customers money to enable them to purchase the bank's shares.

(b) When financial assistance is given to employees to enable them to purchase the company's shares under an employee share scheme. Financial assistance can be either money lent to the employee by the company, or the guaranteeing of a loan by a lender to the employee. The shares acquired by the employee under the company share scheme must be fully paid – s.153(4)(b), Companies Act 1985.

The rules apply to both public and private limited companies. However, for public companies giving assistance as described in (b) above, the assistance must not have the effect of reducing the company's net assets, or must be given out of distributable profits. If these rules are broken then the assistance is a criminal offence.

For a private company, there is an additional proviso for financial assistance to be made in any circumstances and for *any* purpose provided that:

(a) The net assets of the company are not reduced by such assistance, unless the assistance is provided from distributable profits.

(b) The assistance is approved by means of a special resolution passed at a general meeting. The assistance cannot be given within four weeks of the date of the resolution unless *all* members eligible to vote at a general meeting were in favour. (A special resolution only needs 75% of votes cast at a general meeting to be passed.)

(c) The directors must make a statutory declaration of solvency, i.e. the company could pay all its debts due within 12 months if it were to be wound up. The assistance must be given within eight weeks of the statutory declaration. The statutory declaration must be accompanied by an auditor's report confirming the declaration.

(d) The company lodges with the registrar of companies within 15 days:
   (i) a copy of the special resolution;
   (ii) the statutory declaration of solvency;
   (iii) the auditor's report.

Holders of 10% of the nominal value of the issued share capital can apply to the court within 28 days for the special resolution to be cancelled.

For a private company, a common occurrence of needing to provide financial assistance to purchase its shares will arise when a new director is appointed and there is a requirement in the articles of association that a director must have a 'qualification holding'. A qualification holding is the minimum number of shares needed to be a director. Either the company will lend the director the money, or the bank will lend against a guarantee by the company. If the bank has lent to the director, against the company's guarantee, the guarantee will be enforceable provided the above conditions have been met.

11.10.2 Financial assistance to directors and connected persons

A connected person is a person connected to the director: the director's partner or spouse; directors' families; companies with which the director is associated (if he or she controls over 20% of the voting power); the trustee of a trust whose beneficiaries include the director. 'Director' includes a shadow director.

Under s.330, Companies Act 1985, financial assistance to directors and connected persons is prohibited, whether it is by way of a loan or by a guarantee or other security. The loan can be a 'quasi-loan', i.e. a transaction that does not appear to be a loan, but which is one in effect. For example, a company charge card where the company settles the bill and is later reimbursed by the director is a quasi-loan because the company is lending the director money which is later repaid by the director.

Sections 332–8, Companies Act 1985 (as amended by s.138, Companies Act 1989) does provide certain exceptions:

(a) For a relevant company (i.e. a company which is a public company or member of a group of public companies), a 'quasi-loan' can be made for a short term, providing the maximum amount does not exceed £5,000 – s.332, amended by s.138(a), Companies Act 1989.

(b) Any company can make small loans to directors, up to a maximum amount of £5,000 – s.334, amended by s.138(b), Companies Act 1989.

(c) Relevant companies which are money-lending companies can make loans or quasi-loans up to £100,000 to a director – s.338, amended by s.138(c) Companies Act 1989.

   The loan must be made in the ordinary course of business and on terms no more favourable than would be offered for similar facilities to unconnected persons. A bank can lend to its directors on the same terms as to its employees, i.e. at preferential rates. A bank, however, is not subject to a maximum amount of loan as are other money-lending organisations.

(d) When the company is a member of a group of companies, the other members of the group would be classed as 'connected persons'. However, the company is allowed to make loans or quasi-loans to other companies in the group, or to guarantee or give security for the borrowing or quasi-borrowing of the other companies in the group – s.333.

(e) Any company can give financial assistance to enable directors to carry out their duties properly, provided that prior approval has been granted at a general meeting and that all details were disclosed at that meeting.

If a bank lends for any of the purposes specified above as being an 'exception' under ss.332–8, Companies Act 1985 (as amended by s.138, Companies Act 1989), then the lending will be enforceable. If the lending is not for one of these exceptions it will be unenforceable against the company.

Similar considerations apply to the validity of a guarantee given by a limited company to secure the borrowing of a director.

11.11 Interested Directors

Section 137 Companies Act 1985 states that a company director who is interested either directly or indirectly in a contract involving the company must declare the nature of the interest at a meeting of the board of directors. Such an interest could evolve from a director being a guarantor of the company's liabilities with its bankers when it is proposed that additional direct security from the company is to be given to the bank, which obviously would reduce the likelihood of the director being called upon to meet the commitment. Another occasion would be where a company guarantees or gives security for the liabilities of another company and a director voting on the resolution to authorise the giving of this security is also a director or shareholder of the company for whose liabilities the guarantee or security is to be given.

The articles of association of many companies prohibit interested directors from voting on resolutions which cover matters in which they have an interest and also call for an independent quorum of directors to pass the resolution. Banks no longer have any duty to enquire into the authority of directors passing any resolution regarding the giving of a guarantee or other security by the company. However, if a bank is aware that any of the company's directors are 'interested' in the transaction, some enquiry must be made of the company and possibly its legal advisers as to the directors' ability under the company's articles of association to act and vote on the matter concerned despite their interest; or, alternatively, where interested directors are not allowed to vote, that an independent quorum of directors had passed the board resolution. Confirmation of this information should be provided to the bank in writing. Obviously if any matter is *ultra vires* the directors, then a resolution in general meeting should be passed giving the approval of the company. A copy of this would normally be required by the bank.

An important case regarding interested directors was *Victors Ltd* v *Lingard and Others* (1927). The facts of this case were that the directors of the company gave personal guarantees in respect of the company's indebtedness to the bank in 1920. A year later the company gave the bank direct security by means of debentures. Later the company went into liquidation and the liquidator claimed that, as the directors who voted to give the debentures were personally 'interested' in the transaction, the debentures should be declared invalid. The court held that the liquidator's claim was correct but, in view of the fact that the company by its future actions had led the bank to believe that the debentures were valid, it was estopped from denying liability.

It would appear that where direct security from the company and the personal guarantees of the directors are taken simultaneously, then the security will be valid. However, many banks adopt the practice of ensuring that they take the direct security from the company first before completing the formalities regarding the personal guarantees of the directors.

Summary

Now that you have read this unit, you should be able to:

☐ Differentiate between private and public limited companies.

☐ Recognise the effect which the Companies Act 1989 has had on bank procedures when dealing with its company customers.

☐ Be able to follow the procedure for opening a company account.

☐ Recognise the procedure to be followed when there is a dispute between directors.

☐ Identify the exceptions to the rules that companies cannot give financial assistance for the purchase of their own shares or to directors and connected persons.

☐ Recognise the procedures to be followed where directors are interested parties in the giving of company security.

If you can tick all the above boxes with confidence, you are ready to answer the questions which follow on pp.127–29.

List of Cases

Bondina Ltd v *Rollaway Shower Blinds Ltd* (1986)

Brady and Another v *Brady and Another* (1988)

Charterbridge Corporation Ltd v *Lloyds Bank Ltd* (1969)

Chemco Leasing S.p.A v *Rediffusion Ltd* (1987)

Kleinwort Benson Ltd v *Malaysia Mining Corporation Berhad* (1988)

London & Montrose Shipbuilding & Repairing Co Ltd v *Barclays Bank Ltd* (1926)

Salomon v *Salomon & Co Ltd* (1897)

Victors Ltd v *Lingard and Others* (1927)

List of Statutes

Companies Act 1985

Companies Act 1989

Self-assessment Questions

Short-answer questions

1 What is a letter of comfort?

2 Which sections of the Companies Act 1985 generally prohibit the provision of direct or indirect financial assistance by a company to enable an individual to purchase that company's shares?

3 Which section of the Companies Act 1985 generally prohibits financial assistance to directors and connected persons, whether by way of loan, guarantee or other security?

4 John Mower is a director of Landscaping Limited, a company which provides the services of landscape gardeners. He wishes to build a tennis court in his garden. Landscapings Limited are prepared to lend Mr Mower £4,000 towards the cost of the tennis court.

Would such a loan contravene the Companies Act 1985? Give reasons for your answer.

5 Clive Mattox is a director of Maxbank plc. He is moving house and wishes to borrow £150,000 from Maxbank on a mortgage loan. If the bank agrees to the loan, Mr Mattox will receive the same preferential rates of interest which the bank's employees benefit from.

Would such a loan be allowable under the Companies Act 1985?

6 Would your answer in Q5 be different if Mr Mattox was a director of Maxi-Loans Finance Co plc? Give reasons for your answer.

7 Mark Mason is a builder who has had an account in his own name for several years at your branch. The average balance on the account has been £20,000.

He calls in to see you today and advises you that he is in the process of changing his business into a limited company to be known as 'Mark Mason Ltd'. He believes that the formalities should be completed within six weeks but in the meantime he would like to open an account in the limited company's name. He mentions that no borrowing is envisaged and that he will advise you when the incorporation procedures have been finished.

What would be your reaction to your customer's request?

8 D V USS plc has recently received its certificate of incorporation but is still awaiting receipt of its trading certificate. An offer for the sale of its shares is in the process of being made and the company secretary urgently requires to open a bank account.

What action do you take?

(Answers are given in Appendix 2, pp.303–04)

Multiple-choice questions

1 Which case established that when a company gives security there must exist commercial justification for it being given?

(a) *Charterbridge Corporation Ltd* v *Lloyds Bank Ltd* (1969).
(b) *Kleinwort Benson Ltd* v *Malaysia Mining Corporation Berhad* (1988).
(c) *Chemco Leasing S.p.A.* v *Rediffusion Ltd* (1987).

2 The bank receives notice of a dispute between the two sole directors of Tempora Limited which could seriously affect the existence of the company. The mandate held allows for either director to sign. What action would it be prudent for the bank to take?

(a) No action whatsoever.
(b) Give notice to the directors that the bank intends to close the company account on a particular date unless it is advised that the dispute has been resolved.
(c) Advise the company and directors that the bank will only comply with instructions received which bear the signatures of both directors in future.

3 Which of the following types of company are allowed to provide financial assistance for employees to purchase the company's shares when such a purchase is not made under an employee share scheme?

(a) Engineering companies.
(b) Bakeries.
(c) Banks.
(d) Finance companies.

4 Which section of the Companies Act 1985 states that a company director who is either directly or indirectly interested in a contract involving the company must declare the nature of the interest at a meeting of the board of directors?

(a) S.307.
(b) S.317.
(c) S.327.
(d) S.337.

5 Which case established that a debenture taken by a bank could be invalid against the liquidator of a company if the directors of that company who voted to give the debenture were personally 'interested' in the transaction?

(a) *Chemco Leasing S.p.A* v *Rediffusion Ltd* (1987).
(b) *London and Montrose Shipbuilding and Repairing Co Ltd* v *Barclays Bank Ltd* (1926).
(c) *Victors Ltd* v *Lingard and Others* (1927).

(Answers are given in Appendix 2, p.304)

Revision question

You are the manager of a bank which has maintained the account of your valued customer, Telectronics plc, for several years. They are retailers of a wide variety of electrical goods and have a chain of shops throughout the UK.

One of the company's directors calls to see you about the company's future. He tells you that market research has shown that the demand for TV satellite dishes and compact disc players is likely to grow over the next few years and the demand for credit is also likely to grow in proportion. In order to take advantage of this opportunity the company is proposing to set up a subsidiary company which would finance the sales of electrical goods on credit and he asked you what you would require in order to open an account for the new company. He adds that no borrowing from the bank is envisaged by Telectronics plc, although its proposed subsidiary may require a small working capital facility once all the incorporation and account opening formalities have been completed.

Tabulate the account-opening formalities which you would follow. You should ignore any security which may be called for regarding the working capital facility for the subsidiary company.

(Answers are given in Appendix 2, pp.304–05)

Past examination question

You have at your branch of Old Bank the account of Turnbull Ltd, a wholly-owned subsidiary of Wainwright plc.

Today, the directors of Turnbull Ltd approach you for a short-term overdraft facility of £150,000.

They offer as security a letter of comfort from the parent company.

Required

Discuss the enforceability of a letter of comfort as a form of security. You should support your answer by reference to case law.

[6 marks]

(Spring 1992)

(Answers are given in Appendix 2, p.305)

UNIT 12

Bankruptcy of a Customer

Objectives

- Recognise procedures to be followed by banks upon receipt of notice of bankruptcy proceedings against their customers and third party sureties.
- Appreciate the importance of opening wages accounts for financially troubled business customers.
- Identify the circumstances where preferences or transactions at an under-value may affect a bank's position.
- Recognise the effect that dealing with an undischarged bankrupt can have on a bank.
- Identify when a bankrupt can be discharged from bankruptcy.
- Consider the various alternative procedures to bankruptcy proceedings.

Introduction

The Insolvency Act 1986 is the major statute when dealing with bankruptcy.

12.1 Steps in Bankruptcy

(a) Creditor presents a petition to the court requesting the making of a bankruptcy order. Such a petition will normally be based upon an outstanding unsecured debt of £750 or more.

(b) Court hears the petition and decides whether it should be dismissed or if a bankruptcy order should be made.

(c) If a bankruptcy order is made, it should be advertised in the *London Gazette.*

(d) A statement of the debtor's affairs will be forwarded to all creditors.

(e) A meeting of creditors may be held to appoint a trustee in bankruptcy.

(f) While not always necessary, a public examination of the debtor may be held.

(g) Proceeds from the realisation of the debtor's assets will be used to pay a dividend to creditors.

(h) The debtor's discharge from bankruptcy.

12.2   Basis for Presentation of a Petition

(a)   Debtors may present their own petitions if they are unable to pay their debts.

(b)   A creditor can petition where a debtor has failed to satisfy a statutory demand.

(c)   A petition can be brought where a judgment, execution or other process has not been satisfied.

(d)   Under the Criminal Justices Act 1972 or the Criminal Courts Act 1973 a person who has committed a crime and caused damage or loss of £15,000 or more can be adjudicated bankrupt.

(e)   The Supervisor of an individual voluntary arrangement can petition the court if that arrangement fails.

12.3   The Bankruptcy Order

This operates from the day the order is made until such time as the debtor is discharged, which is normally between two and fifteen years later.

Once the bankruptcy order is made, the official receiver acts as the debtor's trustee in bankruptcy, an office which will be held unless or until the creditors appoint a licensed insolvency practitioner as a replacement.

12.4   Advertisement of the Bankruptcy Order

By advertising the bankruptcy order in the *London Gazette* and a local newspaper, it is considered that notice has been given to the whole world. At the same time details of the bankruptcy order will be filed against the debtor's name on the Land Charges Registry and Land Registry. This is to protect creditors' interests, as the lack of such a warning could enable a purchaser of such land to have a good title in the event of being unaware of the bankruptcy petition or bankruptcy order. (Bankruptcy petitions are normally recorded against the debtor's name for similar reasons.)

12.5   Debtor's Statement of Affairs

This should be prepared within 21 days of the date of the bankruptcy order. It should give full details of the debtor's assets and liabilities. A copy of this statement of affairs will be sent to all creditors. Any property which the bankrupt held on trust can be ignored when compiling this information.

12.6   Proof of Debt

Once the bankruptcy order is made, the bank will be able to prove for the debt.

If it holds security lodged by the bankrupt, the bank can take a number of courses of action:

(a) It can release the security to the trustee and prove as an unsecured creditor for the outstanding debt.

(b) It can value its security and prove as an unsecured creditor for any perceived shortfall.

(c) It can realise its security and prove as an unsecured creditor for any shortfall.

(d) It can realise its security, pay off the debt owing and forward any remaining funds to the trustee in bankruptcy.

12.7 Third-Party Security

The decision in *Re Sass* (1896) confirmed that a bank can ignore third-party security when submitting its proof of debt. Thus, any proceeds from third parties can be placed on a suspense account without jeopardising the bank's right to receive all dividends due from the bankrupt's estate as if it were an unsecured creditor.

12.8 Rights of a Third-Party Surety under the Doctrine of Subrogation

Section 5 Mercantile Law Amendment Act 1856 allows a third-party surety to stand in the shoes of the bank, provided that all the outstanding debt owed to the bank has been repaid. A guarantor whose liability was £5,000, and who merely repaid this amount, when the total owing to the bank was £7,000, would not benefit from subrogation. However, if the guarantor repaid £7,000, he or she would benefit from subrogation.

12.9 Debtors' Public Examination

Where more than half in value of creditors, or the official receiver, want a public examination of a debtor, one must be set up. In the case of small bankruptcies, public examination will often not take place due to the financial and time cost.

12.10 Order of Repayment in Bankruptcy

1 Secured creditors. They rank according to the extent of the value of their security.

2 The costs incurred by the bankruptcy proceedings and the expenses of the trustee in bankruptcy.

3 The costs incurred by the petitioning creditor.

4   Preferential creditors. These include payments due for certain taxes, national insurance contributions and wages. With regard to wages, banks open wages accounts for businesses where there are possible financial problems, in order for such payments made by them to be considered as preferential debts in the event of bankruptcy or liquidation in the case of a company. (Further details are given later in this unit).

5   Unsecured creditors.

6   Deferred creditors, which include the bankrupt's spouse.

12.11   Wages Accounts

Student Activity 1

Examine your bank's internal rules and regulations regarding procedures to be followed for opening and operating wages accounts when a business customer is suffering financial difficulties. Compare your findings with the sections which follow.

12.11.1   Why do banks open wages accounts?

Unpaid wages up to a maximum of £800 per employee for a maximum period of four months prior to the liquidation of a company or the bankruptcy of a sole trader or partnership ranks as a preferential creditor (Schedule 6 Insolvency Act 1986). Money lent for the purpose of paying such wages also ranks as a preferential debt.

Therefore, for example in the case of a limited company, a bank will open a wages account for that company where it feels that there is a danger of the company going into liquidation.

12.11.2   How should the wages account be operated?

(a)   Cheques drawn on the wages account should be made payable to 'wages'.

(b)   The directors/partners/sole trader should submit a list of employees and the amount to be paid to each one.

(c)   The bank should prepare an analysis of the balance of the wages account each week to ensure that the balance is made up of only qualifying wages, i.e. maximum of £800 per employee, maximum period four months back.

(d)   After the first four months of operation of the wages account, or when the £800 limit has been attained, credit the wages account with the first amount which was originally debited there and debit the current account.

(e)   If there was an overdraft limit marked upon the current account prior to opening the wages account, amend the bank's records to show the limit now covers the net position on both accounts.

12.11.3 Is it legally necessary to open a wages account to rank as a preferential creditor for advances for wages up to £800 per employee for a maximum of four months prior to liquidation or bankruptcy?

The answer is no, but a bank could have problems if it does not, due to the following reasons:

(a) It may be difficult to prove which parts of a company's borrowing were for qualifying wages advances.

(b) If the current account is active, the rule in *Clayton's* case could ensure that the debit balance consists of items debited later than the four-month qualifying period. Thus the rule in *Clayton's* case would work against the bank's position.

12.11.4 Should a bank open a wages account where it holds security for its business customer's borrowing?

Where a bank holds a fixed charge over security which, if realised, would more than repay the bank borrowing, then a wages account is not essential. However, where there is likely to be a shortfall, the existence of a wages account is obviously an advantage.

12.11.5 Problems which could arise with regard to the preferentiality of wages accounts where the decision in the case of *Re Unit 2 Windows Ltd* (1985) applies

Where a bank operates two or more accounts in addition to a wages account, it may find that the extent of the preferentiality of the balance of the wages account is threatened in the event of bankruptcy/liquidation. The decision in *Re Unit 2 Windows Ltd* (1985) stated that where such circumstances existed, any credit balances must be allocated to debit balances on a pro-rata basis, notwithstanding that some of these balances may be of a preferential nature. An example of this would be as follows:

Balances:

No 1 account £9,000 Credit
Loan account £30,000 Debit (No security held)
Wages account £15,000 Debit

The credit balance would be allocated, in the event of bankruptcy/liquidation, as follows:

Loan account: £6,000
Wages account: £3,000

Thus, the bank would be a preferential creditor for £12,000 and an unsecured creditor for £24,000.

Banks prevent the diminution of possible preference claims in such circumstances by taking written agreement from their customers, when they open wages accounts, that any credit balances should be initially applied to non-preferential debit balances.

12.12 The Bank's Position Regarding Transactions Taking Place on an Account between the Presentation of a Petition and the Granting of a Bankruptcy Order

Under s.284 (4) (5) Insolvency Act 1986 a bank would be protected against any claim from a trustee in bankruptcy for credits received during that period, provided that it had no notice of the petition and had acted in good faith and for value.

Obviously, once a bank has notice of a petition, all relevant accounts should be stopped.

12.13 Preferences

A potential bankrupt may decide to limit the financial damage which the bankruptcy would cause by carrying out certain transactions to favour certain creditors, to the detriment of others. Such actions are known as preferences and could be set aside by the court.

In order for this to take place, s.340 Insolvency Act 1986 states that the desire to produce an advantageous position must be evident, although in the case of an associate of the bankrupt such as a spouse, such a desire can be presumed.

In addition to this, any preference must have occurred within six months prior to the presentation of a petition (or two years in the case of an associate). This period is known as 'a relevant time' (s.341 Insolvency Act 1986). Also, the person concerned must have been insolvent at the time of the transaction, or have become insolvent as a result of it.

Dangers for banks lie principally with this six-month period, particularly in respect of releasing third-party security after repayment of a debt. If such a repayment was deemed by the court to have been a preference, it could make an order to restore the position to what it had been previously. Unfortunately if the released security was subsequently lodged elsewhere in good faith, for value and without notice of the relevant circumstances, the bank would be unable to recover the security. As a consequence, banks incorporate a clause in their charge forms enabling them to retain security for six months after an account has returned to credit.

Banks will only rely on the above clause when the surrounding circumstances warrant it. Obviously, in most cases, banks will release security, when requested, after repayment of the outstanding debt.

12.14 Transactions at an Undervalue

Section 339 Insolvency Act 1986 deals with transactions at an undervalue. These are where assets are sold at less than their true worth or are given as a gift, thus placing creditors at a disadvantage. The trustee can apply to the court to restore the previous position. A transaction at an undervalue can be challenged by the trustee within two years of the petition, irrespective of whether the bankrupt was insolvent at the time or became insolvent as a consequence of it. Such a transaction can be challenged outside this two-year period up to five years from the petition, but in such circumstances the trustee must show insolvency of the bankrupt during years three, four and five.

Student Activity 2

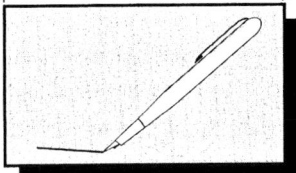

Examine the procedures which your bank follows upon receipt of a bankruptcy order for various types of account holder and compare it with the following.

12.15 Procedures to be Followed by Banks upon Receipt of Notice of a Bankruptcy Order against Various Types of Account Holder

12.15.1 Sole account holder

(a) Stop all accounts.

(b) Return any cheques presented for payment, marked 'Refer to drawer, bankruptcy order made'.

(c) Credits received after notice of the bankruptcy order should be placed to the credit of a suspense account, and the trustee in bankruptcy advised.

(d) Provide details of balances, any preferential claims which the bank may have, and also details of security held, to the trustee when requested.

(e) After setting off any balances held, funds must be forwarded by the bank to the trustee when instructed.

12.15.2 One party to a joint account

(a) Stop the joint account, whether in credit or debit.

(b) Request instructions from the trustee in bankruptcy and solvent party(ies) to the account with regard to the disposal of credit balances and any items held in safe custody.

(c) Discuss with the solvent party the possibility of opening a new account in the solvent party's own name. Take instructions relating to any cheques signed by the solvent party on the joint account being debited to this new account.

(d) Where the solvent party will not agree to cheques drawn on the joint account and signed by him or her being debited to a new account in his or her name, they must be returned marked 'Refer to drawer – joint account holder in bankruptcy proceedings'.

(e) Cheques drawn by the bankrupt party must be returned marked 'Refer to drawer – bankruptcy order made'.

(f) Where the joint account is overdrawn, the bank can prove in the bankrupt's estate for the full amount owing and receive any dividends paid. If it holds security lodged by the bankrupt, the bank has several courses of action open to it as described earlier in this unit.

(g) As regards a solvent party to a joint account in these circumstances, the bank can make demand for repayment under its joint and several liability mandate. Any monies received can be placed to a separate account without affecting any claim which the bank may make against the bankrupt's estate. Likewise, where the bank holds security which was charged by the solvent party, it can realise this and place it to a realisations account without affecting its claim in the bankrupt's estate.

12.16 Procedures to be Followed by Banks upon Receipt of Notice of Winding-Up Orders or Bankruptcy Orders against Partnerships or Individual Partners respectively

Under the Insolvency Act 1986 and the Insolvent Partnership Order 1986, a partnership creditor can choose to begin bankruptcy proceedings against the partnership alone or both the partnership and some or all of the partners.

12.16.1 Winding-up order against a partnership

(a) Stop the partnership account.

(b) Allow either individual partners' accounts to continue as before, whether in credit or debit, *or*, relying on the joint and several liability clause in the partnership mandate, where the partnership account is overdrawn and individual partners' accounts are in credit, stop the partnership account and carry out the bank's right of appropriation.

12.16.2 Winding-up order against a partnership and bankruptcy order(s) against the partners(s)

(a) Stop the partnership account and the accounts of partners named in the bankruptcy orders, whether they are in debit or credit.

(b) Bank can lodge a proof of debt in both the partnership winding up and in the estates of the individual partners.

(c) Bank security forms will allow the bank to realise any assets charged to the bank by individual partners and apply their proceeds as it wishes in repayment of partnership debt or of the individual partner's own borrowing.

(d) Where an individual partner's account has a credit balance (and where a bankruptcy order has been presented against that partner in addition to a winding-up order against the partnership), the bank can set off this balance against any debit balance on the partnership account because of the joint and several liability clause contained in the bank's partnership mandate.

12.16.3   Bankruptcy order against a partner

(a) Where a partnership account has a credit balance, and a bankruptcy order is served upon one of the partners, the account can continue to operate.

(b) Any partnership account cheques signed by the bankrupt partner must be authorised by the remaining partners before being paid. If this is not forthcoming, such cheques must be returned marked 'Refer to drawer – bankruptcy order made against X'.

(c) If security has been provided for the partnership account by the bankrupt partner, the account must be stopped while alternative security is arranged with the remaining partners. This will apply whether the partnership account is in credit or debit unless the bank is prepared to rely either on the financial integrity of the remaining partners or on other security already held.

(d) Where a partnership account has a debit balance and a bankruptcy order has been served upon one of the partners, the account should be stopped, if the bank wishes to preserve its rights against the bankrupt's estate. Failure to do so could lead to the rule in *Clayton's* case operating to the detriment of the bank. If the bank is prepared to release the bankrupt's estate from its liability for the partnership debt, then the bank can allow the partnership account to continue.

12.17   Procedure to be Followed by Banks upon Receipt of Notice of Bankruptcy Proceedings against a Third-Party Surety

The procedure followed by banks should be the same whether it has notice of a bankruptcy petition or bankruptcy order:

(a) Stop the account for which the third-party security has been given. This fixes the surety's liability at that time.

(b) Interview customer to ascertain whether alternative security is available, or whether new borrowing facilities are to be negotiated.

(c) In the event that the bank wishes to preserve its right against the surety, it will prove in the bankrupt's estate; any proceeds received will be placed on a suspense account. In effect, such funds become cash collateral security in support of the customer's indebtedness. When the customer's borrowing is repaid, these funds can be returned to the trustee in bankruptcy.

12.18   Undischarged Bankrupts

Anyone adjudicated bankrupt has certain restrictions placed on their conduct which have implications for banks.

(a) An undischarged bankrupt must not obtain credit in excess of £250 without advising the party concerned of his or her undischarged bankrupt capacity (s.360 Insolvency Act 1986).

(b) An undischarged bankrupt who wishes to trade in other than the name under which he or she was adjudicated bankrupt can only do so provided the undischarged bankruptcy is revealed to the person(s) being traded with (s.360 Insolvency Act 1986).

(c) Section 307(3) Insolvency Act 1986 covers property which may be acquired by or inherited by an undischarged bankrupt after adjudication. Such property vests in the trustee in bankruptcy. As such, should an undischarged bankrupt charge such property to the bank, the latter could have problems in realising the security and applying the proceeds as it wishes. However, s.307(4) Insolvency Act 1986 does offer some protection. It states as follows:

Where, whether before or after the service of a notice under this Section –

(a) a person acquires property in good faith, for value and without notice of the bankruptcy: or

(b) a banker enters into a transaction in good faith and without such notice, the Trustee shall not in respect of the property or transaction be entitled by virtue of this section to any remedy against that person or banker, or any person whose title to any property derives from that person or banker.

(d) Sometimes, a bankrupt spouse may wish to conceal certain business transactions from the trustee in bankruptcy and may use their marriage partner's account for this purpose. If a bank suspects this, it should interview its account holder; should it be established that this is the case, then the account should be stopped and the trustee in bankruptcy advised.

(e) Sections 11 and 13 Company Directors Disqualification Act 1986 prevent undischarged bankrupts from being company directors. If the bank is advised that an undischarged bankrupt has been acting as a director it should confer with the other directors of the company, obtain a new mandate where necessary, and ensure that any company cheques bearing the bankrupt's signature are confirmed by the other directors as being for bona fide company transactions. The company account need not be stopped.

(f) As was seen above, s.307(4) Insolvency Act 1986 protects a bank when it operates an account for an undischarged bankrupt when it has acted in good faith and has no notice of the bankrupt's status. However, if a bank learns that one of its customers may be an undischarged bankrupt, there are certain actions it should take:

(i) Search on the Bankruptcy Register in London or contact the Official Receiver or trustee in bankruptcy (where known).

(ii) If it transpires that the customer is an undischarged bankrupt, stop the customer's account.

(iii) Advise the trustee in bankruptcy of the existence of the account and await instructions. If no claim on the funds in the account is received within 42 days, then the account may continue as usual (s.309(i) Insolvency Act 1986).

12.19 Discharge from Bankruptcy

A bankrupt can be discharged from bankruptcy providing certain time periods have elapsed since the granting of the bankruptcy order (ss.279 and 280 Insolvency Act 1986).

In the case of a person made bankrupt under a bankruptcy order by way of a certificate of summary, discharge will take place two years from the date of the bankruptcy order. (This type of bankruptcy order can be granted in respect of bankruptcies where the bankrupt's assets do not exceed £2,000.)

In the case of criminal bankruptcies, the bankrupt can apply to the court for discharge once five years have passed since the granting of the bankruptcy order.

A bankrupt who has been adjudicated bankrupt on a previous occasion, within 15 years of the date of the current bankruptcy order being granted, can apply to the court for discharge provided that five years have elapsed since the date of the granting of the current bankruptcy order.

Except for those cases mentioned above, a bankrupt will receive an automatic discharge three years after the date of the bankruptcy.

12.20 Alternatives to Normal Bankruptcy Procedures

12.20.1 Individual voluntary arrangements

Where the debt involved is only a small amount, an individual may wish to come to an arrangement with his or her creditors concerning how the liabilities may be met. This is known as an individual voluntary arrangement.

Procedure to be followed in respect of an individual voluntary arrangement

1 Debtor makes an application to the court.

2 The court will make an interim order which will exist for as long as the court stipulates, but is normally 14 days.

3 The effect of this order is to suspend any proceedings which may be pending regarding the applicant's liabilities, e.g. bankruptcy petition hearing.

4 As a result of the interim order, a licensed insolvency practitioner will be appointed as nominee. The nominee will then try to devise, in conjunction with the debtor, an arrangement which will satisfy the debtor's creditors. The nominee will then advise the court of his or her view on this proposed arrangement and will arrange a meeting of creditors. The creditors will then be able to discuss the proposal, amending it where necessary, and finally voting on it. They may also appoint their own nominee, if they wish, to replace the one originally appointed as a result of the interim order. If the proposal to accept the individual voluntary arrangement is passed, then all creditors who had received notice of the creditors' meeting will be bound by the decision, whether they attended or otherwise.

5   Once the proposal has been accepted, the nominee will advise the court; the nominee is then appointed as the supervisor of the arrangement.

When a supervisor advises a bank of his or her appointment, the bank will require sight of a copy of the individual arrangement to determine the supervisor's powers in relation to the debtor's account, e.g. disposal of credit balances, safe custody items, unwanted security.

6   When a bank receives notice of the creditors' meeting, it should stop any overdrawn account in the name of the debtor and also any account for which the debtor is a surety. If the debtor's account has a credit balance, the account can continue to operate until the creditors' meeting approves the arrangement and a supervisor is appointed. If, at that time, the credit balance forms part of the arrangement, then the account should be stopped awaiting instructions from the supervisor.

7   When a bank receives notice of the creditors' meeting and the debtor is a party to a joint account or partnership account, any action taken by the bank will depend upon whether the account has a credit or debit balance and if, in addition, the account has any other liabilities to the bank.

Providing there are no other liabilities, an account in credit can be allowed to continue. However, where an account is overdrawn, and the bank may wish to preserve its right against the party to the account, the account should be stopped. The remaining account holders should be advised and new bank accounts arranged where necessary.

Upon the appointment of a supervisor, any credit balance on a joint account, covered by the individual voluntary arrangement, may only be paid over to the supervisor upon receipt of the joint instructions from the supervisor and the remaining joint account holders. Where the joint account holders wish to continue the account, including the party who has an individual voluntary arrangement with the creditors, guidance should be sought from the supervisor concerning its feasibility.

Obviously, if a bank is prepared to waive its claim in the individual voluntary arrangement against a debtor, and the joint account/partnership account is overdrawn, then the account can continue to operate.

12.20.2   Deeds of arrangement/deeds of assignment

Deeds of arrangement, which are also known as deeds of assignment, are governed by the Deeds of Arrangement Act 1914.

Under such an arrangement a debtor, normally in conjunction with a licensed insolvency practitioner, will advise creditors of an impending meeting to discuss his or her financial position. This advice will often include a detailed analysis of the debtor's assets and liabilities.

At the meeting, the deed of arrangement will have to be agreed to by a majority in value and number of creditors. It must be registered at the Department of Trade and Industry within seven days. (Any creditor who has not agreed to the deed of arrangement can still petition for bankruptcy, if the debtor has not satisfied a statutory demand.) A licensed insolvency practitioner will be appointed a trustee to oversee the arrangement.

Where a bank is a creditor and assents to the deed of arrangement, it will have to analyse its security position in order to ascertain the unsecured debt which would have to be mentioned in the bank's assent.

If a bank is approached by a trustee to open an account for the purpose of dealing with a deed of arrangement, normal account-opening procedures should be followed and the account's name should show its status e.g. 'David Duncan, Trustee for Ian Rankin'.

Summary

Now that you have read this unit, you should be able to:

☐ Recognise procedures to be followed by banks upon receipt of notice of bankruptcy proceedings against their customers and third-party sureties.

☐ Appreciate the importance of opening wages accounts for financially troubled business customers.

☐ Identify the circumstances where preferences or transactions at an undervalue may affect a bank's position.

☐ Recognise the effect that dealing with an undischarged bankrupt can have on a bank.

☐ Identify when a bankrupt can be discharged from bankruptcy.

☐ Consider the various alternative procedures to bankruptcy proceedings.

If you can tick all the above boxes with confidence, you are ready to answer the questions which follow on pp. 143–46.

List of Cases

Devaynes v *Noble* (1816) (*Clayton's* case)

Re Sass (1896)

Re Unit 2 Windows Ltd (1985)

List of Statutes

Company Directors Disqualification Act 1986

Criminal Courts Act 1973

Criminal Justices Act 1972

Deeds of Arrangement Act 1914

Insolvency Act 1986

Insolvent Partnership Order 1986

Mercantile Law Amendment Act 1856

Self-assessment Questions

Short-answer questions

1 George Simmons is a partner in the firm of Simmons, Jay and Dee which maintains a business account with you. You learn today that a bankruptcy order has been made against him. The balance of the partnership account is Cr £9,000.

What action will you take concerning the operation of the account?

2 Would your answer to Q1 differ if the partnership had an unsecured overdraft of £9,000 instead of a credit balance and, if so, why?

3 Would your answer to Q2 differ if the overdraft was secured by a charge over stocks and shares given by Jay, which were currently valued at £30,000?

4 Would your answer to Q3 differ if the stocks and shares were charged by Simmons?

5 Lewis and Fraser has a business account with you and you learn today that a winding-up order has been granted against the partnership. (No bankruptcy orders have been granted against the individual partners.) Lewis has a sole current account with you which is in credit. Must the bank automatically stop this private account?

6 Jack Williams guaranteed a loan of £20,000 which you made to his son, Jim, last week. The guarantee was unsupported. You learn today that Jack Williams is involved in bankruptcy proceedings.

What action will you take concerning the account of Jim Williams?

(Answers are given in Appendix 2, p.305)

Multiple-choice questions

1 Two days ago you were advised that a bankruptcy order had been made against your customer John Dunn. In today's post you receive a banker's draft for £50,000 from a firm of Australian solicitors, Wally Bee and Alice Springs, advising you that Mr Dunn's uncle had died and that he had instructions in his will that the funds enclosed be placed in John Dunn's bank account with you.

What action will you take?

(a) Open a new account for John Dunn and credit the funds to this account under advice to John Dunn. Acknowledge receipt to solicitors.

(b) Acknowledge receipt to solicitors. Credit funds to a suspense account and advise the Official Receiver.

2   Paul and Sheila Savage operate a joint account with you. The balance of the account is Cr £30,000. You are advised this morning that a bankruptcy order has been made against Paul Savage. There is a cheque in this morning's clearing for £25,000 payable to Overseas Property Ltd which is technically in order and signed by Sheila Savage. The account mandate which you hold is for 'either to sign'.

What action would you take concerning this cheque?

(a) Pay the cheque.

(b) Return the cheque marked 'Refer to drawer – joint account holder in bankruptcy proceedings'.

(c) Interview Sheila Savage to ascertain whether a new account can be opened and overdraft facilities agreed so that the cheque can be paid. If unable to do this, act as in (b).

3   Refer to the alternative answers in Q2. What would be your answer if the bank had only received notice of a petition against Paul Savage?

(Answers are given in Appendix 2, p.306)

Past examination questions

1   The account of John Douglas was satisfactorily opened at your branch in January 1989. He is a bookseller who occasionally trades under the name of Maple Books.

In December 1990 you agreed to provide John Douglas with an overdraft facility of £3,500 in his own name to enable him to buy some books at auction. Repayment was to come from the subsequent sale of the books over a period of 12 months. Security was taken in the form of a memorandum of deposit over stock exchange shares (value £5,000) which he had inherited on the death of his widowed mother in June 1990.

Today (13 May 1991), with the account overdrawn £1,625, you receive a letter from the Official Receiver asking whether you hold an account for John Douglas and whether it is overdrawn. Upon further investigation you are surprised to find out that a bankruptcy order was made against John Douglas on 23 June 1988 and that he has not yet received his discharge.

Required

(a) Comment on your bank's position and explain what action you will now take. Give reasons for your answer.

[17 marks]

(b)   State when John Douglas might expect to receive his discharge.

[3 marks]

[Total marks for question – 20]

(Spring 1991)

2   Robert Abel is a valued customer at your branch. Four years ago you lent him £20,000 on loan account to acquire a partnership in a local firm of accountants. Repayment was agreed at a rate of £4,000 per annum, and the loan was secured by a guarantee from his mother supported by an equitable charge over stock exchange securities, current value £28,000. The borrowing is being repaid as arranged and the latest accounts of the partnership, which also banks at your branch, show good profits being made.

Today, you receive a letter from Mr Abel enclosing a cheque for £10,642 issued by a firm of stockbrokers. He tells you that the money is from the sale of some recently inherited shares. Mr Abel asks you to credit the funds to his current account and, following clearance of the cheque, to repay the loan. Once this is done, he requests that you write to his mother confirming her immediate release from the guarantee liability, and returning her share certificates.

Your clerk is reluctant to agree to Mr Abel's request, on the grounds that a preference may have taken place.

Required

(a)   State what you understand by the term 'preference'.

[2 marks]

(b)   Outline the criteria in respect of which any claim for preference against an individual is judged.

[6 marks]

(c)   Having regard to your clerk's comments, discuss fully the considerations you would have in mind in dealing with Mr Abel's request, and explain what action you would take. Give reasons for your answer.

[12 marks]

[Total marks for question – 20]

(Spring 1992)

(Answers are given in Appendix 2, pp. 306–07)

UNIT 13

Company Liquidations

Objectives

- Recognise what action should be taken in the event of a company being compulsorily wound up.
- Differentiate between members' and creditors' voluntary liquidations.
- Detail procedures to be followed upon receipt of notice of voluntary liquidation.
- Identify the difference between an individual and company voluntary arrangement.
- Recognise the differences between company and individual preferences and transactions at an undervalue.
- Differentiate between wrongful trading and fraudulent trading.

Introduction

There are three types of company liquidation:

(a) compulsory winding up;

(b) creditors' voluntary liquidation;

(c) members' voluntary liquidation.

13.1 Compulsory Winding Up

The most common reason for a company to be compulsorily wound up by the court is when a creditor, who is owed £750 or more, presents a petition to the court on the grounds of the company's inability to meet its debts. If a winding-up order is subsequently made by the court, the liquidation is said to have begun on the date of presentation of the petition (s.129 Insolvency Act 1986). Thus any disposition of company assets between the petition and the winding up will be void against the liquidator. Banks therefore scrutinise the *London Gazette* for details of petitions. Upon learning of one, all accounts, whether in debit or credit, will be stopped. Any cheques presented will be returned 'Refer to drawer – petition presented'. The company will be advised of the bank's action. If the company needs certain payments to be made, s.127 Insolvency Act 1986 allows for it to apply for a validation order, which enables certain disbursements to take place while the petition is outstanding. If such an order is produced, the bank can safely deal with a transaction.

Student Activity 1

Examine your bank's rules concerning the action to be taken upon notice of the making of a winding-up order against a company customer. Compare this with the details given below.

13.2 Actions to be Taken upon Making of a Winding-Up Order

1 Company accounts must be stopped. Instructions can no longer be accepted from the directors.

2 The bank must see a copy of the winding-up order.

3 It must give details of account balances, contingent liabilities and direct security held to the liquidator.

4 Safe custody items can be withdrawn by the liquidator, against the liquidator's receipt.

5 Cheques presented for payment must be returned marked 'Refer to drawer – winding-up order made'.

6 Any credit balances should be released to the liquidator.

13.3 Set Off

Credit and debit balances can be set off when a company goes into liquidation. This was confirmed in *National Westminster Bank Ltd* v *Halesowen Presswork and Assemblies Ltd* (1972).

13.4 Security

In the event of a company entering liquidation and the bank holding security in respect of borrowings, the bank has a number of alternative actions which it can take.

(a) Realise the security held itself.

(b) Allow the liquidator to realise the security and account to the bank for the proceeds less expenses.

(c) Where it is difficult to realise security, the bank can merely value it and lodge a proof of debt. This measures any unsecured bank debt upon which a dividend may be paid. Should the security be sold eventually, the bank's claim can be amended up or down accordingly.

13.5 Voluntary Liquidation

Voluntary liquidation normally evolves from a company's extraordinary resolution that due to its liabilities it cannot continue its business and it is advisable to wind up (s.84 Insolvency Act 1986). Liquidation begins upon the passing of this resolution and will be advertised within 14 days in the *London Gazette*. The company will then cease to trade, except to the extent that it is necessary for winding-up purposes.

A voluntary liquidation can be either a members' or creditors' voluntary liquidation.

13.5.1 Members' voluntary liquidation

This occurs when the directors make a statutory declaration, within five weeks prior to the winding-up resolution, that they believe that the company will be able to pay its debts together with interest within 12 months of the commencement of liquidation. This declaration must be filed at Companies House and will include details of the company's liabilities and assets.

13.5.2 Creditors' voluntary liquidation

If the directors of a company do not believe that the company can meet its liabilities in full, then the liquidation will become a creditors' voluntary liquidation.

A meeting of creditors will take place within 14 days of the members' meeting which resolved to wind up the company. The creditors' meeting will be advertised in the *London Gazette* and creditors must receive seven days' notice of the event.

At the meeting, a full statement of affairs will be presented to the creditors. A liquidator will normally be appointed by the creditors, although occasionally the company will be allowed to do this. A creditors' committee will be elected and the liquidator will keep this committee informed of progress. Once a liquidator is appointed, all the directors' powers end unless the creditors' committee agree otherwise.

Sometimes there is a period of time between the passing of the company resolution and the creditors' meeting. During this period any liquidator appointed by the company has limited powers to deal with the company's assets until his or her position is confirmed at the creditors' meeting. Obviously the creditors can replace the liquidator who was appointed initially with an insolvency practitioner of their own choice.

13.5.3 Procedure to be followed upon notice of voluntary liquidation

1 Determine whether liquidation is a members' or creditors' voluntary liquidation.

2 For a creditors' voluntary liquidation, no account credit balances, safe custody items or unwanted security should be released to the liquidator until the appointment has been confirmed at the creditors' meeting and the bank has seen a copy of the resolution.

3   In the case of a members' voluntary liquidation, the bank can allow access to the liquidator upon sight of a copy of the members' resolution.

4   The bank account should be stopped upon notice of the passing of the company resolution to enter voluntary liquidation.

5   Cheques presented after receipt of notice should be returned marked 'Refer to drawer – company in voluntary liquidation'.

6   Details of balances, direct security held, safe custody items and contingent liabilities will be given to the liquidator.

7   As with bankruptcy, the bank can realise any security held or allow the liquidator to realise it and account to the bank for its proceeds or can have it valued and prove in the liquidation for any amount not covered by the security held in order to obtain any declared dividend.

8   Where the company holds more than one account, the bank will exercise its right of set off and will only pay over any net credit balance. If the net position shows a debit balance, it will lodge a claim which will identify any preferential amounts.

13.6   Company Voluntary Arrangement

A company voluntary arrangement will commence with an approach to an insolvency practitioner who becomes known as 'the nominee'. He will then advise the court as to whether a meeting should occur between the company and its creditors.

At such a meeting, creditors will take two votes on proposals made. In order for the first vote to be carried, 75% in value of unsecured creditors must be in favour. If this is carried, a further vote will take place which will exclude connected persons such as directors, and here a 50% majority will suffice.

The difference between this procedure and the appointment of an administrator is that creditors may still continue action against the company when the insolvency practitioner is acting as a nominee. (This obviously differs from voluntary arrangements for individuals whereby the debtor is automatically protected from the action of creditors.)

13.7   Transactions at an Undervalue

Transactions at an undervalue are assets which are sold at less than their true money, or money's-worth value, or are given as a gift. If such a transaction has taken place within two years prior to the commencement of insolvency, the liquidator can apply to the court for the position to be returned to what it was prior to the transaction occurring (s.238 Insolvency Act 1986). In taking such action the liquidator must prove that at the time of the transaction the company was unable to pay its debts, or that as a consequence of the transaction this position resulted. The exception to this is where the transaction was with a connected person, in which case insolvency is presumed unless shown otherwise.

A company is said to be unable to pay its debts if:

(a) It does not pay a written demand for £750 or more.
(b) It is proven to the court that it cannot meet its debts as they fall due.
(c) It is proven to the court that the company's liabilities exceed its assets.
(d) It fails to satisfy an execution by a creditor.

13.8 Preferences

Where a company desires to place a person, e.g. a creditor, in a better position than would otherwise have been the case, to the detriment of other parties, and insolvency arises, a preference can be stated to have taken place. If the transaction took place within six months of the commencement of insolvency for a normal creditor or two years for a connected person, e.g. an associate company, it can be challenged by the liquidator. The liquidator must prove that the company was insolvent (s.239 Insolvency Act 1986).

13.9 Wrongful Trading

Under s.214 Insolvency Act 1986, if a director or shadow director, knowing that a company was insolvent or that it was highly unlikely that it could avoid insolvency, continued to allow that company to trade, the liquidator could apply to the court for a monetary contribution from these parties. This is in order to prevent such people increasing the losses of companies. Obviously , if it can be shown that such steps were taken to minimise losses to the company's creditors, no liability will attach. (A shadow director is a person on whose instructions directors will normally act. Excluded from this definition is advice given in a professional capacity, e.g. by accountants, solicitors, bankers.)

13.10 Fraudulent Trading

Section 213 Insolvency Act 1986 states that where a company enters liquidation and that company has been trading with the intent to defraud creditors, then any party who was knowingly party to this, e.g. a director, can be ordered by the court to make contributions to the company's assets. Such activity is known as 'fraudulent trading' and is a criminal offence.

13.11 *Re M C Bacon Limited* (1989)

The background to this case was that the company lost its main customer, which seriously affected its financial position. As a result the bank insisted that its own head office accountancy investigation team should investigate the company and report back. This report stated that the company was 'virtually insolvent' but could survive if certain steps were taken. Consequently, the bank agreed to renew the overdraft at £250,000, provided that a mortgage debenture was given as security and that the company considered implementing recommendations made by its investigation team.

Subsequently, few of the recommendations were implemented by the company, and despite efforts by the directors a buyer for the business was not forthcoming. The directors therefore took steps to place the company into liquidation and the bank appointed an administrative receiver under its mortgage debenture.

The liquidator sought to show that the bank had acted as a shadow director, and as such, if it could be proven that it had been guilty of wrongful trading, should contribute to the assets of the company in liquidation. The liquidator also sought to show that the giving of the mortgage debenture as security to the bank was a preference and a transaction at an undervalue.

The liquidator abandoned the claim that the bank was a shadow director, and it therefore would seem at present that banks are safe with regard to this type of claim.

As regards the preference claim, it was held that the important test for a preference was whether the company desired to give a preference. The judge stated that 'a man can choose the lesser of two evils without desiring either'. An illustration of this in this case was the statement of one of the directors that either the bank was given a debenture or it would have called in the overdraft. The liquidator's claim therefore failed. The liquidator also failed with a claim regarding the giving of the security as a transaction at an undervalue. The judgment held that by charging its assets, the company had only appropriated them to meet liabilities due which did not reduce their value. The company had given nothing away and the value which the company had received in return was incapable of being measured in 'money or money's-worth'.

Summary

Now that you have read this unit, you should be able to:

☐ Recognise what action should be taken in the event of a company being compulsorily wound up.

☐ Differentiate between members' and creditors' voluntary liquidations.

☐ Detail procedures to be followed upon receipt of notice of voluntary liquidation.

☐ Identify the difference between an individual and company voluntary arrangement.

☐ Recognise the differences between company and individual preferences and transactions at an undervalue.

☐ Differentiate between wrongful trading and fraudulent trading.

If you can tick all the above boxes with confidence, you are ready to answer the questions which follow on pp.153–55.

List of Cases

Re M C Bacon Limited (1989)

National Westminster Bank Ltd v *Halesowen Presswork and Assemblies Ltd* (1972)

List of Statutes

Insolvency Act 1986

Self-assessment Questions

Short-answer questions

1   There are three types of company liquidation. What are they?

2   Megabux Ltd is a good customer of your branch and normally maintains a high credit balance on its account. Today, 23 March, you learn of a petition for the compulsory winding up of the company, which has been presented by a creditor who is owed £1,500.

The company's account has a credit balance of £197,500. In this morning's clearing there is a cheque which is technically in order and dated 28 February drawn on the company's account for £900 payable to 'H.M. Customs and Excise'.

What action would you take concerning this cheque?

3   On 12 February your customer, Havant Allott Ltd, has a winding-up order made against it which you learn of from an article in your local evening newspaper. On 15 February the two directors of the company call and ask you to give them the freehold deeds of the company's factory, which are held in the company's name in safe custody.

How would you respond?

4   Define a 'transaction at an undervalue'.

5   When can insolvency be presumed and not have to be proven in connection with action taken by a liquidator in relation to a transaction at an undervalue?

6   Define when a 'preference' is said to have taken place.

7   Define a 'shadow director'.

8   What is 'wrongful trading'?

9   What is 'fraudulent trading'?

10 If a director is found guilty as a party to a company trading fraudulently, what action can the court take?

11 What section of the Insolvency Act 1986 covers fraudulent trading?

12 What section of the Insolvency Act 1986 confirms that if a director is found guilty of wrongful trading, a liquidator can apply to the court for that director to be made liable for company debts?

(Answers are given in Appendix 2, pp. 307–08)

Multiple-choice questions

1 Credit and debit balances can be set off when a company enters liquidation. Which case confirmed this?

(a) *National Westminster Bank Ltd* v *Halesowen Presswork and Assemblies Ltd* (1972).
(b) *Re M C Bacon Limited* (1989).

2 A transaction at an undervalue can be attacked by a liquidator of a limited company, where such a transaction has taken place within what period prior to the commencement of the insolvency of the company? (s.238 Insolvency Act 1986.)

(a) 3 months.
(b) 4 months.
(c) 6 months.
(d) 1 year.
(e) 2 years.

3 The answer to Q2 applies to:

(a) An ordinary creditor?
(b) A connected person?

4 A preference can be attached by a liquidator of a limited company, provided the transaction took place within what period of the commencement of the insolvency, with the exception of connected persons?

(a) 3 months.
(b) 4 months.
(c) 6 months.
(d) 1 year.
(e) 2 years.

5 For a connected person, what would be the answer to Q4?

(a) 3 months.
(b) 4 months.
(c) 6 months.
(d) 1 year.
(e) 2 years.

6 Ena Fix Ltd, who banks with you, has entered liquidation. The balances on its accounts are as follows:

No 1 account Dr £24,000
No 2 account Cr £6,000
Wages account Dr £12,000

No letter of set off is held. For what amount would the bank have a preferential claim?

(a) £12,000.
(b) £10,000.
(c) £8,000.
(d) £6,000.

(Answers are given in Appendix 2, p. 308)

Past examination question

Your customer, Kidtoys Ltd, a toy manufacturer, has been experiencing trading difficulties through reduced sales. In May 1990 the directors of the company agreed to an investigation into its financial and trading position by a firm of chartered accountants who were instructed by your bank to report and make recommendations. In late June the report was received, and this stated that the company was in great difficulties and possibly almost insolvent but that, with continued bank support at the existing level of £500,000, it could survive, as the directors had taken steps to reduce costs and were to engage in a marketing campaign to raise turnover. The report also recommended that the directors should consider the sale of certain fixed assets, and might like to consider finding a purchaser for the business who could inject capital.

Your bank agreed to continue its support, but only subject to the provision of security, and on 1 July the company executed a debenture incorporating a fixed charge over land, buildings, goodwill, book and other debts, and a floating charge over all the company's other assets.

However, in September, the directors of Kidtoys formed the view that the company was still losing money and, on 15 September, the company's members and creditors voted at separate meetings for the company to be placed immediately into a creditors' voluntary liquidation. On 16 September the bank appointed an administrative receiver under the terms of its security. Later in September the liquidator wrote to both the bank and the receiver claiming that the bank's debenture was invalid as a voidable preference and as a transaction at under value.

Required

State the grounds upon which the liquidator is making his two claims. Indicate what he must prove, and state whether you consider his claims have any merit. Deal with each claim separately.

Give reasons for your answer.

[17 marks]

(Autumn 1990)

(Answer is given in Appendix 2, pp. 308–09)

UNIT 14

Mock Examination

Answer all questions. Time allowed three hours plus 15 minutes' reading time.

1   On 15 February 1989 you learnt by telephone from the Official Receiver that your customer, Mathon Ltd, had gone into compulsory liquidation on that day. Its current account was then £44,341 overdrawn. As security you hold a first legal mortgage over its factory, valued on a forced-sale basis at £110,000, and unlimited joint and several guarantee from two of its directors, Mr Lowe and Mrs Lowe. Whilst you had previously feared that the company might be in difficulties, you were surprised to hear of the liquidation.

Today, 16 October 1989, the liquidator has written to you claiming that all transactions in the company's account since the petition was presented on 3 January 1989 are void. (Details of the account appear below.) He also says he believes the directors to be guilty of wrongful trading for three months prior to the commencement of the liquidation, and he requires to know what they said to you when seeking renewal of the company's overdraft facilities in November 1988.

Mathon Ltd

1989			**Debits** £	**Credits** £	**Balance** £
January	1	Brought Forward	36,310		Dr 36,310
	4	Smith & Co	2,908		Dr 39,218
	5	Cheques		1,119	Dr 38,099
	17	Wages	5,214		Dr 43,313
		Cheques		2,407	Dr 40,906
	28	Electricity	3,910		Dr 44,816
	31	Water	1,109		Dr 45,925
February	8	Thomas	816		Dr 46,741
		Cheques		2,400	Dr 44,341

Required

(a)   Comment on the reasons for the liquidator's claim concerning transactions in the account. What merit (if any) is there in his claim?

[11 marks]

(b)   State what you understand by 'wrongful trading', and indicate the possible consequences if that is proved.

[4 marks]

(c)   State whether you will give the liquidator information concerning the renewal of the overdraft facilities. Give reasons for your answer.

[2 marks]
[Total 17 marks]

(Autumn 1989)

2   As Manager of the Slipshod Bank, you are holding an interview with Gerry Manders who is a jobbing builder and maintains the account of Gerry Manders Builders with you. The business has been suffering recently from cash flow problems largely due to the late payment for jobs completed by Mr Manders. He has brought in a list of these outstanding debts and you are surprised to see that one of the people mentioned is a highly regarded private customer of your branch, Will Enall, who maintains high credit balances on his accounts. Mr Manders explains the background to each debt on the list and it appears that Mr Enall owes Mr Manders £22,000 in respect of a loft extension and erection of a conservatory. Mr Manders advises you that he is going to be pressing for immediate payment from his debtors over the next few weeks and if payment is not forthcoming then he will be seeking restitution through the courts. Coincidentally, Will Enall calls to see you later the same day to discuss with you various investments, which he is contemplating making. During the course of the conversation he mentions about the building work recently carried out by Mr Manders and says that he is in dispute with Mr Manders concerning the quality of the workmanship and materials used but that he hoped to come to some sort of compromise shortly. Two months later you have another interview with Gerry Manders who advises you that he has been very successful in collecting outstanding debts, with the exception of the debt owed by Mr Enall. Despite several attempts to resolve the matter, Mr Manders had been unsuccessful and this had thus resulted in the presentation of a petition to the court a week ago and the hearing of the petition was due to take place in nine weeks' time. (He shows you a letter from the court confirming this.) He expected that by taking this action he would persuade Mr Enall to meet his debt in full prior to the hearing, rather than face the stigma which would be attached should a bankruptcy order be granted against him.

At the end of the interview, you discover that the balance of Mr Enall's current account is £15,600 credit and his high interest current account has a credit balance of £37,500.

Other matters which you discover are as follows:

—   Since the petition was presented to the court, cheques to the value of £27,500 have been paid on the accounts, including five totalling £8,000 which have been cashed by Mr Enall.

—   In today's clearing there are seven cheques totalling £12,500, one of which is payable to 'Inland Revenue' for £11,000, and all drawn on the current account and technically in order.

Required

(a) Define a 'petition' and what are the grounds for presenting one?

[5 marks]

(b) What action should you take with regard to the accounts of Will Enall and the cheques in today's clearing?

[5 marks]

(c) What is the bank's position with regard to the cheques which have already been paid since the petition was presented to court?

[5 marks]

(d) If the bank had no knowledge of the petition and only learnt of the proceedings on the day the bankruptcy order had been adjudicated, what would be its position with regard to any transactions passed through the bankrupt's accounts between the date of the petition and the date of the bankruptcy order?

[5 marks]

[Total 20 marks]

3 Your customer, Day Construction Ltd, went into creditors' voluntary liquidation on 17 April 1990, when the company's balances in your books were:

Current Account	£10,000 Dr
Loan Account	£30,000 Dr
No 2 Account	£18,000 Cr
Wages and Salaries Account	£20,000 Dr

Your bank has no security and, in addition to its lendings, it is at risk because it gave Town Local Authority an 'on demand' bond for £50,000 on 1 April 1989 in respect of a contract relating to roadworks and drainage to be carried out by Day Construction Ltd on an estate in High Lane, Town.

You submitted your claims to the liquidator on 18 April 1990.

Today (14 May 1990) you have received from Town Local Authority a demand for immediate payment of £50,000 and, on checking your records, you see that, although it was understood that Day Construction Ltd would give you a counter-indemnity, this has been overlooked and has never been received.

Required

(a) Set out the bank's various claims in the liquidation of Day Construction Ltd which you should have submitted on 18 April 1990. Base your answer solely on the balances and the facts given above. Give reasons for your answer.

[10 marks]

(b) State what factors you would bear in mind, and explain what actions (if any) you would take, in response to the demand for immediate payment from Town Local Authority.

[7 marks]

[Total 17 marks]

(Spring 1990)

4 What is the position of the bank in the following situations?

(a) Your valued customer, Jack Trasker, has deposited several share certificates with your branch in safe custody. Half of these shares are in the name of your customer and half in the name of Jane Trasker, who is unknown to you.

Today a lady who identifies herself as Jane Trasker calls at your branch and tells you that her husband, Jack Trasker, deposited some of her share certificates with your branch by mistake when he deposited his own for safe keeping. She informs you that she has recently sold these shares and now her stockbroker requires them in order to complete the deal. She advises you that her husband is currently abroad for six months touring the Far East with some friends and cannot be contacted. She asks you to return her share certificates to her.

[12 marks]

(b) The bank vault at your branch was recently flooded when the nearby river burst its banks. This caused several of the boxes stored in safe custody to be immersed in water. One of your customers who has come to examine his box after the flood is your valued customer, Phil Attlee. He shows you the sodden remains of what was apparently his stamp collection which was stored in the box. He tells you that the collection was worth at least £20,000 and that he will be claiming restitution from the bank.

[8 marks]

[Total 20 marks]

5   At 10.30 this morning, 27 April 1987 your Head Office telephoned to advise you that they had been served with an unlimited garnishee order *nisi* made on 24 April naming your customer, Custard Pies Ltd, as the judgment debtor, and Rhubarb Supplies Ltd as the judgment creditor. The judgment debt is shown as £3,237.17, entered by the Court against Custard Pies Ltd on 31 March 1987.

Your customer's account as at last close of business, Friday 24 April, shows a credit balance of £2,911.14 and in today's in-clearings are two cheques and one bank giro credit. The cheques are both dated 11 April 1987, one being for £257.98 in favour of Rhubarb Supplies Ltd, and another for £444.14 in favour of the Inland Revenue. The bank giro credit, for £311.11, was paid in at your Country branch last Thursday, 23 April, and consisted of £200 cash and a cheque for £111.11.

Also in this morning's post is a special presentation of a cheque for £399.19, dated 31 March 1987, drawn by Custard Pies Ltd in favour of Williams & Co. This cheque has been cancelled by one of your clerks, who has prepared a letter of advice of fate to the presenting bank, Downtown Bank Plc.

Immediately after you have completed the telephone call you notice that a director of Custard Pies Ltd is at your counter presenting a cheque for encashment.

Required

State what action you would take in respect of:

(a)   the garnishee proceedings;
(b)   Custard Pie's account;
(c)   the transactions mentioned above.

Give reasons for your answers.

[17 marks]
(Spring 1987)

(Answers are given in Appendix 2, pp. 309–12)

UNIT 15

Bank Security Forms, Clauses and Solicitors' Undertakings

Objectives

- Appreciate the effects of clauses contained in bank security forms.
- Recognise the reasons for and significance of solicitors' undertakings for banks.

15.1   Bank Security Forms

When banks lend money to customers, they will often require the borrower to provide assets which can be mortgaged/charged as security. Such charges are known as direct security. Where security is provided for the borrower's liabilities by other than the borrower, this is known as third-party or indirect security.

In this unit we will be examining the clauses contained in the bank's standard charge form for direct security. (We will examine clauses contained in a bank's indirect security form in Unit 21.)

15.2   Main Clauses found in Direct Security Charge Forms

Student Activity

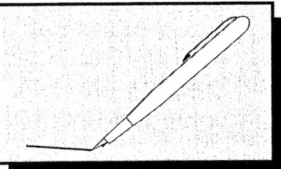

Examine the clauses contained in your bank's direct security charge forms and compare them with those given below.

15.2.1   All moneys clause

This clause is designed to cover all liabilities due either now or in the future, both actual or contingent. A contingent liability could arise where a bank is called upon to pay under an advance payment guarantee which it gave on behalf of its customer. In such circumstances, the bank could seek reimbursement by realising the security given if its customer could not pay.

Often coupled with this clause is a section specifically excluding s.93 Law of Property Act 1925. If this exclusion were not included, and the bank held several mortgages over various assets, then after partial repayment of the borrowing, the borrower could insist that one or more of the charges be released. Obviously depending upon their marketability, this could result in the bank having to release its more saleable security, thus undermining its security position.

This exclusion of s.93 Law of Property Act 1925 is not strictly necessary, as the 'all moneys' clause gives the bank the right to retain all security until all borrowing is repaid. However, it does help to clarify and emphasise the point.

15.2.2   Continuing security clause

This clause prevents a claim from a charger that the security was given for a specific borrowing and that because of the rule in *Clayton's* case, future credits have repaid this original borrowing, thus releasing the security given.

15.2.3   Repayment on demand clause

This clause emphasises the borrower's duty to repay on demand. Once demand has been made by the bank, the time period scheduled under the Limitations Act 1980 begins to run from the date of demand. This means that the bank will have a right of action against the borrower for repayment for six years in respect of a security signed under hand, i.e. a simple contract or 12 years for a security completed under seal. After these times have elapsed, the bank's legal right of recovery ends (*Lloyds Bank Ltd* v *Margolis* (1954)).

Coupled with this clause will be a description of how the demand is to be delivered. This will normally say that it is to be in writing and addressed to the mortgagor's last known address. It will also say that mere service of the demand will make it effective, whether or not it is refused by the addressee or returned by the Post Office.

15.2.4   Power of sale clause

Section 101 Law of Property Act 1925 confirms that any mortgage made by deed entitles the mortgagee to sell that mortgaged property. However, s.103 Law of Property Act 1925 delays a mortgagee's right of sale by stating that it can only be exercised where (a) demand has been made and the borrower is three months in arrears, or (b) interest is two months or more in arrears, or (c) some other term of the mortgage has been breached.

Banks therefore avoid this delay by explicitly excluding s.103 Law of Property Act 1925 in their power of sale clause.

15.2.5   Additional security clause

This clause states that the security is in addition to any other security held now or in the future. As such, it will remain valid where other security is taken or released in the future.

15.2.6   Conclusive evidence clause

This will state that a statement of indebtedness sent to a customer by a bank will be conclusive proof of the amount due unless the amount is questioned by the customer within (normally) 14 days. The clause is designed to prevent any dispute over the amount of the debt and was held to be valid in *Bache and Co (London) Ltd* v *Banque Vernes et Commerciale de Paris* (1973). However, nowadays, the bank would have to act reasonably, otherwise the Unfair Contract Terms Act 1977 could invalidate this clause.

15.2.7 Consideration clause

This clause will say that in consideration for borrowing allowed by the bank, an asset has been charged by the mortgagor to the bank as security.

15.2.8 Successor clause

This states that where the bank may change its name or be taken over, the new owner will take over the rights of the bank concerned with regard to the security given.

15.2.9 Priority protection clause

Where a bank receives notice of a further charge over security which it holds, it will normally stop the relevant account, to prevent the rule in *Clayton's* case operating against the bank and a consequent dilution of the bank's priority position. This clause is designed to protect the bank's position if it fails to stop its customer's account, and was held to be valid in the case of *Westminster Bank Ltd* v *Cond* (1940).

15.3 Solicitors' Undertakings

Banks often have dealings with solicitors, particularly in respect of mortgages or the sale of land which they hold as security.

In such circumstances, the solicitor will be requested to undertake to carry out certain duties for the bank. As the bank will, therefore, be relying upon the integrity of the solicitor, it should carry out a status report with the solicitor's bankers and receive a satisfactory reply. Obviously, if the solicitor is known to the bank already, the need for a status report can be dispensed with.

If a solicitor does default, then the bank can look to the Law Society for compensation, although this event happens extremely rarely. In order to clarify the situation regarding solicitors' undertakings, the Law Society and the Committee of London Clearing Banks agreed standard forms of undertakings, which would mean that there was less chance of misinterpretation or dispute. The main types of solicitors' undertaking are detailed below.

15.3.1 Undertaking to release deeds or land certificate for inspection and return

Customers sometimes require sight of the document(s) of title to their property, perhaps due to a boundary dispute, rights of way or some other reason. This may obviously involve some legal interpretation and the customer may give the bank written instructions to forward the document(s) of title to the customer's solicitor. Providing that a good status report is held, the bank will comply with its customer's instructions against the solicitor's undertaking to hold the document(s) to the bank's order and to return them to the bank immediately, if requested, in the same condition as they were received. The solicitor will also return receipted any schedule of deeds/documents if it is not contained in the original undertaking.

Some banks may retain their mortgage form in respect of unregistered land and even the original of the last conveyance (substituting a photocopy) as a means of safeguarding their security position.

15.3.2 Undertaking relating to release of deeds or land certificate pending sale of property

A customer who wishes to sell property will have to provide the bank with written instruction to forward the documents of title to the solicitor who is dealing with the sale. The bank will require confirmation that contracts have been exchanged, and also details of the sale figure. (Where contracts have not been exchanged, an inspection and return undertaking may be applicable initially.)

The undertaking, if contracts have been exchanged, will give details of a net sum to be paid to the bank after payment of legal costs and estate agents' fees. It will also state that the document(s) of title will be returned to the bank in the same condition as received, if the sale does not occur or at the bank's request. Following receipt of the sale proceeds, the bank will release its charge in the usual way.

This type of undertaking, in addition to being used when a customer wishes to repay bank borrowing, may be used where another lender wishes to take over the bank borrowing. In such a case, the bank will require written confirmation from the lender of the extent of the financial commitment.

15.3.3 Undertaking to use moneys lent by the bank to purchase title to a property

A solicitor will undertake to use moneys advanced to obtain a good and marketable title to a property and to hold the property's title documents to the order of the bank and to complete any mortgage from the purchaser to the bank when the title to the property passes to the purchaser.

If the bank is taking a second or subsequent mortgage, it will require confirmation that written commitment from the first mortgagee with regard to funds advanced has been seen. Obviously, the wording of the undertaking will be altered to take into account the fact that the bank would be a second or subsequent mortgagee, rather than a first mortgagee.

15.3.4 Undertakings relating to bridging facilities

Bridging facilities occur when a bank agrees to lend money to a customer for the acquisition of a property pending the sale of an existing property from which source repayment will be forthcoming. Bridging facilities can be open-ended bridges or closed bridges. Open-ended bridges are far more risky for the lending bank, in that funds will be advanced before contracts have been exchanged with regard to the sale of the existing property. Closed bridges are where contracts have been exchanged for the sale of the existing property.

Undertakings for bridging facilities differ in their content, as bridging facilities vary from transaction to transaction. For example, one transaction may only involve the lending of the full purchase price of the new property. In another, the bank may first lend money to repay the outstanding mortgage on the existing property and take a first mortgage over it as security, and then lend the full purchase price of the new property. Whichever bridging facility is agreed, the clauses contained in the solicitor's undertaking must cover all eventualities.

Such clauses should cover some or all of the following:

(a) Application of sums received to discharge the outstanding mortgage on the existing property.

(b) Application of sums received to obtain a good and marketable title to the new property.

(c) Application of sums received to pay any legal costs and payments due in connection with the purchase.

(d) Confirmation of the purchase price and total amounts involved.

(e) Details of the proposed mortgage and details of the lender.

(f) An undertaking to hold to the order of the bank the documents of title (i) of the existing property pending sale and (ii) of the new property (unless they are subject to any prior mortgage).

(g) Payment to the bank of the net sale proceeds of the existing property.

(h) Details of expected sale proceeds and likely disbursements.

Summary

Now that you have read this unit, you should be able to:

☐ Appreciate the effects of clauses contained in bank security forms.

☐ Recognise the reasons for and significance of solicitors' undertakings for banks.

If you can tick all the above boxes with confidence, you are ready to answer the questions that follow on p. 166.

List of Cases

Bache and Co (London) Ltd v *Banque vernes et Commerciale de Paris* (1973)

Clayton's case *(Devaynes* v *Noble* 1816)

Lloyds Bank Ltd v *Margolis* (1954)

Westminster Bank Ltd v *Cond* (1940)

List of Statutes

Law of Property Act 1925

Unfair Contract Terms Act 1977

Self-assessment Questions

Short-answer questions

1   List the main clauses found in a bank's direct security charge form.

2   James Edwards has taken out several loans with the bank over the last three years and has provided various assets as security. The repayments of these loans has run smoothly and several of the loans have now been repaid. Mr Edwards has therefore requested that the mortgages given at the time that these repaid loans were taken out should now be released and the assets returned to him. He says that this is his right under s.93 Law of Property Act 1925. What is your reaction?

3   In April 1990 your bank agreed an overdraft with your customer Alf Love of £20,000 providing that he gave the bank a first legal mortgage over the deeds of his house which was valued at the time at £150,000. This facility has been renewed annually. In May 1991, Mr Love requested a loan of £30,000 to purchase a small boat. In view of the security held, the bank decided not to request any further security.

Today, Mr Love has called to advise you that he has not had to use his overdraft facility for the past six months and will not need to use it for the foreseeable future. You therefore agree to cancel this facility and Mr Love asks for his security to be released and returned to him. When you remind him that he still has an outstanding loan and that the mortgage will be required to secure that, Mr Love says that he believed that the mortgage which he gave was only to secure the overdraft.

What would be your response?

4   If a solicitor gives an undertaking to a bank in standard form but subsequently defaults, who can the bank look to for compensation?

5   Following recent gales which severely damaged a wall between your customer, Ian Patch's property and his neighbour's land, Mr Patch has written to you requesting that you forward the deeds of his house to his solicitors, Earnest, Frank and Speed so that it can be established who is responsible for repairing the damage. The solicitors are known to you and you have a first legal mortgage over Mr Patch's property.

Detail the procedure which would be followed to meet your customer's request.

(Answers are given in Appendix 2, pp. 312–13)

UNIT 16

Company Securities, Debentures, Administrative Receivers, Administrators and Receivers

---

Objectives

- Identify procedures to be followed regarding registration of company charges in accordance with the 1989 Companies Act.
- Recognise those company securities which do or do not require registration with the registrar of companies.
- Be able to detail the procedures to be followed with regard to the registration of company securities with the registrar of companies.
- Recognise how a registered charge can be cancelled with the registrar of companies.
- Identify the components of a bank debenture.
- Be able to detail the procedures to be followed when taking a debenture as security.
- Appreciate the problems of a floating charge.
- Recognise the complexities of retention of title clauses to goods.
- Identify the remedies available to a debenture holder.
- Differentiate between administrative receivers, administrators and receivers.
- Detail the procedure to be followed to discharge a bank debenture.

16.1 Registration of Charges and the 1989 Companies Act

Companies often provide direct security in order to support their borrowing requirements from the banks. Direct security is where a company executes a charge over some or all of the assets which it owns. The taking of such security will often require registration with the registrar of companies. As at the time of writing, such registration procedures have been amended by the 1989 Companies Act although they have not yet been put into practice. The text will therefore refer to these amended procedures and sections of the Companies Act 1985 as amended by the 1989 Companies Act.

16.1.1 Securities given by companies which require registration

Section 396 details those charges which must be registered with the registrar of companies. These include:

(a) Charges on land or interest in land.

(b) Charges on goods or interests in goods. Excluded from these are money, or occasions where the chargee is entitled to the documents of title to the goods, or even possession of the goods themselves, e.g. produce advances.

(c) Charges on goodwill, intellectual property, book debts, or uncalled share capital.

(d) Floating charges over company property, e.g. stock.

(e) Charges for securing the issue of debentures.

16.1.2 Securities given by companies which do not require registration

The following securities do not need registration with the registrar of companies.

(a) Stocks and shares which are held by the company as assets in its balance sheet. (This does not refer to the company's own stocks and shares which form part of the capital of the company.)

(b) Pledges over goods, e.g. produce advances.

(c) Insurance policies. These will normally be taken out by a company on the life of an individual whose death would adversely affect the company. Such insurance is known as key-person insurance.

(d) Negotiable instruments, e.g. bills of exchange which may be deposited as security against book debts.

(e) Guarantees.

(f) Set off letters. These give a company's formal agreement that a bank can set off two or more of the company's accounts to arrive at a net position.

(Students should note that the first letters of each of these securities provide the mnemonic 'SPINGS', which should help them to remember.)

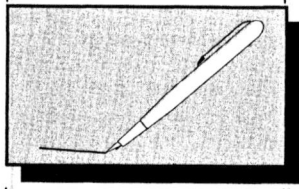

Student Activity 1

Examine your bank's rules concerning the procedures to be followed regarding registration of company security with the registrar of companies. Compare these procedures with the procedure set out in the 1985 Companies Act as amended by the 1989 Companies Act, detailed below.

16.2 Registration of Charges

Under s.396, the registrar of companies must maintain a register of charges over company assets/property which are laid down in this section.

Under s.398(4), particulars of the charge must be recorded and the date upon which the particulars were delivered to the registrar. Under s.398(5), the registrar must forward a certificate containing the particulars of the charge and the date of delivery to the charger (the company) and the chargee (the

bank) and to any person who delivered the particulars who has an interest in the charge.

If the details of a charge have to be altered or added to in any way, then the amended particulars can be forwarded to the registrar with a covering form signed by the company and the chargee (s.401). If the company should refuse to sign this form, then the bank could apply to the courts for dispensation of the company's signature (s.417(1)). It is likely that banks will incorporate a clause in their charge forms which will enable the banks to carry this out on the company's behalf, if the company should refuse to be co-operative.

Although a company is supposed to deliver the particulars of a charge to the registrar for registration in the prescribed form, it is usual for the bank to do this itself. This is allowed under s.398(2). The charge should be registered within 21 days of being created. In the case of a charge over property which is being purchased or acquired this should be registered within 21 days of the date of acquisition (s.398(1)).

If these particulars are not registered within the 21 days stipulated, the charge is not necessarily void. However, if a person should acquire an interest in the property which is the subject of the charge, or insolvency proceedings against the company commence, and these situations occur after the charge has been created but before the particulars have been registered, then such a charge would be considered void. These occurrences are referred to as 'relevant events' in s.399(1) and (2).

As regards the 'relevant event' pertaining to insolvency proceedings, an administrator or liquidator of the company would have to provide evidence that the company was unable to pay its debts at the date when the particulars were delivered, or that as a result of the creation of the charge the company was unable to pay its debts. The administrator/liquidator would also have to show that the insolvency proceedings commenced before the 'relevant period' expired (s.400(2)).

Section 400(3) defines a 'relevant period' as follows:

> In the case of floating charges two years where it is created in favour of a connected person or one year for a non-connected person or six months for any other type of charge.

Under s.416 a person taking a charge is deemed to have notice of any matter requiring registration and disclosed on the register at the time the charge is created. Such information could be the undertaking of the company not to create any future charge, which would rank *pari passu* or ahead of the charge being registered.

If particulars are delivered to the registrar of companies which are either inaccurate or incomplete, then any underlying charge will be void to the extent of these inaccuracies or omissions (s.402(1)).

However, a bank could apply to the courts for the making of an order to validate such a charge. This will normally be granted, provided that the court is satisfied that no unsecured creditor has been materially misled and that no

person has become an unsecured creditor while the registered particulars were incomplete or inaccurate.

16.2.1 Cancellation of registered charge

A completed memorandum signed by, or on behalf of, the company and the charges should be delivered to the registrar (s.403). The registrar will file it and note the date of delivery. The company and the chargee will then be advised by the registrar that this has been carried out, with details of the date of delivery.

16.3 Debentures

The most common security taken by banks from companies is a debenture.

16.3.1 What is a bank debenture?

This will normally be an all-monies debenture which will give a fixed charge over a company's freehold and leasehold property, fixed plant and machinery, goodwill, trademarks, patents, uncalled capital, book debts and other debts. It will also give a floating charge over the remainder of the company's assets.

The validity of the clause giving a fixed charge over book debts was confirmed in the case of *Siebe Gorman and Co Ltd* v *Barclays Bank* (1979). Also as regards book debts the debenture will contain a clause whereby the company covenants to pay all monies collected into its bank account. This seems to indicate that the freedom of use of an asset which the company would enjoy under a floating charge is curtailed by this clause.

The debenture will also show that any real property which the company may acquire in the future will be subject to an equitable charge in favour of the bank.

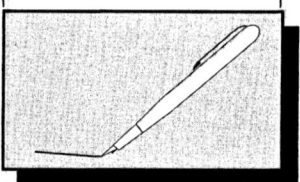

Student Activity 2

Obtain a copy of your bank's debenture form and compare its clauses with those given below.

16.3.2 What clauses will be found in a bank debenture form?

Some or all of the following clauses will be found in a bank debenture form:

(a) The security is to cover all liabilities due now or in the future.

(b) The charge will be expressed as a continuing security.

(c) Monies due will be deemed to be repayable on demand. Section 103 Law of Property Act 1925 will be specifically excluded so that the bank's power of sale and its ability to appoint an administrative receiver become enforceable immediately upon default.

(d) There will be a first charge by way of legal mortgage over property scheduled in the debenture and a first equitable charge on all other company property owned both now and in the future. The company will also undertake to deposit with the bank title documents relating to any acquired property and to complete a legal mortgage if called upon to do so.

(e) A fixed charge will be created over the company's present and future book and other debts.

(f) A fixed charge over goodwill, trademarks, patents and uncalled capital of the company will be granted.

(g) Thereafter the company will undertake to grant to the bank a floating charge over all other company assets.

(h) The company will covenant not to create a mortgage or charge which will rank alongside (*pari passu*) or ahead of the bank's charge.

(i) The company will undertake to maintain a certain ratio of assets cover to the level of its borrowing from the bank.

(j) The company will undertake to maintain the property in good repair and also to keep it adequately insured.

(k) A clause will state that when the security becomes enforceable the bank may appoint an administrative receiver. It will go on to say that the administrative receiver will be an agent of the company, which will be responsible for any actions the receiver might take.

(l) A clause will deal with the administrative receiver's right to remuneration out of any realised proceeds of the company's assets.

(m) The company will undertake to provide any information relating to the business to the bank or any accountant appointed by the bank.

(n) A clause will stipulate that any notice which it is necessary to serve on the company, such as a demand for repayment, may be served at the company's registered office and that such notice shall be deemed to be served whether or not it is accepted or returned.

16.3.3 How do you take a debenture as security?

Some banks will examine the company's memorandum and articles of association to ascertain such matters as whether the company can give security or whether 'interested' directors can vote to give the security. Other banks, in view of the Companies Act 1989, will merely request confirmation from the company or its legal advisers that the giving of the security is in accordance with the memorandum and articles of association of the company.

If the debenture includes a legal mortgage over land, then the normal steps for perfecting such a mortgage should be carried out. The bank should obtain a copy of the board resolution agreeing to the giving of the security and the bank's debenture should be completed and sealed by the company.

Particulars of the debenture should be filed with the registrar of companies within 21 days of creation of the charge. The registrar should be requested to provide a certificate of filing. Searches at Companies Registry should be carried out both before and after the giving of the security to ensure that there are no charges outstanding beforehand, that the particulars of the bank's charge which are filed are accurate, and that no other particulars have been filed during the intervening period. A valuation of the debenture should also be carried out.

The company should deposit its fire policy so that the bank can ensure that there is adequate cover. The bank will also give notice of its interest to the insurance company and request an acknowledgement. In addition, the bank will require sight of all the company's other insurances covering such matters as stock, book debts, and public liability.

The bank will diarise to ensure that fire insurance premium receipts are exhibited annually.

16.4   Floating Charges

A floating charge enables a company to deal freely with both present and future assets covered by such a charge until such time as the floating charge crystallises. A floating charge will crystallise if an administrative receiver is appointed or the company ceases business or enters liquidation, or if there is a breach of the terms of the debenture which causes crystallisation, e.g. default on repayment.

The latter was confirmed in *Re Brightlife Ltd* (1987). This case also established that where there was a clause in the form of floating charge which allowed a chargee to convert a floating charge into a specific charge over particular assets, having given notice to the charger, then the effect of this in practice was to create a fixed charge over these assets. Such action would be valid provided that an administrative receiver had not been appointed, nor was the company being wound up. It is worth remembering at this stage that when a company is wound up or an administrative receiver has been appointed, the holder of a floating charge ranks in priority behind a preferential creditor (ss.40 and 175 Insolvency Act 1986). Thus the decision in *Re Brightlife Ltd* (1987) would work to the advantage of the bank if it had taken action to turn a floating charge into a fixed charge prior to either of the said events taking place. This is because a fixed charge would give a bank priority over all other creditors, whereas assets covered by a floating charge would be required to repay preferential creditors before the floating charge holder would receive any payment from them.

16.4.1   Problems relating to floating charges

In addition to the priority which preferential creditors benefit from ahead of floating charge holders, there are other problems which floating charge holders have to consider.

If a company is insolvent when a floating charge is given and that company enters liquidation within 12 months of the floating charge being created, then the security will only be effective for new monies advanced (s.245 Insolvency Act 1986). Thus applying this criterion means that past advances will not be secured by the floating charge. However, the rule in *Clayton's* case operates to the bank's benefit here, as any future credits will reduce the debt which existed at the time the charge was taken, and any future debits will create new borrowing which will be secured by the floating charge. This was confirmed in the cases of *Re Thomas Mortimer Ltd* (1925) and *Re Yeovil Glove Co Ltd* (1965).

If a bank does not file at Companies Registry that the company is prevented from creating any charge which will rank *pari passu* or ahead of the bank's charge, then any subsequent mortgagee can obtain a valid fixed charge over an asset which would be covered by the bank's floating charge. Thus it is essential that all relevant particulars are checked by the bank as being correctly filed at Companies Registry.

A floating charge?

If a company is in financial trouble it is likely that it will sell off a great deal of its assets, e.g. stock, which would be picked up under the floating charge in order to pay off pressing creditors. Although banks will normally include a clause in their debentures that assets are to be kept within certain ratios to borrowing, by the time that they hear of the reduction in assets it is often too late to do anything about it.

Some creditors, if they are not being paid, may decide to seize assets in lieu of payment. Again these assets would probably be covered by the bank's floating charge, and the chances of recovering these for the bank is normally minimal.

Finally, one of the major problems relating to floating charges is that certain stock in a company's possession may not have been paid for and the underlying commercial contract may contain a retention of title clause. This would mean that the ownership of the goods would not pass to the purchaser until payment had been made and would therefore remain the property of the seller until such time that this contract has been settled. If the goods were on-sold before they were paid for, then any proceeds would still belong to the original seller. This was confirmed in the first case held in England involving retention of title clauses, *Aluminium Industrie Vaassen BV* v *Romalpa Aluminium* (1976). As a result of this case, contracts for sale of goods are now often said to be sold on 'Romalpa terms'. It can be seen from this that if a great deal of stock, work-in-progress or sales proceeds are subject to 'Romalpa terms', then the value of a floating charge over such assets will be greatly diminished.

16.4.2   Further cases relating to goods sold on 'Romalpa terms'

Clough Mill Ltd v *Martin* (1984) established that where goods are identifiable and the sales contract contains an adequately worded retention of title clause, then the seller can reclaim the goods concerned. Contrast this, however, with the decision in *Re Bond Worth Ltd* (1979). In this case the underlying sales contract contained a clause referring to 'equitable and beneficial' ownership of the goods remaining with the seller. The case established that such wording allows the legal title to the goods to pass to the purchaser and as such does not allow the seller to recover the goods, where payment has not been made, in the event of the purchaser's liquidation. This type of clause would therefore be considered to be a charge and would thus require registration at Companies Registry.

Armour v *Thyssen Edelstahlwerke AG* (1990) held that a reservation of title clause in a contract for the sale of goods does not create a right of security in favour of the vendor which is capable of registration under the Companies Act 1985. The House of Lords held that if a reservation of title clause was considered to be good then a vendor's right of security over the goods covered by such a clause could not coexist. It continued by stating that under the 'right of security' principle a creditor is obliged to pay over any surplus proceeds to the debtor once the original debt has been satisfied. However, where a good reservation of title clause exists, if the vendor should repossess the contract goods and sell them elsewhere for more than the original contract price, such monies would remain the property of the original vendor.

Compaq Computers Limited v *Abercorn Group Limited* (1991) held that where a reservation of title clause purports to cover the sale proceeds when goods have been on-sold, it will be void for lack of registration at Companies Registry (where the original purchaser is a limited company).

Borden (UK) Limited v *Scottish Timber Products Limited* (1979) established that where goods which were subject to retention of title clauses had lost their identity in a manufacturing process, then the original seller of these goods cannot lay claim to part of the value of the final manufactured product.

As can be seen, 'Romalpa terms' are a legal minefield and although legislation has been promised to clarify the situation, this has not yet taken place.

16.4.3   Remedies of the debenture holder

(a)   Appoint an administrative receiver.
(b)   Sue the company on its covenant to repay.
(c)   Petition the court for the company to be wound up.
(d)   Sell or transfer the debenture to a third party.

16.5   Differences between Administrative Receivers, Administrators and Receivers

Students often become confused over the roles of administrative receivers, administrators and receivers. It is therefore sensible to clarify these roles at this stage of the course before we progress to the topic of insolvency.

When a company is in financial difficulties and on the verge of possible liquidation, the office of the person who is appointed depends upon who has made the appointment.

16.5.1 Administrative receivers

An administrative receiver is appointed under a floating charge s.29(2) Insolvency Act 1986 and must be a licensed insolvency practitioner (s.230(2) Insolvency Act 1986).

The person is appointed in writing and must accept the appointment by the end of the business day following receipt of the letter of appointment. Written confirmation of this acceptance must be given within seven days.

The administrative receiver must:

(a) advertise his or her appointment in the London Gazette and a local newspaper;

(b) give specific notice of the appointment to creditors within 28 days of the appointment;

(c) ensure that all company stationery contains notice of the appointment.

It is not uncommon for an administrative receiver to continue the business of the company with a view to selling it as a going concern (which will mean that more money will be raised for creditors than would otherwise be the case).

Although it is the bank which appoints the administrative receiver, he or she is in fact an agent of the company until liquidation occurs, with the power to bind the company contractually in any transaction which he or she initiates. However, the administrative receiver will deal with the security held at the bank's instruction.

The administrative receiver will be personally liable on all contracts unless he or she specifically contracts out of liability.

16.5.2 Administrators

An administrator is appointed under a court order which is applied for by a company, its directors or a creditor. The application for an administration order is based on 'the belief that the company is, or is likely to become, unable to pay its debts' – Rule 2.3.1(a) Insolvency Rules 1986.

An application is made to the court to appoint an administrator under s.9 Insolvency Act 1986. The court will give notice to any creditor who is entitled to appoint an administrative receiver. Under Insolvency Rules 2.6 and 2.7, at least five days' notice must be given of the hearing, and if an administrative receiver is appointed in that period, the petition to appoint an administrator will be dismissed.

If the time period of five days has expired without the bank appointing an administrative receiver under its floating charge, the court is free to grant the administration order and appoint an administrator.

The effect of the appointment of an administrator is to prevent winding-up proceedings being started. The implication of this is that the administrator will prevent the bank from realising the asset under its security. The bank will also be deprived of its right to realise assets subject to the floating charge. If the court permits, the administrator can sell assets that are caught under a fixed charge; in doing so, the claim of the secured creditor from the proceeds must be satisfied.

As the bank is deprived of its rights to realise its security under a debenture, it will usually oppose the appointment of an administrator, particularly as the administrator can continue to use assets charged to the bank in the everyday business of the company which the bank would otherwise have sold.

If the bank only holds a fixed charge it is unable to block the appointment of an administrator, unlike the holder of a floating charge. However, the securities can only be realised either with the agreement of the fixed charge holder – s.11(3) (c) and (d), Insolvency Act 1986, or by application to the court. If the court believes that this will benefit the survival of the company, or will achieve a better realisation of assets than would be the case in a liquidation, since the business can be continued and sold as a going concern, then it will allow the administrator to continue the business. There is, however, some protection for the fixed charge holder who has been deprived of the right of sale by an administrator's appointment: the fixed charge holder will receive at least the market price which could be obtained in an unenforced sale – s.11(5) and (6) Insolvency Act 1986. (Forced sale values of assets are almost always far lower than normal market value.) This 'market value' provision only applies to fixed charge holders and not to floating charge holders.

An administrator must provide proposals for creditors within three months and a meeting of creditors must approve these proposals, otherwise the administration order may be discharged. Only creditors whose debt is wholly or partially unsecured can vote on the proposals; a simple majority is all that is required.

16.5.3 Receivers

A receiver is appointed by a fixed charge holder under the Law of Property Act 1925. The receiver's role is to sell the assets caught under a fixed charge and to repay the fixed charge holder from the proceeds. Any surplus proceeds should be returned to the company. The problem with the appointment of a receiver is that if an administrator is subsequently appointed, the administrator can force the receiver to vacate office – s.11(1) and (2) Insolvency Act 1986.

16.6   Discharge of a Bank Debenture

The bank will have the statutory receipt completed on its debenture form. This form can either be given up to the company concerned, or a letter confirming the cancellation of the debenture can be forwarded by the bank to the company. A completed memorandum of satisfaction signed by the bank and the company should be forwarded to the registrar of companies, who will notify both parties that the memorandum has been filed, giving details of the date when this was done. Any other procedures which need to be carried out, e.g. cancellation of a charge over land, should also be processed.

Summary

Now that you have read this unit, you should be able to:

☐ Identify procedures to be followed regarding registration of company charges in accordance with the 1989 Companies Act.

☐ Recognise those company securities which do or do not require registration with the registrar of companies.

☐ Detail the procedures to be followed with regard to the registration of company securities with the registrar of companies.

☐ Recognise how a registered charge can be cancelled with the registrar of companies.

☐ Identify the components of a bank debenture.

☐ Detail the procedures to be followed when taking a debenture as security.

☐ Appreciate the problems of a floating charge.

☐ Recognise the complexities of retention of title clauses to goods.

☐ Identify the remedies available to a debenture holder.

☐ Differentiate between administrative receivers, administrators and receivers.

☐ Detail the procedure to be followed to discharge a bank debenture.

If you can tick all the above boxes with confidence, you are ready to answer the questions which follow on pp. 178–80.

List of Cases

Aluminium Industrie Vaassen BV v *Romalpa Aluminium* (1976)

Armour v *Thyssen Edelstahlwerke AG* (1990)

Re Bond Worth Ltd (1979)

Borden (UK) Limited v *Scottish Timber Products Limited* (1979)

Re Brightlife Ltd (1987)

Clough Mill Ltd v *Martin* (1984)

Compaq Computers Limited v *Abercorn Group Limited* (1991)

Devaynes v *Noble* (1816) (*Clayton's* case)

Re Thomas Mortimer Ltd (1925)

Siebe Gorman and Co Ltd v *Barclays Bank* (1979)

Re Yeovil Glove Co Ltd (1965)

List of Statutes

Companies Act 1985

Companies Act 1989

Insolvency Act 1986

Insolvency Rules 1986

Law of Property Act 1925

Self-assessment Questions

Short-answer questions

1   Under s.398(5), the registrar of companies must send a certificate to the charger and the chargee of a security.

What will be shown on this certificate?

2   Details of a charge can be altered with the registrar of companies – s.401, Companies Act 1985.

How is this effected?

3   Which case confirmed that a fixed charge over book debts was valid?

4   Long Mill Ltd created a debenture over its assets two years ago in favour of South Bank plc. It has recently purchased a derelict site for clearance and erection of a new factory for the company.

(a) Is it likely that this new site will be covered by the debenture?
(b) If your answer to (a) is no, what is South Bank's position as regards this newly acquired property?
(c) If your answer to (a) is yes, what type of charge will South Bank have?

5   Does the bank's debenture form contain a clause which obliges a company to deposit the title documents relating to acquired property with the

bank and to create a legal mortgage in the bank's favour if called upon to do so?

6   Under what conditions can a floating charge crystallise?

7   A retention of title clause in a commercial contract may affect the value of assets covered by a floating charge. Why?

8   What action can a floating charge holder take to prevent the appointment of an administrator?

(Answers are given in Appendix 2, pp. 313–14)

Multiple-choice questions

1   Which of the following securities given by companies require registration with the registrar of companies?

(a)   Guarantees.
(b)   Charges over land.
(c)   Pledges over goods.
(d)   Insurance policies.
(e)   Negotiable instruments.
(f)   Floating charges over a company's assets.
(g)   Stocks and shares.
(h)   Charges over book debts.

2   Morrow Ltd has given a charge over its premises to its bankers, Slapdash Bank plc. Unfortunately, Slapdash Bank Plc has received a certificate from the registrar of companies showing that details of the charge were not delivered to the registrar within the prescribed 21 days.

Is the charge:

(a)   Automatically void?
(b)   Automatically valid?
(c)   Valid, providing that no person has acquired an interest in the property prior to registration of the bank's charge or insolvency proceedings have not commenced?

3   If particulars of a charge are delivered to the registrar of companies which bear omissions or inaccuracies, will the charge be:

(a)   Totally void?
(b)   Void to the extent of the omissions or inaccuracies?

4   Which case established that where goods are identifiable and the sales contract contains a retention of title clause, then the seller can reclaim the goods concerned?

(a)   *Borden (UK) Ltd* v *Scottish Timber Products Ltd* (1979).
(b)   *Clough Mill Ltd* v *Martin* (1984).

5   Which of the following are remedies available to a debenture holder?

(a)   Appoint an administrative receiver.
(b)   Sue the company.

Q

(c) Sell the debenture to a third party.
(d) Petition the court for the company to be wound up.
(e) Transfer the debenture to a third party.

6   Prior to liquidation, an administrative receiver appointed by a debenture holder will be the agent of:

(a) The debenture holder.
(b) The company.

7   An administrative receiver is appointed:

(a) Under a fixed charge.
(b) Under a floating charge.

(Answers are given in Appendix 2, p. 314)

Revision question

Discuss, compare and contrast the advantages of fixed and floating charges.

(Answer is given in Appendix 2, pp. 314–15)

UNIT 17

Land

17.1 Legal Estates in Land

There are two types:

(a) *Freehold*
Stated to be an estate in fee simple, absolute in possession.

(b) *Leasehold*
Term of years absolute granted by the freeholder to the lessee. Value will depend on the terms of the lease and the amount of time which the lease has still to run.

17.2 Legal Mortgage

A legal mortgage can be set up in two ways (Law of Property Act 1925).

17.2.1 By a charge by deed expressed to be by way of legal mortgage

This gives the lender the same rights, protection and remedies as when a mortgage is taken by lease or sub-lease, irrespective of whether the land is freehold or leasehold.

17.2.2 By granting of a lease of the land for a term of years absolute, subject to the proviso that upon repayment the term ceases ('cesser on redemption')

Again, this can apply to either freeholds or leaseholds. In respect of leasehold property, a sub-lease must be created which will expire at least one day earlier than the original lease. One problem concerning leasehold title lies in the fact that most leases contain a clause which requires the agreement of the landlord to any further assignment or sub-let. This often also applies when the mortgage is expressed to be by way of legal mortgage.

Legal mortgages provide additional rights when compared with equitable mortgages. For example, a legal mortgagee will have an automatic right of sale of the property, providing that there is vacant possession and demand for repayment has been made, whereas an equitable mortgagee would have to resort to the courts in the event of the mortgagor failing to co-operate concerning the sale.

17.3 Equitable Mortgage

Under the Law of Property (Miscellaneous Provisions) Act 1989, an equitable mortgage is created over land by the deposit of deeds or a land certificate and the completion and execution of a memorandum of deposit by the mortgagor and mortgagee. The memorandum of deposit will contain clauses whereby the mortgagor will undertake to create a legal mortgage if called upon to do so. If the mortgagor refuses to comply with this request the bank has a number of options. The memorandum of deposit may contain a clause which bestows on the bank an irrevocable power of attorney. This would be the case where it has been completed under seal and would allow the bank to appoint an attorney who could then grant the bank a legal mortgage. In addition to this, the attorney can sell the property or grant leases. Sometimes, instead of including this power of attorney clause, there is a clause which states that the mortgagor is merely holding the property in trust for the bank.

Consequently, the bank can dismiss the mortgagor as trustee and appoint a replacement. Either of these measures will enable the bank to sell the property without having to apply to the court first.

When a bank is aware of subsequent mortgagees, it is likely to create a legal mortgage before instigating sale procedures. This is particularly so when the probable sale price is unlikely to satisfy amounts owing to all mortgagees. If the bank had only been appointed as attorney and had wished to sell the property, this could be prevented by other mortgagees, who could refuse to release their mortgages. However, where the bank wishes to sell and is a legal mortgagee, it can do so without the danger of later mortgagees preventing the sale from going ahead. Obviously, the bank must only sell for a fair market price.

Many equitable mortgages are completed under hands rather than under seal. In such cases, if the mortgagor refuses to create a legal mortgage, the bank will have to apply to the court for a court order, which is both time consuming and costly. Another disadvantage for equitable mortgages is that they are subject to any prior equities. Therefore, if when the bank took its equitable mortgage, there were other equitable interests in the property, these would have priority over the bank.

17.4 A Legal Mortgagee's Remedies if the Mortgagor Fails to meet his Repayment Commitment

17.4.1 Sue the mortgagee for repayment

This remedy would be available whether security was held or not. It is only usually contemplated when the mortgagor is known to have assets which could be used to repay the borrowing but is reluctant to do so.

17.4.2 Sell the property

As we stated in a previous unit, this clause excludes s.103 Law of Property Act 1925, which means that the mortgagee can sell the property once the mortgage moneys are due without having to wait three months which would be the case if this exclusion was not incorporated.

With regard to legal mortgages, the mortgagee will have to apply to the court for an order for sale, unless the security is in respect of a regulated agreement as covered by the Consumer Credit Act 1974. Provided that there is vacant possession the bank will proceed with the sale. However, if this is not the case then the bank will have to apply to the court for a possession order.

When a bank takes possession of a property it will normally be with a view to sale. In such circumstances it owes the mortgagor a duty to obtain the current market price and will usually employ an estate agent to handle the sale.

There are a number of important cases concerning a legal mortgagee's sale of property. In *Cuckmere Brick Co Ltd* v *Mutual Finance Ltd* (1971), the finance company did not mention, when advertising the sale of the land, that planning permission had been obtained for the erection of flats, which would have enhanced the value of the land. Consequently, the finance company was successfully sued for negligence by the mortgagor. A counter-claim for the moneys owed by the mortgagee failed.

One contentious issue which often arises between the mortgagee and mortgagor is the timing of the sale of the mortgaged property. In *Bank of Cyprus (London) Ltd* v *Gill* (1979) it was held that a mortgagee is under no obligation to await an upturn in property prices before selling the mortgaged property. Another important recent case was that of *Palk* v *Mortgage Services Funding Plc* (1992).

Mr Palk obtained a loan for £300,000 secured against a mortgage given by himself and his wife over their home. Unfortunately, Mr Palk's business entered liquidation and he was unable to maintain the repayments. He therefore tried to find a buyer in a deflated housing market and eventually negotiated a sale which did not fully repay the loan and interest accrued. The mortgagees, Mortgage Services Funding plc, therefore refused to rectify the sale and obtained a possession order. The mortgagees did not intend to sell the property at that time because of the depressed state of the market but did, however, intend to let it out on a short-term lease pending an upturn in the housing market when the house could then be sold. The likely return from letting the property would only amount to about 30% of the rate at which the debt would grow due to interest accruing. It therefore seemed inequitable to Mr and Mrs Palk that their position should deteriorate substantially through the mortgagee not exercising its power of sale.

Mr and Mrs Palk applied to the County Court for an order under s.91(2) Law of Property Act 1925 for the house to be sold. The County Court found against the Palks, stating that a sale could only be made against the wishes of the mortgagee if the amount obtained repaid the borrowing covered by the mortgage. Mr Palk subsequently became bankrupt but Mrs Palk appealed against this judgment in the Court of Appeal.

In the Appeal Court it was confirmed that a mortgagee did owe some duties to the mortgagor. While retaining the right to take no action concerning the mortgaged property whatsoever, if the mortgagee decided to exercise its rights over the property then it must act fairly towards the mortgagor. In this case the mortgagee was not acting fairly, but was speculating on a recovery in the housing market, to the detriment of Mrs Palk's financial position. In other words, Mrs Palk was underwriting the mortgagee's speculative risk. The court therefore ordered the house to be sold under s.91(2) Law of Property Act 1925, and pointed out that the mortgagee could, in fact, purchase the property as sale was by court order and not under the mortgagee's remedies contained in its mortgage form. The mortgagee would then be free to wait until there was the upturn in the housing market which it expected.

To summarise this case, it can be stated that a court has the discretion under s.91(2) Law of Property Act 1925 to order the sale of a mortgaged property, even if the sale proceeds do not repay the borrowing fully and even against the wishes of the mortgagor.

When a bank as mortgagee sells a property it may find that the proceeds are in excess of the borrowing and accrued interest. Where the sale relates to unregistered land, the bank should carry out a search at Land Charges Register to ensure that there are no subsequent mortgagees, before paying over any surplus proceeds to the mortgagor. In respect of registered land, a search at the District Land Registry is unnecessary as the bank would have been advised automatically of any subsequent mortgagees.

17.4.3 Appointment of a receiver

A receiver can be appointed under the Law of Property Act 1925 in the same circumstances as for the power of sale. The receiver acts as an agent of the mortgagor and consequently the latter is responsible for the receiver's actions. The receiver is appointed in writing by the bank normally where the mortgaged property is subject to a tenancy and there are rents to be collected.

17.4.4 Take possession of the mortgaged property and grant leases

This right of action is rarely taken, but where it is, any rents collected are used in reduction of the bank debt.

17.4.5 Right to foreclose

Foreclosure transfers the title of a mortgaged property from the mortgagor to the mortgagee. It initially involves a court order for foreclosure *nisi* and the court will normally allow the mortgagor time to repay the debt. If this is not satisfied, the order will be made absolute and the transfer of a title will then be completed. Foreclosure tends to be a last resort, as courts prefer to order the sale of the property, it being felt that this is more equitable. Otherwise, foreclosure could lead to the mortgagee obtaining a property which was worth far more than the debt which was outstanding.

17.5 An Equitable Mortgagee's Remedies if the Mortgagor Fails to meet his Repayment Commitment

An equitable mortgage can be created under hand or under seal. The remedies available to an equitable mortgagee will depend upon which of these two mortgages has been created.

17.5.1 Equitable mortgage under hand

1 Sue on the debt.

2 Obtain a court order for the sale of the property.

3 Where, in one of the clauses, the mortgagor undertakes to complete a legal mortgage if called upon to do so, and then reneges on this, the mortgagee will have to resort to the courts in order to take possession of or sell the property.

17.5.2 Equitable mortgage under seal

Section 101 Law of Property Act 1925 enables mortgagees whose mortgages have been created by deed to appoint a receiver or to have the power of sale. Thus, an equitable mortgagee whose mortgage has been created under seal has similar rights to those held by a legal mortgagee. One major exemption, however, is that the legal mortgagee can enter into possession, whereas the equitable mortgagee cannot.

17.6 Remedies of a Second Mortgagee

A second mortgagee can exercise similar remedies to a first mortgagee. However, if it decides to exercise the power of sale, it must bear in mind that a first mortgagee has a prior claim on the proceeds. It is, therefore, only feasible to follow this course of action if the final proceeds are going to be sufficient to discharge the debt owing to the second mortgagee in addition to the amount owing to the first mortgagee.

17.7 Bank Mortgage Forms

In Unit 15, details were given of charge form clauses contained in direct security forms. In addition to these, there are extra clauses to be found in mortgage forms relating to land. Details of these are given below.

17.7.1 Repair and insure clause

This is an undertaking by the mortgagor to keep the property in good repair and adequately insured. It will also state that the mortgagor will pay premiums when due and will provide sight of the premium receipts to the bank. Additionally, should the mortgagor not maintain the property in good repair, then the mortgagee can arrange for such work to be carried out at the mortgagor's expense.

17.7.2 A clause undertaking not to create or surrender leases

This clause is designed to protect the mortgagee's ability to exercise the power of sale. A property's saleability will often depend upon the mortgagee's ability to offer a property for sale with vacant possession. If a mortgagor was allowed to create tenancies on mortgaged property this would not be possible and would affect the value of the security. Hence, the inclusion of this clause to prevent this situation arising.

17.7.3 A clause preventing a mortgagor creating subsequent mortgages without the bank's consent

17.7.4 A clause stating that the mortgage does not breach a company's memorandum and articles of association

This is needed where registered land is involved. The land registrar will not issue a charge certificate if this statement is not included, unless a separate resolution has been passed to this effect.

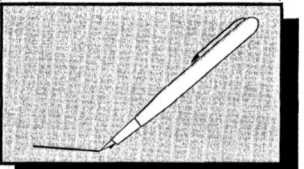

Student Activity 1

Obtain copies of the legal/equitable mortgage forms used by your bank when dealing with land. Examine the clauses included in these and compare them with those shown above and in Unit 15.

17.8 Unregistered Land

Title to unregistered land is evidenced by a bundle of deeds.

17.9 Perfecting a First Mortgage of Freehold Unregistered Land

17.9.1 Valuation

The property should be valued either by a bank official or by a professional estate agent or surveyor. Commercial property should be subject to a professional valuation. The effect of the Environmental Protection Act 1990 on property valuations has been diluted by the government's decision not to introduce contaminated land registers. However, a bank will still check that a property does not have a contamination problem.

17.9.2 Occupants

The bank should always check whether a property is owner-occupied or subject to a tenancy. It should also enquire as to other persons being in occupation of the property at the time when the mortgage was created, as such people may have rights which override those of the bank.

If a property is tenanted at the time when it is mortgaged, then the mortgage will be subject to the prior occupation rights of the tenant (*Universal Permanent Building Society* v *Cooke* (1951)).

An exception to the *Cooke* case was established in *Midland Bank Ltd* v *Farmpride Hatcheries Ltd & Willey* (1980). Here the company granted a bank a mortgage over land which it owned, but the directors did not divulge that part of the land was subject to an existing tenancy to themselves. The court held that the bank was under no obligation to make enquiries but that the directors, who were also the occupiers, should have advised the bank about the tenancy. As the directors failed to do this they were estopped from claiming the priority of their occupation over the rights contained in the bank's mortgage. Therefore, a possession order was granted in favour of the bank.

Dudley and District Benefit Building Society v *Emerson* (1949) looked at the problem for a mortgagee where the mortgagor created a tenancy in breach of the mortgage deed after the mortgage had been established. In this case it was held that such a tenancy would be void against the mortgagee.

In recent times there have been a number of cases relating to persons who were in occupation at the time when a mortgage was created over a property and who were not the registered owners of that property but nevertheless had interests which might override the bank's rights as mortgagee, e.g. sale of the property with vacant possession.

Williams & Glyn's Bank v *Boland* (1980) was a highly important case in relation to overriding interest. It established that if the title of a property is vested in one person's name but another person, e.g. a spouse has contributed money or money's worth to the purchase price of the property, and that person is in occupation at the time of the mortgage to the bank, then that person will have rights which override the bank's mortgage rights to obtain a possession order so that the property could be offered for sale with vacant possession. In this case it was stated that the husband owned the property in trust for himself and his wife and could not therefore sign away his wife's rights. A subsequent case, *Midland Bank* v *Dobson* (1985), ruled that household or domestic duties could not be construed as money's worth.

As a result of the *Boland* case, banks nowadays ensure that all occupants of a property who are adults sign a consent form to the giving of the mortgage over a property in which their name does not appear on the title document but of which they are in occupation. An independent solicitor would normally advise the occupants of the implications of their action prior to signing.

The decision in the case of *City of London Building Society* v *Flegg* (1987), while confirming the verdict in the *Boland* case in respect of sole owners, has actually taken the position a stage further as regards property vested in joint names but where there are other occupants who have contributed to the purchase price and who were in occupation at the time when the mortgage was created.

The *Flegg* case confirmed that where a property vests in one name and another party who has contributed money or money's worth was in occupation at the date of execution of the mortgage, then the court will not grant a possession order unless the occupier has properly completed consent form procedures. This therefore echoed the decision in the *Boland* case. However, the decision went on to say that where a property vests in joint names and a third person has contributed to the purchase price and was in occupation of the property at the time that the mortgage was created, the mortgagee can still exercise the rights, even in the absence of a consent form.

The *Flegg* case therefore held that two or more trustees can sign away the rights of a beneficiary, while confirming that a sole trustee cannot sign away the rights of a beneficiary.

Some recent cases have added to the information regarding overriding interests. *Abbey National Building Society* v *Cann* (1990) held that if a matrimonial home was purchased in the sole name of one of the spouses, the other spouse must have occupation when the bank mortgage was granted in order to have a beneficial interest which overrides that of the bank. It was established that 'occupation' does not necessarily mean that the spouse must be living in the property when the mortgage was granted, but could include the right to enter to have building work carried out, for example. *Lloyds Bank Plc* v *Rosset* (1990) held that a wife cannot prevent a bank from obtaining a possession order in respect of her husband's house by claiming an overriding beneficial interest unless she can show that prior to its purchase her husband agreed that the property should be jointly owned, or that by her conduct she contributed to its acquisition, thus showing the intention that the husband would own the property for their joint benefit.

In *Target Home Loans Limited* v *Clothier* (1992) there was an interesting decision regarding deferral of a possession order. Mr and Mrs Clothier defaulted in meeting the monthly mortgage repayments in respect of a loan for the purchase of a property. Target Home Loans Limited applied to the court for a possession order over the mortgaged property.

The court held that the possession order should be deferred for three months in order to allow the Clothiers the opportunity to try and sell the property. The court's view was that an occupied house is more attractive than a repossessed property to a potential buyer. This postponement of repossession was granted in accordance with s.36 Administration of Justice Act 1970, as amended by s.8 Administration of Justice Act 1973. If, at the end of the three-month period, no sale had been agreed which would discharge the whole debt, Target Home Loans Limited would take immediate repossession of the house.

17.9.3 Report on title

Banks usually ask a solicitor to carry out a report on title for them against the solicitor's undertaking to hold the deeds to the order of the bank and to return them on request. Any defects in title should then be brought to attention of the bank.

17.9.4 Execution of the mortgage

Independent legal advice should be taken where necessary. Where this is the case, the mortgagor will sign the mortgage form in the presence of a solicitor who will witness it. Otherwise, the mortgagor will complete the form on the bank's premises. A copy of the mortgage form will normally be given to the mortgagor.

17.9.5 Official Land Charges Register searches

An official search will be carried out on the name and address of the mortgagor. The search should result in the response of 'no subsisting entries' and should be carried out prior to the mortgage form being executed. The bank will then have a period of 15 working days from the date of the search in which to complete its mortgage, without the worry of another charge achieving priority by being placed upon the register during that interim time period. The bank will normally carry out a further search on the day that the mortgage is executed, as a precaution.

At this stage, it is worth considering the entries which may be revealed as a result of an official search. These can vary from actions in bankruptcy to interests in land. Information relating to land charges will be detailed in classes A to F. The major entries of significance to banks appear in classes C, D and F.

(a) Class C(i) covers legal mortgages which are not protected by deposit of deeds e.g. second mortgages. These are known as puisne mortgages.

(b) Class C(ii) will normally indicate an equitable charge which a tenant has for life.

(c) Class C(iii) is a general equitable charge. It will be registered by an equitable mortgagee who is not protected by the deposit of deeds.

(d) Class C(iv) refers to an estate contract. This entry would be registered by someone who would have an option or contract to purchase a property.

(e) Class D(i) indicates a charge to the Inland Revenue in respect of inheritance tax.

(f) Class D(ii) gives details regarding restrictions on usage of land, although such restrictions between a lessor and lessee would not appear here.

(g) Class D(iii) will indicate rights of way over the property, which are also known as equitable easements.

(h) Class F charges will be registered by spouses concerning their rights of occupation under the Matrimonial Homes Act 1967. Such charges will rank ahead of the rights of subsequent mortgagees unless they are postponed in the mortgagee's favour.

When entries are revealed by an official search, the mortgagor should be interviewed and the circumstances clarified. If, as a result of this, the bank decides to continue with its mortgage, it will have to obtain information relating to the prior mortgage from the mortgagee. Consequently, the mortgagor would have to furnish the bank with an authority, addressed to the mortgagee, requesting the supply of the information required. (This information is detailed later in this unit when discussing second mortgages.)

17.9.6 Local Land Charges Register search

A local search can be effected prior to or after the mortgage has been executed. If any entries are shown, e.g. planning permission for the construction of a new major road, the solicitor acting for the bank and local estate agents can be requested to advise on the significance of these entries with regard to the proposed security, and further enquiries can be made.

17.9.7 Fire insurance

The fire insurance must fully cover the value of the property plus the additional costs involved in the event of a fire e.g. clearance of the site, architect's fees. The bank should give notice of its interest to the insurance company and obtain an acknowledgement. Some banks and insurance companies have come to an agreement whereby notice need not be given where the insurance covers a private property below a certain market valuation. Also, members of the British Insurance Association have stated that where an insurance policy covering a mortgaged property has not been renewed, it will advise the bank and maintain cover on behalf of the mortgagee unless it is advised otherwise.

A bank will need to note in its records when premiums are due and also obtain evidence that premiums are paid. Obviously, if these premiums are paid by standing order or direct debit, this latter requirement will automatically be satisfied.

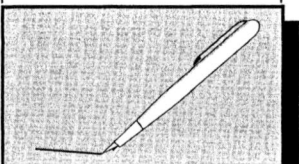

Student Activity 2

Ascertain from your bank's rule book, the current market valuation of a private property below which notice need not be given to an insurance company of a bank's mortgage.

17.10 Additional Procedural Steps to be taken when Perfecting a First Mortgage over Leasehold Unregistered Land

17.10.1 Obtain consent of the lessor

A lease often contains a clause stipulating that the lessor's agreement will be required if the lessee wishes to create a mortgage. In such cases, the bank as intending mortgagor should obtain the written consent of the lessor. This consent should be kept with the relevant mortgage and title deeds.

17.10.2 Give notice of the bank's mortgage to the lessor

Once the mortgage form has been executed, the bank should give notice to the lessor of its charge and also obtain a written acknowledgement.

17.10.3   Obtain sight of ground rent receipts

Lessees have to pay ground rent to the lessor, normally at quarterly or annual intervals. The bank must see the receipts for these payments as they fall due and must mark its security records accordingly. It will therefore diarise when they are due. Failure to pay ground rent by the lessee could lead to forfeiture of the lease, which obviously would create a detrimental position for the bank.

17.10.4   Fire insurance

There may be a clause in the lease stating that the mortgagor is not responsible for the fire insurance but that this is the responsibility of the lessor. It may also stipulate that a particular insurance company must be used. In such cases, the bank should obtain full details of the cover currently in force and give notice to the insurance company concerned of its charge.

17.11   Additional Procedural Steps to be taken when Perfecting a Second Mortgage over Unregistered Land

A second mortgage is a charge over a property which is already the subject of a prior mortgage.

In the case of leasehold land, the mortgage is created either by way of legal mortgage (as it would be for freehold land) or by the creation of a sub-lease which would run for a period one day longer than the term granted to the first mortgagee.

The following amended procedures would be carried out in respect of a second or subsequent mortgage, in addition to procedures mentioned previously.

17.11.1   Valuation

When valuing a property, a second mortgagee must not only take into account the current market value but also the amount outstanding in favour of the first mortgagee. It will therefore apply a safety margin to offset any adverse price movements in the housing market and also to allow for any arrears which might build up between the mortgagor and the first mortgagee.

17.11.2   Fire insurance

The fire insurance policy is unlikely to be held by the mortgagor and will normally be in the hands of the first mortgagee, or in the case of leasehold land, in the hands of the lessor. The bank, as second mortgagee, will obviously wish to ensure that the property is adequately insured and, wherever possible, the bank should peruse the policy if the first mortgagor or lessor are agreeable. If not, full details of the policy should be obtained from the holder.

As usual, the bank should give notice of its interest to the insurance company concerned, unless the latter is a party to the special arrangement agreed between the insurance companies and the banks which was mentioned earlier in this unit. Where written notice has to be given, a written acknowledgement should be obtained from the insurance company concerned.

Two additional actions must be taken in respect of a second mortgage.

17.11.3 Registration of second mortgage on Land Charges Register

As the second mortgagee does not have the title deeds, it must protect its position by registering its charge either as a Class C(i) if it is a legal mortgage, or as a Class C(iii) for an equitable mortgage.

17.11.4 Giving notice of the second mortgage to the prior mortgagee

The bank should obtain the mortgagor's instructions addressed to all prior mortgagees, authorising them to divulge information to the bank concerning the mortgagor's affairs.

The bank will give written notice to the prior mortgagee(s) and request a written acknowledgement. It will also request details of the amount outstanding on the first mortgage and whether the mortgagee is obliged to make further advances. The reason for this latter request is that s.94(1) Law of Property Act 1925 enables a mortgagee to add any further advances to the original advance, which will rank ahead of any subsequent mortgage even if the first mortgagee had received notice of the subsequent mortgage's charge. This course of action is known as tacking. Finally, the bank will wish to know if the first mortgagee has received notice of any other mortgages.

17.12 On What Basis is the Priority of Mortgages over Unregistered Land Decided?

Section 97 Law of Property Act 1925 states that the priority of mortgages depends upon whichever comes first: either the mortgagee had possession of the deeds and a clear search on the Land Charges Register, or the date upon which a mortgage has been registered on the Land Charges Register.

Thus a mortgagee who holds the deeds and has a clear search will maintain priority for as long as possession of the deeds is retained. As such, the mortgagee will not have to register the charge on the Land Charges Register.

Concerning mortgagees who do not have possession of the deeds, priority is settled by the earliest date of registration of the mortgage on the Land Charges Register. Failure to register such a mortgage will invalidate it against purchasers for value, mortgagees and the trustee in bankruptcy – s.13 Land Charges Act 1925, and ss.4–7 Land Charges Act 1972. Mere registration of the charge does not constitute notice to prior mortgagees, and notice is required in order to fix the monetary priority of earlier mortgages.

When discussing priority of mortgages it is necessary to consider what action a bank should take when, as first mortgagee, it receives notice of a second mortgage. Where the bank is lending on current account and there is a volatile fluctuating balance, the rule in *Clayton's* case means that the bank's original lending could be repaid and new borrowing created, which would mean that some or all of the bank's lending would rank in priority after the second mortgage. This was confirmed in *Deeley* v *Lloyds Bank Ltd* (1912). Thus, a bank will normally stop a current account upon receipt of notice of a second mortgage in order to maintain its priority for the existing debt. Bank mortgage forms also include a clause which protects the bank's position if it fails to stop its current account. The authenticity of this clause was confirmed in the case of *Westminster Bank Ltd* v *Cond* (1940). As loan account balances do not fluctuate, these accounts can be allowed to continue.

17.13 Additional Procedural Steps to be Taken when Perfecting a Mortgage over Unregistered Land Offered by a Limited Company

(a) Search at Land Charges Register and Companies House to ascertain whether there are prior mortgages which would rank ahead of the bank's charge.

(b) Ensure that the advance to be granted is in accordance with the objects of the company, particularly where the security is being given for the liabilities of a third party.

(c) Consider whether there is commercial justification for the company charging its assets as security. If this is not evident, then the security could be invalidated.

(d) If the bank is aware that directors have a personal interest in the giving of the company security, e.g. where the directors have previously given guarantees for the company's liabilities, it should check with the company or the company's legal advisers as to whether interested directors can act or vote on the matter concerned. Where such directors are not allowed to vote, the bank should ensure that an independent quorum of directors can pass the necessary resolution.

(e) Providing everything is in order, a copy of the board resolution authorising the giving of the security should be obtained for the bank's records.

(f) After the mortgage has been executed, details of it should be registered at Companies House within 21 days of its creation. A certificate of filing should be requested by the bank from the Registrar.

(g) After the bank's charge has been registered, a further search will normally be carried out at Companies House to make certain that no essential details have been omitted.

17.14 What Action should a Bank Take when it is Offered a Charge over Land Owned by Company Directors but Used by the Company?

The action to be taken applies for both unregistered and registered land.

(a) Who really owns the land? Sometimes the deeds/land certificate are in the name of the directors simply for convenience, but the beneficial owner is the company. This arises when the directors had previously been partners or sole traders who then formed a limited company. In order to save expense, no formal conveyance or transfer would have been executed, and the directors would have held the land as trustees for the company.

(b) In cases of doubt, examine the audited accounts to see if the property appears as a fixed asset. If so the company are the true owners.

(c) If the directors are holding the land as trustees, the bank's mortgage must be executed by both the directors and the company. Register under s.398 Companies Act 1985.

(d) If the property is still owned by the directors, but is leased to the company, the directors can mortgage the freehold, and the company can mortgage the lease. The bank can then value it on a with-possession basis.

17.15   Sub-Mortgages

A sub-mortgage is a mortgage of a mortgage. Although rarely seen, sub-mortgages are often taken where alternative security is unavailable. Sub-mortgages can be legal or equitable. However, where the original mortgage is an equitable mortgage, the sub-mortgage must also be an equitable sub-mortgage.

If a sub-mortgagor defaults, the sub-mortgagee can sue or alternatively he can sell or assign the mortgage debt. If the mortgagor of the original mortgage defaults, the bank as sub-mortgagee will have the same remedies as the original mortgagee, which will be detailed in the original mortgage.

17.16   Procedural Steps to be taken when Perfecting a Sub-Mortgage over Unregistered Land

17.16.1   Report on title

The bank will have its solicitors check that the mortgagor of the original charge (known as the head mortgagor) has a good title to the property. The solicitors will also check that the mortgage given to the bank's customer (known as the head mortgagee) was perfected correctly, as any discrepancy could affect the validity of the proposed sub-mortgage.

17.16.2   Valuation

The value of a sub-mortgage is dependent upon the debt outstanding on the original charge. As repayments on the original debt are made, the value of the sub-mortgage will diminish accordingly.

17.16.3 Occupation

Whoever is in occupation of the property has a significant effect upon the bank's remedies under its charge. (See earlier section in this unit relating to occupancy and overriding interests.)

17.16.4 Execution of the sub-mortgage charge form

The sub-mortgage charge form will be signed and witnessed. It will contain details of the original mortgage, including reference to the property concerned.

17.16.5 Official search at Land Charges Register

An official search will be made upon the names of both the head mortgagor and the head mortgagee. If it transpires that the head mortgagor has created a further charge, then the bank's priority position with regard to the sub-mortgage will depend upon the priority position of the original mortgage.

A sub-mortgage?

17.16.6 Fire insurance

Adequate cover must be apparent. The bank should give written notice of its sub-mortgage to the insurance company concerned and obtain an acknowledgement.

17.16.7 Notice to head mortgagor

Written notice of the bank's sub-mortgage should be given to the head mortgagor and an acknowledgement obtained. Details of the amount outstanding and an agreement by the head mortgagor to make further repayments direct to the bank must also be obtained. As repayments are received, the value of the bank's security should be amended in the bank's records.

17.17 Unregistered Land – Release of Security

17.17.1 First legal mortgage

(a) Bank completes receipt on mortgage form.

(b) Discharged mortgage form together with title deeds returned to title holder, against a receipt. Alternatively, where the bank has received notice of a second charge, these documents must be given up to the second mortgagee against its receipt.

(c) Any notice given to insurance company withdrawn.

17.17.2 Second or subsequent legal mortgage

(a) Bank completes form K11 and forwards it with the relevant fee to the Land Charges Register for Class C(i) charge to be deleted from register.

(b) Bank completes receipt on charge form and forwards it to the first mortgagee against its receipt.

(c) Notice should be given to the first mortgagee and the insurance company, where appropriate, of the bank's action.

17.17.3 Equitable mortgage

(a) Where a bank holds deeds, it can merely write 'cancelled' on its memorandum of deposit, which can then be placed with obsolete security papers.

(b) Where the bank does not hold deeds and has registered its charge as a Class C(iii), it can forward a completed form K11 with the relevant fee to the Land Charges Register for it to be deleted.

(c) Notice of the bank's action should be given to the first mortgagee, and to the insurance company where appropriate.

17.18 Registered Land

When a registered title is granted, the District Land Registry issues a document evidencing title known as a land certificate. It is divided into three parts:

(a) *Property register* – This describes the address of the property or its location.

(b) *Proprietorship register* – This gives details of the owner(s) of the property.

(c) *Charges register* – This details parties who have an interest in the land, e.g. mortgagees.

17.19 How Can a Bank be Certain that the Details Contained in the Land Certificate are up to date?

There are three possible ways of ensuring that details contained in a land certificate are correct and up to date.

(a) The land certificate can be sent to the District Land Registry to be made up to date.

(b) If a bank is considering taking a second mortgage, it can obtain an office copy of the register using form 109.

(c) An official search can be applied for. This will request particulars of any adverse entries either since the land certificate was last made up to date or from the date of the last office copy of the register.

17.20 How is the Priority of Mortgages Over Registered Land Determined?

The crucial date with regard to the priority of mortgages of registered land is the date when a mortgage is registered at the District Land Registry.

As with unregistered land, a would-be mortgagee can obtain a protective period in which to perfect and register its mortgage. This is done by carrying out an official search at the District Land Registry, which then gives 30 working days' protection. Once a mortgagee's mortgage has been registered, the registrar will advise it of any attempts which may be made to place further entries on the register.

17.21 Perfecting a First Legal Mortgage over Freehold or Leasehold Registered Land

(a) Value property.

(b) Send land certificate to District Land Registry to be made up to date.

(c) Carry out official search.

(d) Have mortgage form completed.

(e) Forward completed mortgage form, a certified copy, the land certificate, and the relevant District Land Registry form to the District Land Registry. In addition, a fee should be forwarded which will be based upon the amount of the advance or the value of the property, whichever is the smaller.

(f) District Land Registry will forward a charge certificate to the mortgagee which will have the mortgage form stitched inside. (As stated earlier, the mortgagee will have a protective period of 30 working days in which to register a mortgage.)

(g) If the mortgagor is a limited company, the charge must also be registered at Companies House within 21 days of its creation.

(h) A report on title is normally unnecessary, as title is guaranteed by the state. However, this step will be carried out where there is mention of other interests in the land certificate.

(i) Carry out local searches to ascertain whether there are any local developments which could affect the security, e.g. permission for open-cast mining.

(j) Obtain the fire insurance policy and ensure that the property is adequately insured. The same provisos regarding giving notice of the bank's interest to the insurance company apply as for unregistered land.

In the case of leasehold land, the following additional steps must be taken. They are the same as those mentioned earlier in this unit for Unregistered Land.

(k) Where indicated in the terms of the lease, the written consent of the lessor should be obtained regarding creation of the mortgage.

(l) Give notice of the bank's mortgage to the lessor and obtain a written acknowledgement.

(m) Obtain sight of ground rent receipts.

(n) Diarise for regular exhibition of ground rent receipts as they fall due.

(o) Ascertain who is liable to pay the fire insurance premiums. Ensure that the cover is adequate. Give notice to the insurance company concerned of the bank's charge and obtain a written acknowledgement. Where the mortgagor is responsible for the fire insurance, the policy should be deposited with the mortgagee.

17.22 Obtaining a Mortgage over Registered Land Using the Notice of Deposit System

An alternative way of perfecting a mortgage over registered land is by using the notice of deposit system.

Under this the bank will have its mortgage form executed in the normal way but will not complete registration of it at the District Land Registry.

Instead, it will forward form 85A in duplicate to the District Land Registry with the land certificate. This acts as notice of deposit of the land certificate for security purposes, and the bank's interest will be noted in the charges register of the land certificate. The land certificate is then returned to the bank. (It is possible to give notice without the entry being shown on the land certificate if the customer so wishes. This is effected by not sending the land certificate along with form 85A.)

The notice of deposit procedure protects the bank in the event that any attempt is made to register an interest which could affect the bank's security position. In such circumstances, the registrar will notify the bank, which will then have 14 days in which to fully register its legal mortgage.

This procedure is of particular use when land is being registered for the first time or when the land certificate is unavailable until the transfer of ownership is completed. In the former case, form 85B is used, which indicates notice of intended deposit once the land certificate is produced. In the latter case, form 85C is used to indicate notice of intended deposit; in both situations, the bank's security position is protection by such actions.

17.23 Equitable Mortgage of Registered Land

Under the Law of Property (Miscellaneous Provisions) Act 1989 an equitable mortgage is created by the deposit of a land certificate and the execution of a memorandum of deposit by the mortgagor and mortgagee. The bank will then use the notice of deposit procedure.

17.24 Perfecting a Second Mortgage over Registered Land

(a) Using form 109, request an office copy of the land certificate from the District Land Registry.

(b) Carry out an official search from the date of the office copy in order to establish the 30 working days protective period.

(c) Have mortgage form completed and executed. Details of the land title number and prior mortgage should be scheduled in this document.

(d) Send executed mortgage form, a certified copy, the relevant District Land Registry form and the fee to the District Land Registry. A certificate of second charge will then be forwarded to the bank.

(e) All other procedures which would be carried out for a second mortgage over unregistered land apply similarly for registered land. These include valuation, local searches, notice to prior mortgagees and fire insurance.

17.25 Perfecting a Sub-Mortgage over Registered Land

(a) Obtain the original charge certificate from the head mortgagee, i.e. the bank's customer.

(b) Carry out an official search at District Land Registry.

(c) Have the bank's form of sub-charge executed.

(d) Send the executed sub-charge form, a certified copy, charge certificate and the relevant fee to the District Land Registry. A certificate of sub-charge will then be forwarded to the bank.

(e) Other procedures as detailed earlier in this unit for a sub-mortgage over unregistered land will then be similarly followed with regard to registered land, with the exception of a search at the Land Charges Register.

17.26 Perfecting a Mortgage over Registered Land offered by a Limited Company

Similar considerations and actions will exist for the taking of a mortgage over registered land as were detailed earlier in this unit for unregistered land, with the exception of official searches at Land Charges Register. It is normal to register the charge with Companies House within 21 days of creation initially, before registering the charge at the District Land Registry which will require sight of the certificate of filing at Companies House.

17.27 Registered Land – Release of Security

17.27.1 A registered mortgage

(a) Forward the charge certificate together with the relevant District Land Registry form, duly sealed or signed, to the District Land Registry.

(b) The land certificate will then either be returned to the proprietor or, at the bank's request, to the mortgagee for onward transmission to the proprietor. This applies where the charge is a first mortgage.

(c) In the case of second or subsequent mortgages, the District Land Registry will advise the bank that details of its mortgage have been deleted.

17.27.2 Mortgage by means of notice of deposit procedure

(a) Complete the withdrawal of the notice of deposit form 86 and send it with the land certificate to the District Land Registry.

(b) The land certificate will be sent back to the bank with its notice of deposit details deleted unless another charge exists.

(c) Release the land certificate to customer against a receipt.

(d) Mark the legal mortgage form or memorandum of deposit 'Cancelled' and place it with obsolete security papers.

Summary

Now that you have read this unit, you should be able to:

☐ Identify the legal estates in land.

☐ Differentiate between legal and equitable mortgages and the remedies available under each.

☐ Recognise the significance of the clauses contained in a bank's standard mortgage form.

☐ Appreciate the procedures to be followed when perfecting charges over unregistered or registered land.

☐ Recognise the procedures to be followed when releasing security.

☐ Identify the difference in procedures between unregistered and registered land when dealing with surplus proceeds which arise under the mortgagee's power of sale.

If you can tick all the above with confidence, you are ready to answer the questions which follow on pp. 201–04.

List of Cases

Abbey National Building Society v *Cann* (1990)

Bank of Cyprus (London) Ltd v *Gill* (1979)

City of London Building Society v *Flegg* (1987)

Clayton's case *(Devaynes* v *Noble* (1816))

Cuckmere Brick Co Ltd v *Mutual Finance Ltd* (1971)

Deeley v *Lloyds Bank Ltd* (1912)

Dudley and District Benefit Building Society v *Emerson* (1949)

Lloyds Bank Plc v *Rosset* (1990)

Midland Bank Ltd v *Dobson* (1985)

Midland Bank Ltd v *Farmpride Hatcheries Ltd & Willey* (1980)

Palk v *Mortgage Services Funding Plc* (1992)

Target Home Loans Limited v *Clothier* (1992)

Universal Permanent Building Society v *Cooke* (1951)

Westminster Bank Ltd v *Cond* (1940)

Williams & Glyn's Bank v *Boland* (1980)

List of Statutes

Administration of Justice Act 1970

Administration of Justice Act 1973

Companies Act 1985

Environmental Protection Act 1990

Land Charges Act 1925

Land Charges Act 1972

Law of Property Act 1925

Law of Property (Miscellaneous Provisions) Act 1989

Self-assessment Questions

Short-answer questions

1 Neil Ames defaulted on his mortgage loan to Ezee Bank Plc. The bank held a first mortgage over his domestic property and also held the house's deeds. The bank exercised its right to sell the property as detailed in its mortgage form. After repayment of the amount owing together with bank charges and accrued interest there were surplus proceeds of £10,000. Since it took the first mortgage over the property the bank had not received any notice from any subsequent mortgagees of their interest in the property.

Q

Can the bank pay these surplus proceeds to Neil Ames immediately? Give reasons for your answer.

2   An inherent disadvantage of a sub-mortgage is that it is of diminishing value. Explain this statement.

3   If an equitable mortgage over unregistered land is discharged, does the cancelled memorandum of deposit form part of the chain of title?

4   Name three methods by which a bank can ensure that the details in a land certificate are up to date.

5   One of the methods in Q4 is normally restricted to when a bank is taking a second or subsequent mortgage. Which is this?

(Answers are given in Appendix 2, p. 315)

Multiple-choice questions

1   The title to unregistered land is evidenced by:

(a)   a land certificate?
(b)   a bundle of deeds?

2   Which case established that if a property is tenanted at the time when it is mortgaged, then the mortgage will be subject to the prior rights of the occupation of the tenant?

(a)   *Williams and Glyn's Bank* v *Boland* (1980).
(b)   *Dudley & District Benefit Building Society* v *Emerson* (1949).
(c)   *Universal Permanent Building Society* v *Cooke* (1951).

3   Who is responsible for the repayment of fire insurance premiums relating to leasehold property?

(a)   Head lessor.
(b)   Lessee.
(c)   Either (a) or (b), depending upon the terms of the lease.

4   What is a sub-mortgage?

(a)   A subsequent mortgage where a first mortgage has been executed over a property.
(b)   A mortgage over a submersible craft.
(c)   A mortgage of a mortgage.

5   An intending mortgagee of registered land can obtain a period of protection by carrying out an official search. How long does this period last for?

(a)   15 working days.
(b)   21 working days.
(c)   30 working days.

6   You have an overdraft secured by a legal mortgage of registered land. You receive notice of a second mortgage, but take no action. The customer's account can be summarised as follows:

Balance of account upon receipt of notice of second mortgage – £10,000 Dr

Credit turnover since receipt of notice of second mortgage – £16,000

Debit turnover since receipt of notice of second mortgage – £15,000

Current balance of account – £9,000 Dr

What is the position?

(a) The bank's mortgage is totally void.
(b) The bank's mortgage is valid for £10,000 but has lost priority to the other mortgage.
(c) The bank's mortgage is valid for £9,000 but has lost priority to the other mortgage.

7 Your customer has a current account which is maintained in credit and a loan account. Your security is a first mortgage of registered land.

What action do you take on receipt of the notice of a second mortgage?

(a) Break the account to prevent *Clayton's* case from operating against the bank.
(b) Mark securities records.
(c) Interview customer.
(d) Reply to the notice.

(Answers are given in Appendix 2, p. 315)

Past examination questions

1 (*Note to students: assume that today's date is 7 April 1983.*)
You are the officer in charge of the securities section of your branch of Telford's Clearing Bank plc and you have a new trainee clerk, Miss Gordon. She is engaged in taking a second mortgage over the house of one of your customers, Paul Fillington. The house is at 17 Rose Lane, Sutton, Surrey, land title number LX127946 and it was bought for £95,000 two years ago with the help of a building society mortgage.

Miss Gordon approaches you for help, saying that she has searched the Land Charges Register, and the search has been returned with the answer 'No subsisting entries – Protection expires 30.4.83'. She asks you why the first mortgagee's name does not appear on the search and what the entry means. Miss Gordon also refers to the fire insurance position, mentioning that she understands that for domestic property no action is necessary by the bank.

What would you tell her and why?

[16 marks]

(Spring 1983)

2 For several years you have extended overdraft facilities to your good customers, Pinetree Ltd, ranging up to £80,000 on occasions, against the security of deeds of the factory premises at Oldsway from which they trade. Title to this factory was at one time in the name of John Pinetree (present director and guarantor) when he traded as an individual before the

incorporation of the company. Upon the formation of the company in 1978, he simply became trustee of the property for the company, thereby avoiding costs which would have arisen in a conveyance of the title. You retained your first mortgage from John Pinetree and ensured that you were fully protected as regards the company's interest.

The company now intends to move to new premises at 1 New Street, and you have agreed to certain rearrangements of the bank's security. The old factory will be sold for £90,000 and a new one will be bought by the company for £120,000. Pinetree Ltd have arranged a long-term loan of £60,000 from Mercury Finance plc, who will hold the deeds, and the bank will be given a second mortgage by the company over this new factory at 1 New Street. There will be a delay of one month between the completion of the two transactions to enable Pinetree Ltd to move their business without difficulties and you have agreed to provide the additional short-term bridging facilities.

Required

Prepare a brief note, in tabulated form, of all the steps involved in this rearrangement to ensure that the bank will be fully protected throughout.

[17 marks]

(Autumn 1983)

(Answers are given in Appendix 2, pp. 316–17)

UNIT 18

Life Policies

Objectives

- Appreciate the advantages of life policies as security.
- Identify the main types of policy offered as security.
- Recognise the problem relating to trust or settlement policies as security.
- Appreciate the problems surrounding duplicate policies as security.
- Be able to detail the procedures to be followed when taking an assignment over a life policy.
- Recognise the procedures to be followed in releasing an assignment over a life policy.
- Appreciate how an assignment over a life policy can be realised.

Introduction

Life policies are contracts *uberrimae fidei* (of the utmost good faith). As such, any misrepresentation or non-disclosure of material facts would seriously affect the validity or value of any policy concerned.

18.1 Advantages as Security

(a) They are simple and cheap to charge and realise.

(b) They are an appreciating security. As the customer pays the premiums, the surrender value of the policy increases.

(c) In the event of the death of the mortgagor the repayment of any borrowings can be met from the capital value of the policy concerned.

18.2 What Action can the Bank Take if the Mortgagor is Unable to Continue to Pay the Premiums due on the Policy?

(a) If the policy has a surrender value which is higher than the bank borrowing, then the bank can surrender the policy, repay its borrowing and pay any residue to its customer.

(b) If the policy is nearing its maturity date, the bank may decide to continue to meet the premiums and then obtain repayment from the maturity proceeds.

(c) The bank may decide to convert the policy into a paid-up policy, in which case it will retain a reduced value until the maturity date.

18.3 Types of Policy

There are two types of policy which are normally offered as security. These are endowment policies and whole life policies. Either type can be issued 'with profits' or 'without profits'. Profits are those bonuses which have been declared by the assurance company during the lifetime of the policy and will normally be added to the capital value of the policy at the maturity of a 'with profits policy'. The difference between endowment and whole life policies is that the former is payable at a fixed future time or on the life assured's earlier death, whereas the latter is only payable upon the death of the assured.

Industrial policies are sometimes offered as security. However, they normally have a low capital value and often have restraints on assignment. Premiums are normally paid on a weekly or monthly basis to collectors. Where an assignment over an industrial policy is taken, the bank will require sight of the premium receipt book at regular intervals to ensure that premiums are paid up to date.

18.4 Action to be Taken when the Name of the Beneficiary under a Life Policy Differs from that of the Person who has Taken out that Policy

Sometimes a husband will take out a policy on his own life in favour of his wife. In such a case, where the policy is to be assigned to the bank, both the wife (beneficiary) and the husband (proposer) must join in the policy. Such policies are often drawn up under s.11 Married Women's Property Act 1882 with either spouse being the proposer or beneficiary. In addition, such policies can be for the benefit of the spouse's children. (Where the beneficiary is only referred to in the policy as 'my wife' or 'my children', it is not possible for that policy to be assigned.)

Students should note that where a limited company takes out a policy on the life of one of its employees for its own benefit, then should it assign this policy to the bank it is only necessary for the limited company to complete the bank's assignment form, as the name of the proposer and beneficiary are the same.

18.5 Duplicate Policies

Banks are normally offered the original policies as security, but occasionally a duplicate one is proffered. Banks must be careful, as in such a situation constructive notice is deemed to have been given of an earlier assignment (*Spencer* v *Clarke* (1878)). In such a case the bank's assignment would rank after the earlier assignment.

In the event of an assignee having notice of an earlier assignment and that earlier assignee not having advised the assurance company of its interest, the latter assignee cannot obtain priority by notifying the charge ahead of the prior assignee (*Newman* v *Newman* (1885)).

18.6 Procedure for Taking a First Legal Assignment over a Life Policy

(a) *Examine the policy*
Ensure that the policy has been issued by a reputable assurance company and is payable in the UK. Check that there are no restrictive covenants which could affect the validity of the policy, e.g. restriction on participation in certain sports or pastimes.

(b) *Check whether the age of the life assured has been admitted*
This means that the assurance company has had sight of evidence of date of birth. It is essential that this is provided, otherwise if the date of birth is wrongly stated on the policy, it could be declared void or an adjustment in the amount paid out under the policy could be made.

(c) *Identify the assignors*
Where the proposer and beneficiary of a policy are one and the same person, the assignment form will be merely completed by that person. However, where a policy is proposed by one person for the benefit of another, both parties must join in the form of assignment. In such cases, the bank must decide whether independent legal advice is required.

(d) *Complete the charge form*
The mortgage form must be dated and signed by the assignor(s) and witnessed by a bank official or a solicitor, where independent legal advice was considered necessary. It should clearly identify the policy covered and include the policy number and its date.

(e) *Give notice of assignment to the assurance company*
Notice of the assignment will be given to the assurance company. It will contain a request for details of any other charges granted to third parties or whether the company itself has any charge over the policy.

(f) *Ascertain the surrender value of the policy*
This is required to ensure that the policy provides adequate security. It is normal for banks to regularly update the surrender value, often on an annual basis.

(g) *Obtain evidence of payment of premiums*
Premium payments by standing order or direct debit are easily monitored. However, where this is not the case regular examination of premium receipts must be diarised to ensure that premiums are paid up to date.

18.7 Subsequent Assignments of a Life Policy

If there is any equity in the surrender value of a life policy after allowing for the amount due under a first mortgage, a bank may decide to take a second charge.

The procedure for taking a subsequent charge is similar to that for completing a first assignment, with slight variations. As the bank will not have the original policy it should make arrangements to examine it at the offices of the first assignee, or to obtain full details of the policy.

The mortgage form should give details of prior assignments. The bank must give notice of its assignment to all prior assignees. It will enquire as to the amount secured by the earlier assignments in order to arrive at the equity value of the policy. By giving notice, the bank will automatically receive any surplus funds following the surrender or maturity of the policy. Alternatively, the policy will be forwarded to the bank together with relevant assignments by the prior assignee if it has been repaid and the bank is the next assignee in line.

If the bank itself is the first assignee and it receives notice of a subsequent assignee and the bank is lending on current account, it should stop that account in order to prevent the rule in *Clayton's* case from operating against the bank's priority.

18.8 Assignments by Limited Companies

Limited companies often take out life cover on key members of staff or directors. In such cases the company is both proposer and beneficiary and the same security procedure as for an individual must be followed. In addition, a copy of the resolution to charge the policy as security must be placed with the assignment, which should have been executed under seal by the company. Such assignments do not need registering at Companies House.

18.9 Equitable Assignment of Life Policies

An equitable assignment can be created by the mere deposit of the life policy with the intent that it is to be held as security. Such intent should be recorded in its records by the bank. This intent can be strengthened by the completion of a memorandum of deposit which contains beneficial clauses for the bank, e.g. an undertaking to complete a legal mortgage if called upon to do so.

Banks normally give notice to the assurance company of the creation of an equitable charge in order to ensure that they have priority over any prior assignees who have taken an assignment and not given notice. This assumes that the banks do not have notice of such a prior assignment.

If notice of an equitable assignment is not given and there exist similar equitable assignments of which notice has not been given, priority will be based on the date of the charge. This applies whether a memorandum of deposit is used or not.

The prime problem with an equitable assignment is that a bank will normally have to obtain a court order before it can obtain the policy proceeds.

18.10 Realisation of the Security

When an endowment policy matures, the assignee will forward a completed claim form, the policy, all previously released assignments and bonus notices and its charge form to the assurance company. In the event of death, a copy of the death certificate should accompany these papers.

Sometimes it becomes necessary to surrender a policy before it matures. The procedure followed will depend upon the surrounding circumstances. If the customer has failed to repay borrowings, the borrowing will be called in and upon default the bank will normally take one of the following three steps:

(a) The mortgagor will arrange a loan from the assurance company against the surrender value of the policy (normally up to 90%). The bank will ensure that the proceeds are paid to it in exchange for the discharged assignment form.

(b) The bank could sell the policy to a specialist company.

(c) The bank could surrender the policy. In this instance the bank will forward the policy and form of assignment to the assurance company, which will then draft a form of receipt to be executed by the bank. This is the most common procedure and is quick and simple.

Where a bank's charge is an equitable one and the assignor dies, it will be necessary to obtain the help of the executors or administrators in order to obtain the maturity proceeds as they will have to join in the receipt required by the assurance company. Where the equitably charged policy has merely matured, the beneficiary will normally have to complete the assurance company's papers in order that the proceeds can be obtained. In either case the bank should have the proceeds sent direct to it. Obviously, if the assignor or personal representatives will not co-operate in the collection of the proceeds, the bank will have to seek a court order.

18.11 Release of the Assignment

A bank's form of assignment normally contains a form of release and reassignment. If the security is no longer required, this form will be completed and the assignment will be sealed by the bank. The policy, together with the assignment form, will then be released to the assignor against a receipt. Obviously if the bank has notice of a second charge, these documents will be released to the later assignee. Once the bank's charge has been released, notice of this is given to the assurance company concerned. Where the bank merely has an equitable charge under a memorandum of deposit, it can simply mark the memorandum 'Cancelled' and give it up together with the policy to the assignor against a receipt. Again, the bank should give notice that its interest has ceased to the assurance company concerned.

Summary

Now that you have read this unit, you should be able to:

☐ Appreciate the advantages of life policies as security.

☐ Identify the main types of policy offered as security.

☐ Recognise the problem relating to trust or settlement policies as security.

☐ Appreciate the problems surrounding duplicate policies as security.

☐ Be able to detail the procedures to be followed when taking an assignment over a life policy.

☐ Recognise the procedures to be followed in releasing an assignment over a life policy.

☐ Appreciate how an assignment over a life policy can be realised.

If you can tick all the above boxes with confidence, you are ready to answer the questions which follow on pp. 210–13.

List of Cases

Clayton's case (*Devaynes* v *Noble* (1816))

Newman v *Newman* (1885)

Spencer v *Clarke* (1878)

List of Statutes

Married Women's Property Act 1882

Self-assessment Questions

Short-answer questions

1   What action can the bank take if the mortgagor is unable to continue to pay the premiums due on the policy?

2   Jim McGill has taken out a policy on his own life which is stated in the policy as being for the benefit of 'my wife'. Can the bank take an assignment over such a policy?

3   Jane Smith has taken out a policy on her own life which is stated in the policy as being for the benefit 'of my daughter', Jill Smith. Can the bank take an assignment over such a policy?

4   Slapdash Bank Plc have decided to surrender a life policy charged to them by Jack Beale. You notice that age has not been admitted on the policy and subsequently discover that your customer was born on 23 March 1945, and not 23 March 1954 as stated on the policy.

What effect could this have on the bank's security position?

5   Martin Jax Ltd has taken out life cover on its chairman and director, Jack Milton, for the benefit of the company. The bank is to take an assignment over this policy. Who will complete the bank's assignment form?

(Answers are given in Appendix 2, pp. 317–18)

Multiple-choice questions

1   Which of the following statements is correct?

(a)   A life policy is a contract of the utmost good faith.
(b)   A life policy is not a contract of the utmost good faith.

2   The failure of an assignor to produce the original policy would be constructive notice of an earlier assignment. This was established in which case?

(a)   *Devaynes* v *Noble* (1816).
(b)   *Newman* v *Newman* (1885).
(c)   *Spencer* v *Clarke* (1878).

3   Where an assignee has notice of a prior assignment, the second assignee cannot obtain priority over the prior assignment by giving notice of his charge ahead of the other assignee. This was confirmed in which case?

(a)   *Devaynes* v *Noble* (1816).
(b)   *Newman* v *Newman* (1885).
(c)   *Spencer* v *Clarke* (1878).

4   If a bank receives notice of a subsequent charge over a policy of which it is the first assignee and it is lending on current account, what action should it take?

(a)   Continue lending on the current account as before.
(b)   Stop the account, to prevent the rule in *Clayton's* case from operating to the detriment of the bank's position.

5   If a bank takes an equitable assignment of a life policy and has no knowledge of any prior assignments and gives notice to the assurance company, what will its priority position in respect of other assignments depend upon?

(a)   The date when notice was received by the assurance company.
(b)   The date of the assignment.

Q

6   An equitable mortgage can be created by:

(a)   Mere deposit of a life policy with the intention that it be held as security.

(b)   Deposit of a life policy together with a completed memorandum of deposit.

(Answers are given in Appendix 2, p. 318)

Specimen examination question

Henry Hepworth has banked with your branch for many years. He has an overdraft limit on current account of £18,000 for which you hold as security a legal assignment over a life policy on Mr Hepworth's life. Its nominal value is £30,000 with profits.

Seven months ago, with the balance of the account reaching £20,000 Dr you wrote to Mr Hepworth requesting that the overdraft be returned to within the agreed limit. No action resulted, and despite further letters, the account did not revert to within the agreed limit, although no further transactions went through the account to worsen the situation except for the bank's regular interest charges.

The bank finally decided that, because of the lack of response, it would surrender the policy in order to repay the borrowing. Its surrender value was £23,000, which just about covered the bank's indebtedness. The bank therefore surrendered the policy and returned the account into credit and cancelled the overdraft limit. A letter was sent to Mr Hepworth detailing the bank's action.

Two weeks after this, Mr Hepworth's son, Ian, calls at the branch. He advises you that his father went to visit him in Australia several months ago. Unfortunately his father was involved in a road accident and had been in a coma for five months before dying approximately four weeks ago. Ian Hepworth shows you the relevant death certificate and his father's will which names him as sole executor and beneficiary. He tells you that he has come over from Australia, where he is now resident, in order to wind up his father's estate.

Mr Hepworth has with him the bank correspondence relating to his father's account and the realisation of his father's life policy. He says that the bank failed to exercise reasonable care in establishing why his father had not responded to the bank's letters. He also says that the bank has deprived his father's estate of the capital value of the life policy, as when the bank surrendered the policy, his father had already died. He added that he also felt that the bank was at fault due to the speed of surrendering the policy within a matter of weeks. He said that he believed by statute the bank had to give three months' notice before realising its security. He therefore says that unless the bank compensates him as beneficiary, he will resort to the courts.

Required

What do you consider is the bank's position with regard to Mr Hepworth's claims?

(Answer is given in Appendix 2, p. 318)

Past examination question

You have agreed to lend your customer, Billy Budd, £10,000 on loan account repayable over three years to buy a car; he has promised to give you a legal assignment over one of his life policies as security.

When this policy is brought into the bank by Billy Budd you discover that it is drawn up under the provisions of the Married Women's Property Act 1882, naming his wife, Laura Budd, as beneficiary. The policy, dated 1 July 1979, is for £15,000 payable on 1 July 2011 or on the earlier death of Billy Budd. Billy Budd is now aged 37.

Required

Explain the problems that have now arisen in the light of this information. Assuming that these problems can be overcome by co-operation, state how the bank's documentation for making the loan and perfecting the security will change from that originally envisaged.

[16 marks]
(Autumn 1988)

(Answer is given in Appendix 2, p. 319)

UNIT 19

Stocks and Shares and Similar Investments

Objectives

- Identify the procedures required to effect a charge or pledge over the following:
  - Stocks and shares
  - Gilt-edged securities
  - Bearer securities
  - American and Canadian securities
  - Unit trusts
  - National Savings Certificates and Premium Savings Bonds
  - Shares covered by an allotment letter.
- Recognise the procedure required to release shares held as security.
- Identify the methods required to realise shares held as security.

19.1 Registered Stocks and Shares

These can be shares quoted on the Stock Exchange or the Unlisted Securities Market. Alternatively they can be unquoted. The latter are normally issued by private limited companies, whereas the former are issued by public limited companies.

When a company issues shares, the company registrar keeps a register of the owners of those shares and issues a certificate which details the type of shares, the number issued and the name of the owner. When shares are sold the share certificate is returned to the registrar, together with a signed stock transfer form. The registrar then amends the name of the owner of the shares in the register and issues a new share certificate in the name of their new owner.

19.2 Problems with Unquoted Stocks and Shares as Security

Unquoted stocks and shares are not listed on the Stock Exchange and therefore have a major problem concerning valuation. Various methods can be used to ascertain this, e.g. the bank could ask the company secretary for the most up to date valuation based upon the last sale of the shares. However, this valuation is difficult to rely upon as it does not reflect the daily fluctuations in the company's fortunes, and banks can only usually consider unquoted shares as evidence of means.

Other problems with regard to unquoted shares can be enshrined in the articles of association of private companies. These can restrict the sale of shares, which is quite common when the company concerned is a family business. They can also prevent shares being given as security for borrowing facilities. Another problem can be where a private limited company states in its articles that it has a 'first and paramount lien' over its shares. This means that the shares of a shareholder who has a debt to the company can be forfeited in payment. An example of this would be where the landlord of a pub is a shareholder of the brewery from which he purchases his beer. Where such a clause is encapsulated in the brewery's articles of association, it could cancel the landlord's shareholding as a set-off against monies owed for the beer. This problem is not encountered with public quoted companies as they are prevented from having a lien over their own shares by the rules of the Stock Exchange.

'I'm sorry, Mr Bates, these aren't exactly the type of stocks which I was looking for as security.'

19.3 Gilt-Edged Securities

The UK government raises funds by the issue of loan stocks on the Stock Exchange. These will offer various interest rates and maturity dates, reflected in the stock market price quoted. If a bank decides to accept these as security it will follow the same procedure for perfecting its charge as for quoted shares.

19.4 Bearer Securities

Often known as bearer share warrants, or bearer bonds, these are fully negotiable instruments and are issued by companies and governments. This means that ownership of these securities transfers by mere delivery. It also means that the new holder can acquire a better title to the securities than that held by the transferor, provided that they have been taken in good faith, for value and without any notice of a defect in the transferor's title. This satisfies the requirements of s.29 Bills of Exchange Act 1882 and was confirmed in *London Joint Stock Bank Ltd* v *Simmons* (1892).

As an up-to-date ownership register is not maintained, these securities will normally have sheets of numbered coupons attached. When a dividend is declared, the relevant coupon will be forwarded by the holder to the company or government concerned, and payment will be made.

19.5 American and Canadian Securities

Share certificates which are issued by American and Canadian companies which are quoted on the UK Stock Exchange have similarities to bearer securities.

The name of the registered owner is given on the face of the certificate and on the reverse there is a form of transfer together with a power of attorney. Once this has been signed, in blank, the shares become transferable by delivery, like bearer securities. However, unlike bearer securities, American and Canadian share certificates are not fully negotiable but can merely be considered as quasi-negotiable. As such, the new holder of these securities cannot obtain a better title than the transferor.

When the new holder receives the certificate, it should be forwarded to the company so that the new holder's name may be registered. This can be done by using the power of attorney, so that an attorney can register the change of name in the USA or Canada. If the new holder fails to register his or her own name, the dividend will be paid to the registered owner and the new owner would have to apply to this person for it, having first provided evidence of ownership.

American and Canadian share certificates are registered in 'marking names', but banks will normally only consider them for security if they are registered in 'good marking names'. ('Good marking names' are listed by the Stock Exchange and include banks, finance houses and stockbrokers). This is because in order for a good delivery to be completed, the Stock Exchange requires such certificates to be in 'good marking names' and to be properly endorsed. Also, there can be some difficulties in contacting other than 'good marking names' with regard to dividend payments.

19.6 Unit Trusts

Unit trusts are managed by professional investment managers who maintain a general portfolio of shares. Investors contribute to the funds which are used in the sale and purchase of these shares and in return have a certain number of units allocated to them, which is evidenced by the issue of a certificate. Dividends are declared periodically and the managers announce to unit holders details concerning investments made and any material policy decisions in the previous accounting period.

19.7 National Savings Certificates and Premium Savings Bonds

The above are government securities issued through the Department for National Savings.

National Savings Certificates attract tax-free interest on sums invested for a number of years, normally five. The investor is issued with a holder's registered card and certificates for the amounts invested. Each certificate will bear the holder's registered number. If the certificates are encashed prior to their maturity date, they will attract some interest, unless they have been held for less than a year.

Premium Savings Bonds are issued in minimum amounts of £100. As with National Savings Certificates, holders' registered cards are issued to investors along with the bonds. Each bond will bear the holder's registered number. No interest is payable on these bonds, but they are entered in weekly and monthly draws for varying amounts in prizes. They are, therefore, not an appreciating investment but are merely worth their nominal value.

It is not possible for either of these securities to be transferred into the name of the bank. Therefore if the bank decides to accept them as security, it can only effect an equitable charge.

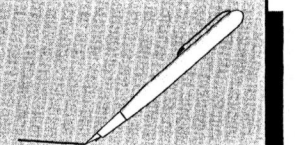

Student Activity 1

Refer back to Unit 15 and refresh your memory regarding the standard clauses contained in bank security forms.

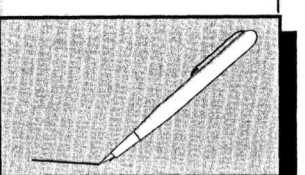

Student Activity 2

Obtain copies of the memorandum of deposit which your bank uses when taking a charge or pledge over shares and similar securities.

19.8 Clauses Contained in a Bank's Memorandum of Deposit which Relate particularly to Shares

19.8.1 Bonus and rights issues

The mortgagor agrees to deposit with the bank any shares received under a bonus issue. Where the bank is a legal mortgagee, it will be entitled to take up any shares issued under a rights issue, or to sell them without contacting the mortgagor. All costs incurred would be for the mortgagor's account.

19.8.2 Extension of security

The security will cover all interest and dividend payment. In addition, it will also cover shares issued under rights or bonus issues.

19.8.3 Undertaking to create a legal mortgage

This clause is an undertaking by an equitable mortgagor to complete a legal mortgage over shares if called upon to do so.

19.8.4 Power of attorney clause

This clause aids the bank if it wishes to realise its security and avoids the need to resort to the courts for an order of sale.

Where a memorandum of deposit covers equitable mortgages, and contains a power of attorney clause, it must be executed under seal.

The bank is then appointed as attorney of the mortgagor and can sell the shares or create a legal mortgage in its own favour if it so wishes.

19.8.5 Margin clause

The mortgagor will agree to maintain a specific margin of cover in shares in respect of his or her borrowing. This enables the bank to ask the mortgagor to provide additional security, should the value of the shares decrease.

19.8.6 Completion of blank stock transfer form

The mortgagor authorises the bank to complete the missing details at any time in the future and thus realise its security if it so wishes.

19.9 Taking an Equitable Charge over Registered Stocks and Shares

An equitable charge over registered stocks and shares can be established by the mere lodgement of the relevant share certificate, provided that there was the intention that it should be held by the bank as security. This was confirmed in *Harrold* v *Plenty* (1901). This intent can, of course, be shown by recording the fact in the bank's records. However, it is more usual to have the customer complete a memorandum of deposit, as this strengthens the bank's position considerably because of the clauses contained therein. It must also be remembered that a memorandum of deposit must be completed where third-party security is involved.

Banks use two types of memorandum of deposit. Where a customer is active in the buying and selling of stocks and shares, an omnibus memorandum of deposit will be taken which will cover any shares which the bank should handle now or in the future. Where only a couple of shareholdings are lodged, another type, which will refer specifically to these holdings, will be used.

Many banks will also ask their customer to sign a stock transfer form. The name of the transferee will be left blank and the form will be undated. If the bank has to realise its security in the future it can complete the missing information, entering its own name as transferee, and can then sell the shares without having to resort to the courts for an order to sell.

Obviously, before taking an equitable charge, the bank will value the shares and ensure that there is an adequate margin.

19.10 Advantages of an Equitable Mortgage over Registered Stocks and Shares

(a) Easy and quick to set up.

(b) The bank's customer carries the risk with regard to the liability under partly-paid shares, rather than the bank.

(c) A director's position with regard to having to hold a certain number of his or her company's shares in order to qualify as a director is unaffected.

(d) As mentioned above, the bank can convert its equitable mortgage into a legal mortgage by holding and completing a stock transfer from.

19.11 Disadvantages of an Equitable Mortgage over Registered Stocks and Shares

(a) As with all equitable mortgages, they are subject to prior equities. If the bank learns of a prior equitable interest or charge, it cannot then convert its mortgage into a legal charge in order to rank ahead of the prior equitable mortgagee or interested party (*Coleman* v *London County and Westminster Bank Ltd* (1916)).

(b) The customer may obtain a duplicate share certificate and sell the shares. It was confirmed in *Rainford* v *James Keith & Blackman Co Ltd* (1905) that, in such circumstances, the bank's security would be worthless. Such happenings can be avoided by serving a 'stop notice' through the Supreme Court on the company. The company must then give the bank eight days' notice before any transactions can take place regarding a transfer of ownership. This will allow the bank time to obtain a court injunction or restraining order to prevent such a transfer taking place.

(c) Any shares issued under rights or bonus issues will be forwarded direct to the customer and not to the bank.

Rights issues of shares are where a company offers shares to existing shareholders pro rata to their current shareholding, at an advantageous price.

Bonus issues of shares occur where a company wishes to capitalise its reserves. It then issues 'free' shares to existing shareholders pro rata to their current shareholding.

The effect of rights or bonus issues is normally to reduce the share market price. A customer is supposed to deposit such shares with the bank; if the customer does not, or should sell them, this could seriously affect the value of the bank's security.

19.12 Taking a Legal Mortgage over Registered Stocks and Shares

(a) Value the shares and ensure that there is an adequate margin.

(b) Obtain share certificate and have customer complete a memorandum of deposit and stock transfer form with the transferee named as the bank's nominee company.

(c) Forward share certificate and stock transfer form to the company registrar.

(d) The company registrar will send a new share certificate to the bank which will name the bank's nominee company as the registered owner.

(e) Ensure that dividends from the shares will be credited to the correct account.

It is worth mentioning here that legal or equitable mortgages over gilt-edged securities require the same procedures as for registered stocks and shares.

19.13 Advantages of a Legal Mortgage over Registered Stocks and Shares

All documentation relating to the shares is sent direct to the bank. The bank therefore has complete control.

By having a legal mortgage, the bank is not affected by any prior equitable interests unless it was aware of them when it took its legal charge.

19.14 Disadvantages of a Legal Mortgage over Registered Stocks and Shares

(a) This takes longer to complete than an equitable mortgage.

(b) A major problem occurs when the bank has a legal charge over partly-paid shares. As the registered owner, the bank's nominee company is liable for any calls made on these shares. It will also remain liable on these shares for up to 12 months after they have been transferred from the bank nominee company's name to a subsequent shareholder, where that shareholder does not pay the calls made upon him or her.

(c) If the transferor's signature was forged then the bank, as transferee, is liable to indemnify the company registrar if any loss is suffered as a result of the latter acting on such a forged transfer form. This is because a transferee implies that the transferor's signature is genuine. This was confirmed in *Sheffield Corporation v Barclay* (1905) and *Yeung Kai Yung v Hong Kong and Shanghai Banking Corporation* (1980).

(d) If the mortgagor is a director of the company whose shares are being taken as security, then the shares may represent his or her qualification holding. If a legal mortgage is completed over these shares, it could disqualify your customer as a director and he or she would then be forced to resign. In such cases, an equitable mortgage is usually taken to prevent this happening.

19.15 Equitable Mortgage over Unquoted Shares

The bank would follow the same steps as for quoted shares. However, it will also give notice in duplicate to the company. This additional step helps the bank as follows:

(a) If the company notes the bank's interest, it would be forewarned if the customer attempted to obtain a duplicate share certificate.

(b) If the customer owed money to the company, the company's lending up to the date when it received notice of the bank's interest would take priority. However, any further advances would rank after the bank's mortgage.

19.16 Legal Mortgage over Unquoted Shares

The same procedure, as for a legal mortgage over quoted shares, is followed.

19.17 Taking a Pledge over Bearer Securities

(a) Bearer securities will be deposited as security, and a memorandum of deposit completed.

(b) Diarise when coupons are to be submitted.

(c) Ensure that all relevant coupons are provided.

It should be noted that bearer securities cannot be pledged for borrowing which falls within the auspices of the Consumer Credit Act 1974, as they are negotiable instruments.

19.18 Taking a Charge over American and Canadian Securities

(a) Refer to Stock Exchange Year Book and ensure that shares are in good marking names. Where this is not the case, then the bank should insist that they are transferred into a good marking name before proceeding with the perfection of the security. This is because shares which are not in good marking names have limited saleability.

(b) Make sure that the certificate is endorsed in blank.

(c) Have memorandum of deposit completed by customer.

(d) Diarise when dividends are to be claimed from the marking name.

19.19 Taking an Equitable Charge over National Savings Certificates and Premium Savings Bonds

These investments cannot be registered in the bank's nominee company name and therefore a legal charge cannot be effected.

(a) Compare the certificates with the holder's registered card. This will bear the holder's registered number (as will the certificates) and the registered owner's signature.

(b) Customer should complete a memorandum of deposit and a repayment form. The latter should be left undated and should authorise payment to the bank.

(c) All documents will be held by the bank.

As it is possible for customers to obtain duplicate certificates, the bank should only contemplate such security for customers who are considered undoubted.

19.20 Taking a Charge over Shares covered by an Allotment Letter

Allotment letters are issued to applicants who wish to take up rights issues or new issues of shares. They are basically rights to acquire a set number of shares and can be fully or partly paid.

(a) Ensure that the bank can comply with the terms of the allotment letter.

(b) Make sure that the customer has completed the form of renunciation.

(c) If the bank wishes to effect a legal charge, then the shares must be registered in the bank's nominee company name.

(d) If the shares are partly paid, obtain customer's authority to debit the cost of any calls on the shares to the customer's account.

(e) Diarise when payments are due.

(f) Once calls are paid, the company registrar will forward the relevant certificate to the bank.

(g) If the bank is taking an equitable charge, it should obtain its customer's authority to forward the certificate to the bank when available.

(h) Diarise when certificate should be received.

(i) Customer should complete the normal formalities when the certificate arrives.

(j) A memorandum of deposit should be completed in all cases.

19.21 Taking a Charge over Unit Trusts

A legal or equitable mortgage can be established. No stock transfer form is required.

(a) Memorandum of deposit will be completed.

(b) Share certificate will be endorsed by the customer and handed to the bank.

(c) If a legal mortgage is to be taken, the certificate should be sent to the unit trust managers. They, in turn, will issue a new certificate in the name of the bank nominee company.

(d) If an equitable mortgage is to be taken, the bank will hold the endorsed certificate and give notice of its charge to the unit trust managers.

19.22 Release of Mortgages held over Shares

In respect of equitable mortgages, the procedure is as follows:

(a) Where notice of the bank's charge has been given, an advice should be forwarded to the company registrar or unit trust managers confirming that the bank's interest has ended.

(b) Mark memorandum of deposit 'Cancelled' and place with obsolete security forms.

(c) Return certificate to customer against his or her receipt.

In respect of legal mortgages, the procedure is as follows:

(a) Complete stock transfer form naming customer as transferee.

(b) Forward stock transfer form and share certificate to the company registrar.

(c) Company registrar will send new certificate in customer's name either to the customer direct or via the bank.

(d) Mark memorandum of deposit 'Cancelled' and place with obsolete security forms.

19.23   Realisation of Shares held as Security

If a bank has to realise its security to repay borrowing after the necessary demand for repayment has been made, it will carry out the following procedures:

(a) If the bank holds a legal mortgage, it can authorise its brokers to sell the shares and can thus obtain repayment. As usual it will complete a stock transfer form.

(b) If the bank has an equitable mortgage, unless its memorandum of deposit contains a power of attorney or the bank holds an undated signed blank stock transfer form, it will have to rely on the co-operation of its customer in selling the shares. If such assistance is not forthcoming, the bank will have to apply for a court order. This will be exhibited to the company registrar and the shares will be sold in the normal way.

For both types of mortgage, the memorandum of deposit will be marked 'Cancelled' and placed with obsolete security papers.

Students should remember that a bank may decide to delay realising the shares, on the premise that they may rise in value. This may be the case where there is likely to be shortfall between the customer's debt and the value of the security. Obviously, while the bank is taking no action, the share price may decline and the bank may eventually realise a smaller amount than originally envisaged. However, providing that the bank was not directly instrumental in the decline in the value of the shares, it will not be liable to any third party e.g a guarantor who may have to be responsible for any shortfall. This was confirmed in the case of *China and South Sea Bank Ltd* v *Tan* (1990).

19.24 What Action should a Bank take if Dealings in Shares, which the Bank holds as Security, are Suspended?

The bank should not act hastily and should await the outcome of the suspension. It may be that a take-over bid is imminent, in which case the shares may rise. Thus, the bank's security position could be enhanced.

However, should the bank's security position be undermined, the bank should then contact its customer regarding the position and attempt to obtain alternative security. Further action would depend upon the outcome of these talks.

Any action taken prematurely, before the reason for the suspension in dealings is known, could lead to legal action against the bank, particularly if cheques have been dishonoured.

Banks should, therefore, proceed with caution when dealings are suspended in shares which they hold as security.

19.25 What Action should a Bank take when a Take-over Bid is made for a Company, Shares in which the Bank holds as Security?

(a) Obtain a stockbroker's opinion on the offer and pass this on to the bank's customer.

(b) If the customer wishes to accept or reject the offer, the bank will carry out its customer's wishes where it holds a legal charge or, in the case of an equitable mortgage, the customer will convey his or her wishes directly.

(c) If the take-over bid is successful, the bank will have to send the share certificate, which it holds as security, to the institution which is handling the issue of the new shares. In the case of an equitable mortgage, it will require its customer's authority to do this. (Offers made under take-over bids normally involve the exchange of shares in one company for the shares in the other company, sometimes also with a cash payment.)

(d) Diarise when new certificate due.

(e) When new certificate arrives, enter in security records and delete details of previous certificate.

(f) A new security form need not be completed by the customer where an omnibus memorandum of deposit is held.

(g) If a payment of cash is made as part of the take-over, it should be credited to the customer's account and the customer's future borrowing requirements discussed.

Summary

Now that you have read this unit, you should be able to:

☐ Identify the procedures required to effect a charge or pledge over the following:

—stocks and shares;

—gilt-edged securities;

—bearer securities;

—American and Canadian securities;

—unit trusts;

—National Savings Certificates and Premium Savings Bonds;

—shares covered by an allotment letter.

☐ Recognise the procedure required to release shares held as security.

☐ Identify the methods required to realise shares held as security.

If you can tick all the above boxes with confidence, you are ready to answer the questions which follow on pp. 226–30.

List of Cases

China and South Sea Bank Ltd v *Tan* (1990)

Coleman v *London County and Westminster Bank Ltd* (1916)

Harrold v *Plenty* (1901)

London Joint Stock Bank Ltd v *Simmons* (1892)

Rainford v *James Keith & Blackman Co Ltd* (1905)

Sheffield Corporation v *Barclay* (1905)

Yeung Kai Yung v *Hong Kong and Shanghai Banking Corporation* (1980)

List of Statutes

Bills of Exchange Act 1882

Consumer Credit Act 1974

Self-assessment Questions

Short-answer questions

1   Your customer, Mel Heffernan, requests a loan of £5,000 repayable over three years towards the purchase price of a car. He offers bearer bonds as security for the loan. The current value of these is £15,000.

Would you accept these bonds as security?

2   What are the problems in taking unquoted stocks and shares as security?

3   Why must a bank ensure that American or Canadian securities are in good marking names when offered as security?

4   Can a bank take a legal charge over National Savings Certificates?

5   Your bank has recently taken an equitable charge over shares in Bates International (BIMBO) plc. What action can the bank take to prevent its customer obtaining a duplicate share certificate and then selling the shares?

(Answers are given in Appendix 2, p. 319)

Multiple-choice questions

1   Glen Richards pledges bearer bonds as security for a £30,000 overdraft. You have been advised today that Mr Richards stole these bonds from Graham Wilson.

What is the bank's position?

(a)   As the bearer bonds were stolen, the bank's pledge is invalid.
(b)   As the bank took the bearer bonds in good faith, for value and without notice of any defect in the transferor's title, the bank has a valid pledge.

2   Which case or statute confirmed your answer in Q1?

(a)   S.60 Bills of Exchange Act 1882.
(b)   S.80 Bills of Exchange Act 1882.
(c)   S.29 Bills of Exchange Act 1882.
(d)   *London Joint Stock Bank Ltd* v *Simmons* (1892).
(e)   *Sheffield Corporation* v *Barclay* (1905).

3   An equitable mortgage can be created by the mere deposit of a share certificate with the intention that it be held as security by the bank. Which case confirmed this?

(a)   *Harrold* v *Plenty* (1901).
(b)   *Sheffield Corporation* v *Barclay* (1905).
(c)   *China and South Sea Bank Ltd* v *Tan* (1990).
(d)   *Coleman* v *London County and Westminster Bank Ltd* (1916).

4   The bank has an equitable mortgage of registered shares, and the company makes a bonus issue. What is the position?

(a)   The bonus shares are sent to the bank.
(b)   The bonus shares are sent to the customer.
(c)   The price per share falls.
(d)   The value of the bank's security will fall unless the customer sends the bonus certificate to the bank.

5   The bank has a legal mortgage over registered shares for which a bonus issue is made. What is the position?

(a)   The bonus shares are sent to the bank.

(b) The bonus shares are sent to the customer.
(c) The price per share falls.
(d) The value of the bank's security will not be affected.

6   You learn that dealings have been suspended in shares which the bank holds as security. What action do you take?

(a) Seek alternative security at once.
(b) Ascertain the reason for the suspension.

7   You hold a guarantee for £5,000, supported by shares currently worth £1,000. What is your maximum claim against the guarantor?

(a) £5,000.
(b) £1,000.
(c) £6,000.

(Answers are given in Appendix 2, p. 320)

Revision questions

1   You hold the business accounts of Tony Bryant, a self-employed printer. He established his business some five years ago. At the present time, the bank has granted him loan facilities of £25,000 against the security of a legal mortgage over 10,000 ordinary shares in Lake Communications plc owned by Tony Bryant and an unsupported guarantee given by Tony Bryant's cousin, Brian Powell, which is limited to £25,000.

Tony Bryant's business has fallen on hard times in recent months and the bank on several occasions has had to dishonour cheques drawn on the main business account, which has been kept strictly in credit. Despite meetings with the customer and promises by him that the financial side of his business would improve, you have been unable to make the last two repayments to the loan account and have therefore made formal demand for repayment of the loan.

Unfortunately, your customer has been unable to meet his liabilities and you have therefore called upon Brian Powell to meet his guarantee liability. Having consulted the bank's stockbroking department, you decided to delay selling the shares held in Lake Communications plc as they were currently appreciating in the stock market due to a rumour that the company was poised to make a take-over bid for a prominent Australian conglomerate. At that time the shares were trading at between 115p and 120p per share. Seven days later, trading in the shares was suspended and insolvency proceedings were begun against the company by several creditors. It soon became apparent that no rescue bid would be launched and that the shares were virtually worthless.

Tony Bryant owed the bank £17,500 gross and you have today received a letter from Brian Powell's solicitor. In the letter the solicitor stated that although his client did not deny liability under his guarantee, he did feel that the bank was guilty of a breach of duty of care to him as guarantor. This was because the value of the mortgaged shares collapsed after default by Tony Bryant and that the bank owed him (Brian Powell) a duty of care to sell the shares before their value collapsed. As such the solicitor suggests that it would perhaps be equitable in the circumstances if his client only paid £6,000 under his guarantee liability.

What is the bank's position?

2   David Alcock has operated a private account with you for over 20 years. Five years ago, he was made redundant and using his redundancy money and an overdraft facility from the bank he rented a small lock-up shop and started an antiques business. As security for the overdraft, David Alcock gave the bank an equitable charge by way of memorandum of deposit over various quoted shares. These were registered in his name and were valued recently at £28,000. Mr Alcock signed undated, blank stock transfer forms at the time when the security was taken.

Despite initial success, the shop trade has steadily declined during the last two years and the business has finally failed, with Alcock having a present bank overdraft of £16,000.

The bank has therefore made formal demand for repayment of the debt. Mr Alcock calls to see you and advises you that he is unable to meet this liability. When you mention that the bank would therefore look to the sale of the shares for repayment, Mr Alcock tells you that they do not really belong to him and are merely held by him as trustee for his children.

(a)   What is the bank's position as regards its security?
(b)   Would the bank's position have been any different if, in similar circumstances, it had taken a legal charge over the shares and they had been registered in the name of the bank's nominee company?

(Answers are given in Appendix 2, p. 320)

Past examination question

Mr Robert Frost has a current account at your branch. There is also a current account in the name of his wife, Mary. Mary Frost, whom you have never met, owns shares in a number of different companies, and the certificates are held by you in safe custody.

Recently Mr Frost, who runs an antique stall in the local market, approached you for a loan of £30,000 to enable him to purchase some items at auction. You agreed to assist, subject to a guarantee from Mrs Frost supported by a legal charge over her shares to a value of £40,000.

Mr Frost subsequently called at your branch with a lady whom he introduced as his wife. She signed the security and stock transfer forms, and a respected local solicitor, who had been called in by Mr Frost for the purpose, witnessed her signature. The solicitor also added to each charge form a certificate stating, 'I certify that I have explained the nature and purpose of the within document to Mary Frost and that she has signed under her own free will.'

In due course, the completed stock exchange transfer forms were submitted to the appropriate company registrars and the shares transferred into the name of the bank's nominee company.

Mr Frost then withdrew the amount of the loan and disappeared. It has subsequently transpired that the lady in question was not Mrs Frost and that the signature on the security and stock transfer forms bore no resemblance to that of the real Mrs Frost.

Required

(a) Giving reasons for your answers, discuss the respective positions of:
    (i)   Mrs Frost;
    (ii)   the local solicitor;
    (iii)   the company registrars;
    (iv)   the bank.

[15 marks]

(b) Indicate what steps, if any, the bank should now take.

[5 marks]

[Total marks for question – 20]

(Autumn 1991)

(Answer is given in Appendix 2, p. 321)

UNIT 20

Guarantees

Objectives

- Identify a bank's obligations to a guarantor.
- Recognise the effect of undue influence on a guarantee.
- Detail the clauses contained in a standard bank guarantee form.
- Ascertain the effects of various occurrences on joint and several guarantees.
- Recognise how the cross-guarantee structure of limited companies operates.
- Identify the procedure for taking a guarantee as security.
- Recognise the circumstances which determine a guarantee and the action which banks must take.

Introduction

The Statute of Frauds 1677 defines a guarantee as 'a written promise made by one person to be collaterally answerable for the debt, default, or miscarriage of another.'

A bank's guarantee form is drawn up as an indemnity. This means that a bank can in effect make demand upon the guarantor without first calling upon the principal debtor; only if the debtor failed to meet the agreed obligations would the guarantor be called upon.

Guarantees can be executed under seal or under hand. In the latter case, a guarantee must be supported by some form of consideration. Such consideration in a bank's case would be the granting of loan facilities or the continuance of facilities for a further period.

A guarantee, of course, is third-party security and as such the bank can ignore it when proving for a debt in a bankrupt's estate.

Banks often take personal guarantees from directors of a limited company when lending to that company. This is to reinforce the commitment of the directors to the success of the company, as they are less likely to walk away from an awkward situation, should one develop, if they are personally liable for any debt which may evolve.

20.1 A Bank's Obligations to a Would-be Guarantor

A would-be guarantor will often have a number of questions for the bank. It is therefore better if the bank's customer is present with the proposed guarantor so that the bank can answer questions with its customer's permission and so that any misconceptions can be cleared up at the outset. Failing the attendance of the bank's customer, the bank should obtain the customer's authority to answer any questions posed by the would-be guarantor. If the bank does not have this permission and it is obvious that the guarantor is likely to be misled, then the bank should refer the matter back to its customer.

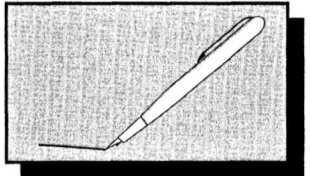

Student Activity 1

Does your bank request all would-be guarantors to take independent legal advice? Check your bank's rules concerning this and undue influence. Compare your findings with what is detailed below.

20.2 Undue Influence

Undue influence occurs where a person is influenced in taking on an obligation by another and is unable to act on his own free will. This situation can arise where there is a personal or fiduciary relationship, such as a husband and wife. In such circumstances it is usual for a bank to ask a potential guarantor to take independent legal advice, normally from a solicitor, so that the party is aware of the obligation being entered into.

A side letter or an endorsement on the actual bank guarantee signed by the solicitor concerned will attest that the meaning of the document and the implications of the liability have been explained to the guarantor. Failure to take this course of action could render the guarantee voidable.

20.3 Important Cases Relating to Undue Influence and Guarantees

20.3.1 Lloyds Bank Ltd v Bundy (1975)

Mr Bundy, a customer of the bank, gave a series of guarantees supported by a legal mortgage over his farm to cover the liabilities of his son's company. Later, Mr Bundy was called upon to pay and upon his default, the bank arranged to sell the farm. Mr Bundy claimed non-liability, due to 'undue influence'. The court held that the relationship between the bank and Mr Bundy was one of trust and confidence and that Mr Bundy relied upon the bank. As such, there had been a conflict of interest on the bank's part and independent advice should therefore have been insisted upon by the bank when the final security had been taken. As such advice had not been given, the guarantee and the mortgage were set aside.

The decision in this case caused a ripple of similar cases. However, subsequent case decisions seem to indicate that the circumstances regarding the Bundy case were exceptional.

20.3.2   *National Westminster Bank v Morgan* (1985)

In this case it was held that, in order for a security to be voidable on a later claim of undue influence, it must be established that as a result of the transaction an unfair advantage would be given to one party over another. Thus the relationship between the bank and the guarantor would have to show that the guarantor was dominated by the bank. Normally, such an occurrence would not happen in a banking situation. Thus the court found for the bank.

20.3.3   *Avon Finance Co Ltd v Bridger* (1985)

Elderly parents completed security forms in respect of their son's obligations to Avon. The forms had been given by Avon to the son for his parents' signatures. The court held that these signatures were obtained by undue influence.

20.3.4   *Barclays Bank Plc v O'Brien* (1992)

The Appeal Court held that where a married woman acts as surety for her husband's debts, the creditor must ensure that she understands the transaction which she is entering into.

As a result of this decision, banks should insist that a married woman, who is providing security for her husband's debts, receives independent legal advice in order that she fully understands the nature and effect of her liability and to avoid the possibility that she has been unduly influenced to sign by her husband.

20.4   Other Important Cases Relating to Guarantees

20.4.1   *Cooper v National Provincial Bank Ltd* (1946)

The customer's husband was an undischarged bankrupt and had signing rights on her account. Cooper felt that the bank should have told him about this and that therefore his guarantees should be set aside. The court held that the bank had no obligation to disclose the information about the customer's account and therefore the guarantees were valid.

20.4.2   *O'Hara v Allied Irish Banks Ltd and another* (1984)

The court held that where the prospective guarantor was a stranger to the bank, the latter is under no obligation to explain the terms and effects of the guarantee nor the maximum liability under it.

20.4.3   *Barclays Bank Plc v Khaira and Another* (1991)

This case confirmed that a bank has no duty to explain the clauses in a guarantee to a customer of another branch of that bank.

20.4.4 *Lloyds Bank Plc* v *Waterhouse* (1990)

The court held that an illiterate person would not be liable under a bank guarantee which he had signed without reading or indicating that he could not read if he had in fact asked questions to ascertain the nature and extent of his liability and the bank's employees had, by their words and conduct, caused him to believe that he was signing something other than what he did in fact sign.

This would seem to be a rare decision where a contract was set aside on a plea of *non est factum*.

20.5 Information which can be Disclosed to a Guarantor after the Guarantee has been Signed

When the principal borrowing exceeds £15,000 and is therefore beyond the ambit of the Consumer Credit Act 1974, the only disclosure which may be given to a guarantor, after that person has signed the guarantee, is the extent to which his or her liability is relied upon. If the guarantee is for a limited amount and the customer's borrowing exceeds the limit of the guarantee, the guarantor should be advised that the guarantee is fully relied upon. If, however, the borrowing is for less than the amount of the guarantee, or the guarantee is for an unlimited amount, the guarantor should be advised of the balance of the account which is secured.

Where the borrowing, for which the guarantee has been given as security, is covered by the Consumer Credit Act 1974, the guarantor has additional rights concerning disclosure of information. In Unit 2, we looked at the effect which consumer credit legislation has had on third-party security for regulated agreements; students should refer back to this in order to remind themselves of this information. At this stage, however, it is worth mentioning that under s.107 Consumer Credit Act 1974, the guarantor, upon payment of a fee, can obtain details of the total amount outstanding and the total amount paid by the debtor under the agreement, together with an analysis of these figures. The guarantor can also obtain another copy of the executed agreement and any security document.

In respect of overdraft, s.108 Consumer Credit Act 1974 says that a guarantor must be given a signed statement detailing the state of the account, any amount currently due and amounts which will become due, together with the dates when they are payable, if no more drawings are made.

20.6 Misrepresentations and Guarantees

A guarantor may attempt to avoid liability by claiming that the document which he or she signed was purported to be different to what it actually was. Banks have always relied upon the decision in *Saunders* v *Anglia Building Society* (1970) in which the plea of *non est factum* was defeated. However, the decision in the case of *Lloyds Bank Plc* v *Waterhouse* (1990) (see above) has cast some doubts on this judgment.

In another case relating to misrepresentation, *Mackenzie* v *Royal Bank of Canada* (1934), Mrs Mackenzie was able to avoid her liability under a guarantee given to the bank, as when she had executed the guarantee the bank had inadvertently intimated that the transaction was a way of obtaining the return of share certificates which had previously been lodged as security.

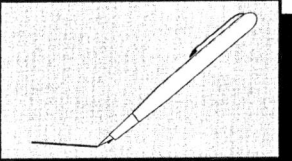

Student Activity 2

Obtain a copy of your bank's standard guarantee form and compare its clauses with those detailed below.

20.7 Clauses Contained in the Standard Bank Guarantee Form

20.7.1 Continuing security

There will be a clause stating that the guarantee will be a continuing security. This statement is included so that all future advances will be covered by the guarantee. Failure to include such a clause would mean that the rule in *Clayton's* case would operate to the detriment of the bank, as all future credits to the account would eventually extinguish the original borrowing and further borrowings would then not be covered.

20.7.2 Whole debt

This clause states that the whole debt due from the principal debtor to the bank is guaranteed by the surety, provided that the maximum sum recoverable does not exceed a certain amount plus interest. The effect of this clause is to prevent the guarantor from taking certain actions unless he clears off the whole debt, even if this exceeds any limit stated in the guarantee form. The actions which the guarantor would be prevented from taking include:

(a) Suing the principal debtor in order to recover the amount paid up.

(b) Claiming alongside the bank in the event of the debtor's bankruptcy.

(c) Claiming a contribution from any fellow joint and several guarantors.

(d) Using the doctrine of subrogation, i.e. claiming securities from the bank deposited either by third parties or the debtor.

The importance of this clause to the bank can best be understood by the following examples.

(a) *Whole debt clause included in the bank guarantee form*
A customer is adjudicated bankrupt owing the bank £30,000. The only security which the bank holds is a guarantee for £20,000. The guarantor is called upon to meet his guarantee liability which he duly does, and £20,000 is credited to a suspense account. The bank proves in the debtor's estate for £30,000. A 33p in the £ dividend is paid to the bankrupt's creditors. The bank will then receive a further £10,000 which, together with the sum from the guarantor, will repay the bank. As the guarantor is unable to prove in the debtor's estate at the same time as the bank, he will receive nothing.

(b) *Whole debt clause excluded from the bank guarantee form*
Given the same details regarding the customer, the bank would have to deduct the guarantor's £20,000 from the debt of £30,000 and could only prove for £10,000. The guarantor would be able to prove for £20,000 alongside the bank. If a dividend of 33p in the £ was paid, the bank would receive £3,333.33 and the guarantor would receive £3,666.66. Thus the bank would have to write off £6,666.66.

20.7.3   Consideration

A clause stating that some consideration has been given will appear in the bank's guarantee form. As stated earlier, any guarantee executed under hand must be supported by some form of consideration.

20.7.4   Indemnity

The aim of this clause is to make the guarantor principally liable for the debt. Its inclusion has had less significance recently, following the abolition of the *ultra vires* doctrine under the 1989 Companies Act. However, it is still of benefit when lending is made to an unincorporated entity such as a club or society.

20.7.5   Payment 'on demand'

The payment 'on demand' clause prevents the Limitations Act (1980) working against the bank until a demand for repayment has been made on the guarantor (*Bradford Old Bank Ltd* v *Sutcliffe* (1918)). Under the Limitations Act, any action on a simple contract must be taken within six years of the date when the cause of action occurred. With regard to a guarantee under seal this time limit is extended to 12 years.

20.7.6   Clause to prevent *Clayton's* case operating to the bank's detriment

This clause protects the bank if it fails to stop the debtor's account when a guarantee has been determined by law, the debtor or the guarantor. The effectiveness of this clause was confirmed in *Westminster Bank* v *Cond* (1940).

20.7.7   Right to set up new account(s) for the principal debtor upon determination of the guarantee

This clause allows the bank to open a new account for the principal debtor after determining the guarantor's liability, without affecting the guarantor's liability.

20.7.8   Power to vary arrangements

The bank can vary arrangements with the principal debtor or release security without affecting the validity of the guarantee, by the inclusion of this clause.

20.7.9   Determination of the guarantee by the guarantor

The guarantor or guarantor's personal representatives will give the requisite amount of notice in writing to the bank to determine his or her liability. This notice will normally be one or three months. The guarantor's liability will not be crystallised until this notice elapses. (There will normally be a further clause, stating that the guarantee will not be determined by the receipt of the notice of death of the guarantor.)

In the event of the guarantor's death, his or her personal representatives must give the requisite amount of notice in order to determine the estate's liability. In practice, the bank will attempt to establish alternative security arrangements with the principal debtor, but obviously it will retain its right to look to the deceased's estate for restitution if no agreement can be reached.

20.7.10   Preference clause

This clause enables the bank to retain any security for a given period. This is to protect the bank in relation to any claim against the bank regarding preference under the Insolvency Act 1986.

20.7.11   Clause preventing the guarantor receiving security from the principal debtor

If a guarantor were allowed to accept security from the principal debtor, then in the event of the latter becoming bankrupt, any dividend received by the bank would be reduced (*Re Sass* (1896)).

Where a guarantor, contrary to this clause, accepts security from the guarantor, he is deemed to be holding this security in trust for the bank. (This is enshrined in another clause.)

20.7.12   Guarantee is in addition to any other security

By taking a further guarantee, a bank is not affecting its position with regard to any earlier guarantee or security which may have been taken.

20.7.13   Retained liability of guarantor despite the change of name or constitution of a bank or firm

Where the name or constitution of the principal debtor alters, a guarantee given in respect of the debtor's liability will not be affected.

20.7.14   Conclusive evidence clause

Under this clause the guarantor agrees to accept as binding any admission of the extent of his or her liability to the bank which is made either by the bank or the principal debtor (*Bache and Co (London) Ltd* v *Banque Vernes et Commerciale de Paris SA* (1973)).

20.7.15   The guarantee will be subject to English law

20.7.16   Costs and charges

All costs and charges are to be met by the guarantor for the enforcement of the security, if they are not met by the principal debtor.

20.7.17 Guarantor's payment to be placed in a suspense account

This clause confirms the decision in *Re Sass* (1896), whereby any payment made under a guarantee can be placed in a suspense account. This statement is often linked with a clause which says that any such moneys do not have to be considered when proving in the principal debtor's bankruptcy.

20.7.18 Guarantee to remain the property of the bank

In order to retain the protection of its clauses, a bank can retain its guarantee form uncancelled.

20.8 Joint and Several Guarantees

Where more than one person signs a bank's guarantee, the guarantee form will state that any liability incurred by the guarantors will be joint and several. This means that should the bank need to look to the guarantors for repayment, it can sue each one individually for the full amount, or jointly.

20.8.1 When does a joint and several guarantee come into effect?

Where, say, four guarantors are intended to sign the bank's guarantee form, the guarantee will not become operative until the fourth guarantor has signed the form. (*National Provincial Bank of England Ltd* v *Brackenbury* (1906)).

It is worth mentioning at this stage the *James Graham & Co Ltd* v *Southgate-Sands and Others* (1985) case. Here it was confirmed that all joint and several guarantors are released from their liability when one of the guarantors signatures has been forged.

20.8.2 The effect of the *Ellesmere Brewery Co* v *Cooper* (1896) case

The above case established that where a bank wishes to take a joint and several guarantee, an intending guarantor should not be permitted to alter the terms of the guarantee in any way, as to do so would discharge the guarantor and all the other guarantors from their liability.

When, however, the guarantee has been signed, the bank can release any guarantor from liability or release their supporting security without first referring to the other guarantors. A clause within the guarantee allows this.

Without such a clause the guarantee would be void if the bank varied arrangements with certain signatories to the guarantee and did not obtain the permission of all guarantors (*Barclays Bank Ltd* v *Trevanion* (1933)).

20.8.3 What action (if any) should a bank take upon learning of the death of a joint and several guarantor?

The death of a joint and several guarantor does not release his or her estate from liability. As mentioned previously, banks normally include a clause in their guarantee forms which requires a period of notice before liability is determined. When a bank receives notice, the remaining guarantors are still liable for any further monies lent and thus a new guarantee is unnecessary. If a current account is overdrawn, it should be stopped on the expiry of notice, in order to prevent the rule in *Clayton's* case operating against the bank.

20.8.4 What action should a bank take when it receives notice to determine a joint and several guarantee?

Banks normally include a clause in their guarantees requiring all joint and several guarantors to give notice of determination in order for such determination to be effective. Should one joint and several guarantor wish to determine his or her liability, the bank will normally arrange a meeting involving itself, its customer, and all guarantors so that a new security arrangement which is acceptable to all parties can be established. The outcome of this may be that the one joint and several guarantor can be released from the liability, particularly where the other guarantors are people of substance. In such cases, it is usual practice to take new guarantees from such guarantors. Obviously, if no agreement can be reached, the bank may call in the debts, or could call on all the guarantors to meet their liabilities, or could rely on the clause mentioned above.

20.8.5 What action should a bank take when it receives notice of the mental incapacity of a joint and several guarantor?

Upon notice of the mental incapacity of a joint and several guarantor, a bank should stop its customer's account if it is overdrawn in order to prevent the rule in *Clayton's* case operating against the bank. A new account would be opened for the customer which would either work in credit or within agreed overdraft limits, dependent upon security held. It is normal banking practice to arrange a meeting between the bank, its customer and the remaining sane guarantors so that fresh security arrangements can be settled.

20.8.6 What action should a bank take if it receives notice of bankruptcy proceedings involving a joint and several guarantor?

If a bank is advised of a bankruptcy order or has notice of a petition against a joint and several guarantor, it should stop its customer's account if it wishes to claim against the bankrupt's estate in respect of the guarantee liability. Such action would not preclude the bank from taking action against the bankrupt's co-guarantors in the future. It must also be remembered that the bank may be prepared to merely rely upon the other guarantors and as such would be able to release the bankrupt's estate from its liability.

20.9 Cross-Guarantee Structure of Limited Companies

Limited companies often expand by buying other companies or creating new subsidiaries. This has serious implications for banks where a company cross-guarantee security structure exists. Cross-guarantees are where every company in the group gives a guarantee to cover the liabilities of every company in the group. The *Ford & Carter* v *Midland Bank Ltd* (1979) case established that where a company is to be brought within an existing cross-guarantee structure, all group member companies must join in the security documentation in order for it to be valid.

Another important case is *Bank of Scotland* v *Wright* (1990). Here it was stated that the guarantor of a holding company's liability to a bank could also be liable for the debts of the holding company's subsidiary if the guarantee was intended to secure an inter-available facility as between companies in the group and not merely a direct facility to the holding company. Other security held for the company's debts also included a cross-guarantee structure, and the judge pointed out that as demands under these guarantees had been made prior to demand being made on Mr Wright, the indebtedness of the holding company included the indebtedness of the subsidiary company.

20.10   Guarantees by Specific Entities or Parties

20.10.1   Guarantees by partnerships

It is normal banking practice to obtain all partners' signatures on a guarantee form given on behalf of a partnership. Under s.5 Partnership Act 1890 a partner does not have an implied authority to bind a partnership by giving a guarantee, unless this is part of that partnership's normal business.

20.10.2   Guarantees by minors

Such guarantees are not normally acceptable, as they are considered to be unenforceable.

20.10.3   Guarantees by women

Banks must consider the possibility of undue influence being present, particularly where a husband's account is being guaranteed (see *Barclays Bank Plc* v *O'Brien* (1992) above).

20.10.4   Guarantees by foreign nationals or companies

A UK bank will ensure that a guarantee liability is allowable under the laws of the country concerned before taking such security, otherwise it could be unenforceable.

20.11   Procedure for Taking a Guarantee as Security

1   Ensure that the guarantor's financial standing is sufficient to meet any liability entered into. If the guarantor does not hold an account with the bank, a status enquiry must be sought from the guarantor's bankers. Follow-up enquiries are normally carried out every six or 12 months. A courtesy reminder of the guarantor's liability is usually sent out at three- to five-yearly intervals by the bank and an acknowledgement requested.

2   Ascertain whether independent legal advice is necessary. If this is the case, the prospective guarantor should receive independent advice from a solicitor. The latter will normally attest on the guarantee that the guarantee was explained to the guarantor and understood. If a prospective guarantor refuses to take independent legal advice when the bank suggests it, the bank may

decide not to go ahead with the guarantee and seek alternative security from its customer.

3   The guarantor should sign the bank's form of guarantee on the bank's premises. In the event of being unable to call at the bank, the guarantor could sign it at his or her own bank, which will witness the signature. The guarantee will then be returned to the account-holding bank. A copy of the guarantee will be given to the guarantor and a receipt obtained. When the guarantee is to secure a regulated agreement under the Consumer Credit Act 1974, the guarantor must be given a copy of the agreement itself in addition to the copy of the guarantee.

20.12   Termination of a Guarantee

20.12.1   Demand by the bank

Only after failure of the bank's customer to repay borrowing, when called upon to do so, will the bank look to the guarantor to meet his or her guarantee liability. In the event of failing to pay immediately, the guarantor will be liable for the payment of interest as stipulated in the guarantee. When a payment is received from the guarantor this will normally be credited to a suspense account (*Re Sass* (1896)) and will only be used to meet any shortfall.

20.12.2   Notice of determination by the guarantor or the guarantor's executors/administrators

As mentioned previously, the guarantee will contain a clause which states what period of notice will be required by the bank from the guarantor in order to determine his or her liability. This period of notice can vary but is often one, three or six months.

When the bank receives such notice it will contact its customer in order to review the security position for any borrowing. This may result in alternative security being provided, or it may be decided that the customer's account should remain in credit in future, in which case alternative security will not be needed. If the customer's account was overdrawn at the end of the period of notice, and no alternative security arrangements had been agreed, then the account should be stopped in order to crystallise the guarantor's liability and a new account should be opened and operated in credit.

The guarantor remains liable for the crystallised sum for a period of six years – the bank can make demand for this amount at any time during that period. It is a misconception that if a bank does not make demand upon the guarantor to pay prior to the expiry of the notice, then the guarantor is released from the liability. This was confirmed in *National Westminster Bank Ltd v French* (1977).

20.12.3   Death of a guarantor

As mentioned previously, the personal representatives of a guarantor who dies have to give written notice in order to determine the guarantee liability.

This period of notice is normally for one or three months. A bank will usually try to agree arrangements with its customer and the guarantor's representatives as soon as possible, and this will sometimes result in the release of the guarantor's estate from liability. However, if alternative arrangements cannot be agreed, the bank will retain its right against the deceased's estate for the guarantee liability.

In the case of a joint and several guarantee, when one guarantor dies there is usually a clause which retains the deceased's liability while allowing the bank to look to the remaining guarantors for future advances. An alternative to this is to take a new guarantee from the remaining guarantors and to lend on a new account.

20.12.4   Death of a joint account holder

When a joint account holder dies and the account is overdrawn the account should be stopped to retain the rights of the bank against the deceased's estate, the surviving account holder and the guarantor. (It is not considered that a guarantee is a good continuing security for the liabilities of the surviving account holder.)

20.12.5   Insolvency or mental incapacity of a guarantor

The bank should stop its customer's account in the following circumstances:

(a) receipt of notice of a petition or bankruptcy order against the guarantor;

(b) receipt of notice of a petition for liquidation of a limited company guarantor;

(c) learning of a winding-up order against a limited company guarantor;

(d) learning of the appointment of an administrative receiver against a limited company guarantor;

(e) presentation of a petition for an administrative order against a limited company guarantor;

(f) where a voluntary arrangement is proposed by a limited company guarantor and a supervisor has been appointed;

(g) confirmation of the mental incapacity of a guarantor. This could be by written advice by the guarantor's medical advisors or by sight of the appointment of a receiver under a court of protection order or evidence that an enduring power of attorney is in force.

20.13   What are a Guarantor's Rights of Subrogation and Contribution?

Section 5 Mercantile Law Amendment Act 1856 enables a guarantor to claim all securities lodged with the bank by its customer, provided that the guarantor fully repays the customer's debt. This is known as the right of subrogation.

Where there are several guarantors or providers of third-party security who have contributed to the repayment of a customer's debt, they will all have their own rights of subrogation. In such a case, it is best if all parties can agree as to how any security lodged by the customer with the bank is to be distributed and to advise the bank in writing. Where agreement cannot be reached, the courts must decide.

20.14 Discharge of the Guarantee

When a guarantor has met the guarantee liability, the bank will normally retain the guarantee document as it is usually stated in the guarantee form that it remains the property of the bank. Thus the bank can refuse a guarantor's request for the guarantee form, although a bank will often give a written acknowledgement of receipt of funds received from the guarantor.

20.15 Preferences

A customer who is in financial difficulties might try to help his or her guarantor by repaying bank borrowing voluntarily (to the detriment of other creditors) and requesting the release of the guarantor from the liability. Such an act could lead to a preference being established and the bank being liable to a trustee in bankruptcy or a liquidator. Where the bank suspects a preference, it can pre-empt this by insisting that the guarantor give the requisite amount of notice stipulated in the guarantee form. Normally any bankruptcy or insolvency proceedings will have begun before such notice has elapsed.

Summary

Now that you have read this unit, you should be able to:

☐ Identify a bank's obligations to a guarantor.

☐ Recognise the effect of undue influence on a guarantee.

☐ Detail the clauses contained in a standard bank guarantee form.

☐ Ascertain the effects of various occurrences on joint and several guarantees.

☐ Recognise how the cross-guarantee structure of limited companies operates.

☐ Identify the procedure for taking a guarantee as security.

☐ Recognise the circumstances which determine a guarantee and the action which banks must take.

If you can tick all the above boxes with confidence, you are ready to answer the questions which follow on pp. 245–48.

List of Cases

Avon Finance Co Ltd v Bridger (1985)

Bache and Co (London) Ltd v Banque Vernes et Commerciale de Paris SA (1973)

Bank of Scotland v Wright (1990)

Barclays Bank Plc v Khairi and Another (1991)

Barclays Bank Plc v O'Brien (1992)

Barclays Bank Ltd v Trevanion (1933)

Bradford Old Bank Ltd v Sutcliffe (1918)

Clayton's case *(Devaynes v Noble* (1816))

Cooper v National Provincial Bank Ltd (1946)

Ellesmere Brewery Co v Cooper (1896)

Ford & Carter v Midland Bank Ltd (1979)

James Graham & Co Ltd v Southgate-Sands and Others (1985)

Lloyds Bank Ltd v Bundy (1975)

Lloyds Bank Plc v Waterhouse (1990)

Mackenzie v Royal Bank of Canada (1934)

National Provincial Bank of England Ltd v Brackenbury (1906)

National Westminster Bank Ltd v French (1977)

National Westminster Bank v Morgan (1985)

O'Hara v Allied Irish Banks Ltd and another (1984)

Re Sass (1896)

Westminster Bank v Cond (1940)

List of Statutes

Companies Act 1989

Consumer Credit Act 1974

Insolvency Act 1986

Limitations Act 1980

Mercantile Law Amendment Act 1856

Partnership Act 1890

Statute of Frauds 1677

Self-assessment Questions

Short-answer questions

1   Jane Kelly has been adjudicated bankrupt. Her current account balance is £18,000 debit. You hold an unlimited guarantee for Jane Kelly's liabilities given by her brother Robert Rees.

What action will your bank take?

2   Alan Birch, the trustee in bankruptcy of your customer Frank Pine, has repaid in full £10,000 owing to the bank. The bank already holds £10,000 on a suspense account, which has been deposited by Jack Spruce, who was the guarantor of Frank Pine's accounts.

What action will the bank take? (Ignore bank interest.)

3   Arrow, Bow and Quiver agree to sign a joint and several guarantee for £21,000 as security for the accounts of Archer. Arrow and Bow both sign the guarantee document but Quiver becomes ill and dies before he can sign.

Is the guarantee valid in respect of Arrow and Bow?

4   Brice, Briggs, Bragg and Bright completed an unlimited joint and several guarantee as security for the accounts of Brill. It subsequently transpires that the person purporting to be Bright is an impostor and has therefore forged Bright's signature on the guarantee document.

Are Brice, Briggs and Bragg still liable under the guarantee?

5   Mark King has given a guarantee limited to £20,000 to cover the liabilities of Steve Prince. Prince's current account balance is £5,212 debit as at the start of business today.

Mark King calls at your branch today and asks the extent of his liability under his guarantee at present.

How would you respond?

(Answers are given in Appendix 2, pp. 321–22)

Multiple-choice questions

1   Which of the following statements are true?

(a) A bank must volunteer information to a prospective guarantor concerning the present and past conduct of its customer's account.

(b) If an undischarged bankrupt is allowed to sign on his wife's account, this must be divulged to a prospective guarantor by the bank before he executes the guarantee form, even without its customer's express authority.

(c) A guarantor can avoid liability under the guarantee if material facts have been innocently or fraudulently misrepresented to him by the bank either in the course of direct negotiations or by silent acquiescence to something either said or written which clearly showed that the guarantor was under a misunderstanding.

2   Ash, Beech, Cedar and Forest have signed a joint and several guarantee limited to £8,000 to cover the liabilities of Elm.

For what amount will Ash, Beech, Cedar and Forest be liable?

(a)   Up to £2,000 each.
(b)   £8,000 in total.
(c)   £8,000 each up to a maximum of £32,000.
(d)   Up to £8,000 each.

3   Alan, Brian and Carl have signed an unlimited joint and several guarantee in respect of the accounts of Derek. Alan dies.

Which of the following statements are correct?

(a)   The guarantee becomes invalid upon the death of Alan for all guarantors.
(b)   Brian and Carl are still liable but Alan's estate is released under the rule of survivorship.
(c)   Alan's estate, Brian and Carl are still liable.
(d)   If Alan's estate wishes to determine its liability under the guarantee, the executors must give the requisite amount of notice as laid down in the guarantee document.

4   Bolt, Nut and Washer are joint and several guarantors of the account of Spanner. Bolt gives three months' notice to the bank that he wishes to be released from his guarantee liability. What is the bank's position?

(a)   The bank can accept that notice from Bolt.
(b)   The bank can insist that Nut and Washer also give notice of determination before Bolt's notice can become effective.

5   When a limited company gives a guarantee to the bank, what is the position regarding registration of the guarantee?

(a)   It must register the guarantee at Companies House within 21 days.
(b)   It must register the guarantee at Companies House within 30 days.
(c)   Registration of the guarantee at Companies House is unnecessary.

(Answers are given in Appendix 2, p. 322)

Revision questions

1   You are the manager of Topsy Turvy Bank plc, Lawnswood branch. Your branch has recently made demand on the following guarantors who all deny liability. Each of the guarantees is on the bank's standard form and none of the guarantors were customers of your branch when they signed the guarantee document.

(a)   Mr Atkinson banks at your Daisy Lane branch and denies liability, as the clauses of the guarantee form were not explained to him when he called at your branch to sign that document. He says that you would have done so if his account were held at your branch. As both branches are part of the same bank you must therefore owe the same duty to customers of other branches. Thus the bank have been negligent and he is not liable under the guarantee.

(b) Mrs Bassett banks at your Hillside branch. She gave the guarantee as security for a loan which you agreed for her husband's business. She states that when she called at your branch regarding the guarantee she was merely asked to sign the guarantee form by your security clerk and no explanation as to the nature or extent of her liability was offered. She says that if she had realised what her liability entailed she would never have agreed to sign the guarantee. She therefore denies liability as she feels that the bank should have ensured that she fully understood the nature and extent of the liability which she was entering into. Your security clerk confirms that no explanation of the guarantee was offered when Mrs Bassett signed it.

(c) Mr Clough says that, when he signed the guarantee, he was not aware that the principal debtor's husband, who was in fact an undischarged bankrupt, had power to sign on the principal debtor's account. He therefore claims the guarantee is invalid.

(d) Mr Dalglish says that, although the bank demanded repayment from him on 4 November, in the sum of £1,500, the principal debtor's account was allowed to continue unbroken. Since the date of demand, sufficient credits have gone through the account to pay off the debt as it existed on that date. He therefore claims that he is no longer liable, and that he cannot be responsible for any indebtedness created by cheques since 4 November.

(e) Mr Evans says that when he signed the guarantee, he was illiterate, and thus had no idea of the written terms of the form. He continues that, before he signed the guarantee, he asked about its terms and had been told that it covered one specific advance. Had he known that its terms made him liable for all the borrowings of the principal debtor, he would not have signed the form. Accordingly he claims that the bank is unable to rely on the guarantee.

Discuss the bank's position with regard to the above situations. Give reasons for your answers.

2 In 1987 your customer Mr Lee Choo acquired a company called Eatery Holdings Ltd. Eatery Holdings Ltd in turn purchased the business of Eatery Kwikfoods Ltd and Eatery Kwikfoods Ltd therefore became a subsidiary of Eatery Holdings Ltd.

The subsidiary company was initially successful and Choo approached the bank for a £75,000 facility for the group in order to facilitate expansion. The bank agreed to this provided that inter-company guarantees were forthcoming and that the directors in addition provided personal guarantees. The cross-guarantees were completed by the companies and the directors completed personal guarantees of the holding company, Eatery Holdings Ltd.

In September 1989 draft management accounts showed net losses of £300,000 for the group, but despite this the bank increased the facility to £200,000.

By 10 December 1989 the situation had not improved so the bank made a demand on Eatery Holdings Ltd for £15,529 and on Eatery Kwikfoods Ltd for £189,548. On 11 December 1989 the bank made a demand on each

Q

company for the other's liability, pursuant to the cross-guarantees. On 14 December 1989 it made a £205,387 demand on Mr Choo under his guarantee liability, which included interest.

Mr Choo contacted the bank and admitted his liability in relation to the debt of Eatery Holdings Ltd but disputed his liability as regards Eatery Kwikfoods Ltd's debt, as his guarantee was given only in respect of the holding company.

What is the bank's position concerning Mr Choo's claim?

(Answers are given in Appendix 2, pp. 322–23)

UNIT 21

Miscellaneous Securities

Objectives

- Recognise the powers and undertakings given by a letter of pledge.
- Identify the documents involved and their importance to the bank when taking a letter of pledge.
- Detail the procedure required to complete a letter of pledge over goods.
- Detail the procedure for taking an assignment over specific book debts or contract moneys.
- Ascertain the advantages and disadvantages of taking an assignment over book debts or contract moneys as security.
- Detail the procedure involved in taking an agricultural charge as security.
- Ascertain the advantages and disadvantages of taking an agricultural charge as security.

21.1　Produce Loans

Produce loans arise when a bank makes a loan to a customer against the security of underlying goods which, upon sale, will repay the loan. They are normally only made available to undoubted customers.

21.2　Bank's Form of Charge

The form used by a bank is a letter of pledge. This can be a specific letter of pledge where the transaction is a one-off situation. Where there is likely to be regular use of produce loan facilities, the form will be a general letter of pledge.

Under a letter of pledge, both present or future goods or the documents of title to the goods are pledged to the bank as security.

The customer will undertake:

(a)　To store and insure the goods.

(b)　To pay the proceeds from any claim under the insurance directly to the bank.

(c)　To pay all rents and other warehouse costs when due.

The bank is given a power of sale over the goods which can be exercised at its discretion.

21.3 Documentation which is Important to a Bank when Taking a Letter of Pledge

21.3.1 Warehouse-keeper's receipt

When goods are imported they are often stored in a warehouse. Upon delivery to the warehouse, the warehouse-keeper will issue a receipt to the depositor.

A depositor who wishes to give a pledge over these goods to the bank will have to complete a transfer order in favour of the bank and deliver this together with the original receipt to the warehouse-keeper so that a new receipt in the bank's name can be issued.

21.3.2 Warehouse-keeper's warrant

There are two types of warehouse-keeper's warrant. The first has a very similar role to the warehouse-keeper's receipt mentioned above. A warrant is issued by the warehouse-keeper to the depositor of the goods. If these goods are subsequently to be subject to a letter of pledge then the depositor must complete a transfer order and forward this together with the original warrant to the warehouse-keeper so that a replacement warrant can be issued in the bank's name.

The second type of warehouse-keeper's warrant is one which has been issued under a private Act of Parliament. These warrants are virtually fully negotiable instruments and are transferable. They state that the goods are to be delivered to the person named and title can be transferred by endorsement of the warrant.

21.3.3 Delivery order

This is a document signed by the person in whose name the goods are warehoused, instructing the warehouse-keeper to deliver the goods to a named party. Thus if the goods are pledged to the bank, the bank will sign such an order directing the goods to be delivered to its customer. However, before a bank will issue such an order it will require its customer to complete a trust receipt or trust letter.

21.3.4 Trust receipt (trust letter)

A trust receipt is devised to maintain a bank's rights with regard to title to pledged goods when the goods have been released to a bank's customer. It basically states that the customer is acting as a trustee for the bank, and contains the following undertakings by the customer:

(a) To hold in trust for the bank the following:

    (i) The goods and/or documents of title pertaining to these goods.
    (ii) Any sales proceeds and upon receipt of such, to pay them into the bank account.
    (iii) Any insurance claim moneys, which will be paid to the bank.

(b) To insure and store the goods adequately.

(c) To return any unsold goods into the bank's control.

(d) If required by the bank, to produce a signed authority addressed to the buyer of the goods, instructing that party to forward payment for those goods to the bank.

The establishment of the customer as a trustee is very important in relation to bankruptcy. If the goods were released to the bank's customer, who was then made bankrupt, because the customer was acting as the bank's trustee, the Trustee in Bankruptcy is unable to lay claim either to the goods or the sale proceeds (s.283(3) Insolvency Act 1986.)

21.3.5 Bills of lading

In the trust receipt section above, mention was made of documents of title. With regard to goods imported by ship, title will normally be evidenced by bills of lading. A bank will normally require a full set of clean, on-board, bills of lading which have been drawn to order and have been endorsed in blank and marked 'freight paid'. These will be issued by the shipper. When bills of lading are referred to as 'clean' it means that there are no indications that the goods were not in good condition when received on board ship. Bills of lading are quasi-negotiable documents.

Students should note that there is no equivalent to bills of lading when goods are transported by air. Air consignment notes/way bills are only documents of movement and not documents of title. The only way that banks can retain control of goods sent by air is for the goods to be consigned to the bank, i.e. for the bank to be named as consignee. It can then give the relevant instructions to the airport authorities for their delivery and storage or warehousing in the bank's name.

21.3.6 Supplier's invoice

This is issued by the supplier and will be signed by him. It will indicate the type, value and nature of goods. With regard to exports, the correct incoterm will be quoted, e.g. c.f.r., c.i.f., to show what price basis had been agreed between buyer and seller.

21.3.7 Insurance policy or certificate

Insurance policies are normally issued in favour of the shipper. If a bank has an interest in the goods being shipped, it should ensure that the shipper endorses the policy in blank. This is so that the bank will have recourse to the policy proceeds, in the event of damage or loss in transit of the goods.

Occasionally, a bank may be prepared to accept an insurance certificate rather than an insurance policy. However, should the bank wish to tender a claim under the policy, mere delivery of such a certificate to the insurance company would be insufficient evidence of title and the policy itself would then have to be produced.

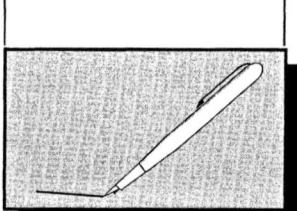

Student Activity 1

What procedure does your bank follow when taking a letter of pledge over goods as security? Compare this with the procedure given below.

21.4 Procedure to be Followed to Complete a Letter of Pledge over Goods as Acceptable Bank Security

(a) Satisfactory status reports should be received concerning the supplier, warehouse-keeper and ultimate buyer. Produce loans should only be considered for customers who are considered undoubted.

(b) The customer will complete the bank's standard form of pledge and his or her signature will be witnessed by a bank official.

(c) The goods covered by such a pledge will normally be stored in a warehouse in the bank's name. The bank will receive a relevant warehouse-keeper's receipt or warrant.

(d) The insurance policy pertaining to the goods must be examined to ensure that the cover is adequate.

(e) Insurance premiums should be paid up to date. The bank should diarise to monitor payment of these premiums as they fall due.

(f) Notice of the bank's interest should be sent to the insurance company and an acknowledgement obtained.

(g) Rent receipts and receipts for any warehouse charges must be exhibited to the bank when payments have been made. The bank should diarise when these are due.

21.5 Produce Lending Control

Produce lending is normally done on loan account for ease of control. The important point concerning goods as security is their valuation. Adequate margins between amounts lent and security valuations must be maintained. This is particularly critical where perishable goods are concerned. Regular inspections should be made by the bank to ensure that goods are not deteriorating.

21.6 Different Produce Loan Circumstances

The circumstances described previously for the storing of goods related to them being kept in a warehouse in the bank's name. This is not always the case and some examples are given below.

21.6.1 Goods stored on a customer's own premises

This can be a particularly difficult situation for a bank, as such goods need to be separate from other merchandise which the customer may have. Ideally such goods should be locked in a separate room or building, which should be clearly marked with the bank's name and to which the bank should have the only keys. The bank will normally take an inventory of the goods which the customer will sign. Full details of the circumstances in which the goods are stored should be kept in the bank's records.

21.6.2 Goods pledged in import/export trade

Goods often may be in transit to a bank's customer, and this customer may have to pay for the goods prior to receipt even though there may be an ultimate buyer to whom the goods are to be delivered from the quay. In such circumstances the bank may advance the purchase price while retaining control over the goods by taking possession of the documents of title, e.g. bills of lading. The bank can then authorise delivery of the goods by use of a delivery order or collection of the goods by the ultimate buyer in return for payment by banker's draft, cash or cheque (where the buyer is undoubted).

21.6.3 Goods deposited with third parties

Goods sometimes may be deposited with third parties for additional processing or packaging prior to sale. Where these goods are pledged to the bank, the bank's customer must instruct the third party to provide a written undertaking to the bank that the goods are being held to the order of the bank as bailee and that the third party has no rights of lien over these goods. This prevents the third party from withholding the goods, should any dispute arise between the third party and the bank's customer.

21.7 Important Case relating to Goods Pledged to a Bank as Security for a Produce Loan

The case of *Lloyds Bank Ltd* v *Bank of America National Trust and Savings Association* (1938) dealt with a dishonest company customer who pledged the documents of title to goods to Bank of America National Trust and Savings Association in return for a produce loan. These documents of title had previously been pledged to Lloyds Bank Ltd for another produce loan and these documents had only been released to the bank's customer against a completed trust receipt. When Lloyds Bank's customer became insolvent, the bank sued Bank of America for the return of the documents of title to the goods over which it believed it had a priority claim.

The Court held that as Bank of America had taken the documents of title in good faith and for value, and a valid letter of pledge had been completed, then it had priority over Lloyds Bank's claim.

This case emphasised the need to offer produce loans only to customers whose status is considered undoubted.

21.8 Assignment of Book Debts and Contract Moneys

The assignment of book debts and contract moneys as security is normally only contemplated when other suitable security is unavailable.

One of the main occasions when bankers will encounter this type of security is with regard to dairy farmers. They sell their milk to the Milk Marketing Board and are paid on a monthly basis. (The Milk Marketing Board is soon to be replaced by Milk Mark and a free market in milk sales will develop.) The bank can have moneys due under such contract assigned to itself. This is achieved by the bank's customers executing the necessary charge form.

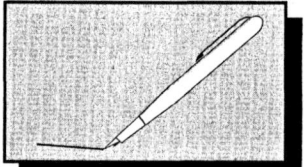

Student Activity 2

Has your bank taken an assignment over book debts or contract moneys recently? If so, what steps did it take to perfect its assignment? Compare this procedure with the one given below.

21.8.1 Procedure for taking an assignment over specific book debts and/or contract moneys

(a) Examine a copy of the contract to ensure that there are no onerous clauses which could affect the bank's position as assignee. An example of such a clause would be where contract moneys can be withheld due to non-completion of part of the contract within a given timescale.

(b) Once satisfied with the underlying contract, the bank will prepare its standard form of legal assignment. This will identify the security offered, e.g. by the date of contract and its reference number. The bank's customer will sign the document and the signature will be witnessed by a bank official or, where independent legal advice is deemed necessary, by a solicitor.

(c) Give notice in duplicate to the debtor of the assignment. The notice will request confirmation of the amount of the debt and also whether any right of set off exists between the debtor and the bank's customer. It will also ask for details of any prior charges and for an undertaking to forward all moneys due direct to the bank. The debtor will sign and return a copy of the notice to the bank as acknowledgement.

(d) Obtain a status report on the debtor if he or she is unknown to the bank.

(e) Where, by the nature of the contract, insurance is expected to be needed, e.g. a building demolition contract, the bank should check that the amount of cover is sufficient and should give notice of its interest to the insurance company concerned.

(f) Where the assignor is a limited company, the charge will be registered at Companies House within 21 days of its creation (s.398 Companies Act 1985). (Prior to taking the security, the bank will have carried out a search at Companies House to ensure that there were no earlier charges.)

In *Re Kent and Sussex Sawmills Ltd* (1947), the bank's customer charged moneys due under contracts to a government department to the bank. When the bank's customer entered liquidation, moneys were due under the contracts. The liquidator opposed the bank's claim to these funds, on the grounds that such charges should have been registered at Companies House, otherwise they were invalid, as would be the claim for the moneys emanating from the contracts. The court found for the liquidator. However, the subsequent decision in *Siebe Gorman & Co Ltd v Barclays Bank Ltd* (1978) stated that the assignment of book debts need not be registered at Companies House.

Nevertheless, banks have tended to treat the *Siebe Gorman* case decision with caution and have therefore continued to register such assignments at Companies House.

21.8.2 Advantages of this security for the bank

(a) The security is simple and easy to perfect.

(b) The bank will be protected from the claims of a trustee in bankruptcy for moneys covered by the bank's charge. It is worth noting here that the bank's charge will cover specific debts and not general debts, as the latter would involve registration under the Bills of Sale Act 1878. Such action is avoided by banks, as it is felt that this could seriously affect the standing and credit-worthiness of their customers.

21.8.3 Disadvantages of this security for the bank

(a) Payments relating to specific debts and contract moneys covered by the bank's charge may not be forthcoming, due to conflict between the debtor and the bank's customer over performance of the contract. Such disputes often have to be resolved in the courts and the delay can seriously undermine the financial stability of the customer concerned.

(b) Payment of moneys due largely depends upon the ability of the debtor to pay. A bank would therefore require a status report if the debtor was unknown.

21.9 Agricultural Charges

Under the Agricultural Credits Act 1928, individual farmers can give an agricultural charge over their farming stock and other agricultural assets (including a tenant's right to compensation under the Agricultural Holdings Act 1923). Such a charge can be fixed, floating, or both. It should be noted that an agricultural charge will not cover land, book debts or non-farming assets, e.g. life policies, which must be charged separately.

Assets covered by a fixed charge will be specified in the charge form. Assets covered by a floating charge are items which may come into the possession of the farmer from time to time. Assets do not include land, which must be mortgaged in the usual manner, nor do they include debts due, e.g. under a Milk Marketing Board contract.

Student Activity 3

Obtain a copy of your bank's agricultural charge form and compare its clauses with those given below.

21.9.1 The bank's agricultural charge form

As stated previously, any assets covered by a fixed charge will be specified in the charge form.

Details of the circumstances under which a floating charge will become a fixed charge will be contained in a clause in the form. Such occurrences would normally include the following:

(a) Death or mental incapacity.

(b) A bankruptcy order being made against the farmer.

(c) Dissolution of the farming partnership.

(d) Failure by the farmer to repay, having received a demand from the bank.

(e) Where the farmer enters into a composite arrangement with his or her creditors.

(f) Where creditors have obtained an execution against the farmer.

Other clauses in the form will include undertakings from the farmer:

(a) To maintain all farm property in good repair.

(b) To fully insure all farm property and keep premiums paid up to date.

(c) To manage the farm in a good and proper manner.

(d) To allow inspection by the bank at any time.

An agricultural charge?

21.9.2 Procedure for taking an agricultural charge

(a) The priority of agricultural charges depends upon the date when they were registered at the Agricultural Credits Department of the Land Charges Registry. The bank will normally carry out a search using form AC6 to ascertain whether any agricultural assets are subject to prior charges.

(b) The farmer will complete the bank's agricultural charge form and will also sign form AC1.

(c) Form AC1 is used to register the bank's charge. Registration must be completed within seven days of execution. (If a farmer subsequently begins farming at a different location, the bank will have to search against that address and will then register its charge using form AC7.)

(d) A further search should then be carried out. This is to ensure that no other charges have been registered and also that the bank's charge has been recorded correctly. (A search, prior to taking an agricultural charge, does not provide any period of protection in which the bank can register its charge.)

(e) The bank should ensure that adequate insurance has been taken out over the assets charged. It should give notice to the insurance company of its interest, which should be acknowledged. Premiums should be paid up to date and a diary note should be made to ensure that this continues to be the case.

21.9.3 Realisation of an agricultural charge

If a bank makes demand for repayment and the farmer fails to meet this demand, then the bank can appoint a receiver. The receiver can either sell the farmer's assets covered by the charge or manage the farm, if it is felt to be viable.

21.9.4 Release of an agricultural charge

(a) The bank should forward a form AC3 to the Agricultural Credits Department.

(b) Advise the insurance company that the bank does not have any further interest in any policy covering assets picked up by the charge.

(c) The agricultural charge form will be kept by the bank with its cancelled security forms.

21.9.5 Advantages of an agricultural charge

(a) It is simple and inexpensive to set up.

(b) Once the bank is aware that the farmer is in financial difficulty, it can appoint a receiver to safeguard the bank's position.

(c) Where the bank holds a floating charge, any future fixed charge will not rank ahead of the bank's interest.

21.9.6 Disadvantages of an agricultural charge

(a) By the time that the bank is aware that the farmer has problems and has appointed a receiver, the number and value of any assets may have been severely reduced.

(b) Preferential creditors must be satisfied prior to the bank from the proceeds of the sale of assets.

(c) Under s.8(5) Agricultural Credits Act 1928, if a farmer becomes bankrupt as a result of a petition presented within three months of an agricultural fixed or floating charge being created and was insolvent when such a charge was created, then the charge is only valid for advances made subsequent to its completion. Thus the rule in *Clayton's* case does not apply and cannot help the bank's position when lending on overdraft.

Summary

Now that you have read this unit, you should be able to:

☐ Recognise the powers and undertakings given by a letter of pledge.

☐ Identify the documents involved and their importance to the bank when taking a letter of pledge.

☐ Detail the procedure required to complete a letter of pledge over goods.

☐ Detail the procedure for taking an assignment over specific book debts or contract moneys.

☐ Ascertain the advantages and disadvantages of taking an assignment over book debts or contract moneys as security.

☐ Detail the procedure involved in taking an agricultural charge.

☐ Ascertain the advantages and disadvantages of taking an agricultural charge as security.

If you can tick all the above boxes with confidence, you are ready to answer the questions which follow on pp. 259–61.

List of Cases

Lloyds Bank Ltd v *Bank of America National Trust and Savings Association* (1938)

Clayton's case *(Devaynes* v *Noble* (1816))

Re Kent and Sussex Sawmills Ltd (1947)

Siebe Gorman & Co Ltd v *Barclays Bank Ltd* (1978)

List of Statutes

Agricultural Credits Act 1928

Agricultural Holdings Act 1923

Bills of Sale Act 1878

Companies Act 1985

Insolvency Act 1986

Self-assessment Questions

Short-answer questions

1   What bank form is used to provide goods as security for a produce loan?

2   Does a letter of pledge give the bank a power of sale?

3   Barry Griffiths has been granted a produce loan by his bank. He has completed a trust receipt and has obtained the underlying goods from the warehouse where they were kept, in order to take them to the ultimate buyer. Before delivery can take place, Mr Griffiths is made bankrupt.

What is the bank's position?

4   Your customer offers you an assignment over moneys due under a contract as security for a loan. When you examine the contract you notice a clause stating that any moneys owed by the creditor to the debtor will be set off against the moneys due under the contract.

Will you accept this as security without further enquiry?

5   How is the priority of agricultural charges determined?

6   Does a search at the Agricultural Credits Department provide a period of protection in which the bank can register its agricultural charge?

(Answers are given in Appendix 2, pp. 323–24)

Multiple-choice questions

1   Which of the following can be negotiable instruments?

(a)   Warehouse-keeper's receipt.
(b)   Warehouse-keeper's warrant.
(c)   Delivery order.

2   Your customer is importing goods and the bank wishes to take the goods and their sale proceeds as security. Which documents are required:

(a)   When the goods are imported by sea?

    (i)   Complete set of clean bills of lading, blank endorsed.
    (ii)   An air way bill with goods consigned to the customer.
    (iii)   An air way bill with goods consigned to the bank.

(b)   When the goods are imported by air?

    (i)   Complete set of clean bills of lading, blank endorsed.
    (ii)   An air way bill with goods consigned to the customer.
    (iii)   An air way bill with goods consigned to the bank.

3   When a limited company assigns its book debts to a bank as security, *in practice* the bank:

(a)   Will register the assignment at Companies House within 30 days of its creation.

(b) Will register the assignment at Companies House within 21 days of its creation.

(c) Will not register the assignment at Companies House.

4 Which case stated that the assignment of book debts by a limited company need not be registered at Companies House?

(a) *Siebe Gorman & Co Ltd* v *Barclays Bank Ltd* (1978)

(b) *Re Kent and Sussex Sawmills Ltd* (1947)

(c) *Lloyds Bank Ltd* v *Bank of America National Trust and Savings Association* (1938)

5 Which of the following would be covered by an agricultural charge?

(a) Life policy.
(b) Poultry.
(c) Honey bees.
(d) Tractors.
(e) Land.
(f) Debtors.
(g) Wheat crop.

6 Within how many days must a bank register its agricultural charge at Agricultural Credits Department?

(a) 5 days.
(b) 7 days.
(c) 10 days.
(d) 14 days.
(e) 21 days.
(f) 30 days

(Answers are given in Appendix 2, p. 324)

Revision question

Your customer, James Bailey, is a tenant farmer. On 1 March, with his current account balance at £20,000 debit, Mr Bailey gave the bank a fixed and floating agricultural charge as security.

On 14 June, the bank was advised of a bankruptcy order made against Mr Bailey. The balance of the account at that time was £35,000 debit. The bankruptcy order was based upon a petition which was presented on 21 April. The balance of Mr Bailey's account as at 21 April was £22,000 debit. (The bank was unaware of the bankruptcy proceedings until 14 June.) What is the bank's position as regards its security?

(Answer is given in Appendix 2, p. 324)

Past examination questions

1 Your customers, Tom Plum and Alan Pear, traded as Golden Fruits and were importers of tinned fruit until they went into bankruptcy recently. Two years ago, when they had the opportunity of supplying a large supermarket chain on a regular basis, you advanced moneys to them as the supermarket insisted on taking six weeks' credit between delivery of supplies and payment.

The tinned fruit was to be imported from several European countries and you were told that the overseas exporters required early payment. Because of the amounts involved you called for security, but the only security the partners could give was a charge over the stocks of goods themselves held from time to time in warehouses to the order of the partnership. You accepted this position and took the usual steps to perfect your security.

Now, however, following the failure of the firm, you have heard from another bank with which, unknown to you, Golden Fruits had an account. Finance Bank Ltd claims to have a charge over a consignment of tinned fruit which you believed formed part of your security. These goods have been inadvertently released from the warehouse and pledged to Finance Bank Ltd.

A German supplier has also written claiming that two of his consignments to Golden Fruits had not been paid for, and that he is therefore entitled to either the tinned fruit or the sale proceeds.

Required

(a) A statement, in note form, of the steps originally taken by the bank to perfect its security.

[7 marks]

(b) Comments on the bank's position in respect of the claims which have now arisen.

[9 marks]

[Total marks for question – 16]

(Spring 1982)

2 You are worried that your customers, Headhunters plc, wholesalers and importers of woollens and cottons from abroad, may be over-trading. However, since they have recently acquired good contracts to supply two major retail outlets, Alpha Shops Ltd and Warm Knitwear Ltd, you are prepared to increase their overdraft provided they give you a charge over each contract. You already hold the directors' joint and several unlimited guarantee. Payment will be made to the overseas vendors on arrival of the goods in this country and receipts under the revolving contracts will be 60 days after delivery.

Required

State how the security would be perfected and controlled. What benefits would it give the branch?

(16 marks)

(Autumn 1984)

(Answers are given in Appendix 2, pp. 324–26)

UNIT 22

Mock Examination

Answer all questions. Time allowed three hours plus 15 minutes' reading time.

1   You took up your new appointment as Manager of Black Bank on 1 March 1990, upon the retirement of Peter Smith. On 10 April, a winding-up order was made against your customer, Trubull Ltd, which owes the bank £210,000. As security you hold a legal mortgage given by the company over its factory and head office, dated 17 October 1988 and valued at £150,000. You also hold the joint and several guarantee of the two directors, Alan Trubull and Mary Trubull, dated 14 January 1985.

Today (14 May 1990) the Liquidator has written to you, saying that, following investigations, he is of the opinion that Black Bank and Peter Smith, its former Manager, acted as shadow directors of Trubull Ltd in the three months before its collapse. He says that Peter Smith attended board meetings and gave advice to the company and that, whenever cheques were presented to the bank which would have taken the company's borrowing over its agreed borrowing limit, Peter Smith, the Manager, would telephone the company and discuss with Alan Trubull which cheques should be paid and which should be dishonoured. The Liquidator goes on to say that he is of the opinion that the company was guilty of wrongful trading from the beginning of 1990, since it is clear from the balance sheet as at 31 December 1989 that the company was insolvent at that date. Accordingly, he claims Black Bank and/or Mr Smith must contribute to the assets of the company in liquidation.

Required

(a)   State what you understand by the term 'shadow director'. [4 marks]

(b)   State what you understand by the term 'wrongful trading'. [4 marks]

(c)   State your reactions to the reasons advanced by the Liquidator of Trubull Ltd for his claims and state what steps you would take before responding.

[9 marks]

[Total marks – 17]

(Spring 1990)

2   Two years ago your customer, John Temple, asked whether your bank would be prepared to grant him a loan of £27,000 to repay a mortgage to the Lowdown Building Society. He explained that he had been experiencing financial difficulties and that the building society, which had a charge over the family home, was threatening possession proceedings. He said that these financial problems were temporary and that his business prospects had recently improved and that as a result, he would be able to repay the loan from company drawings within six

months. You therefore agreed to his loan request subject to a charge over the family home, the deeds of which were in the joint names of John and Ann Temple (Ann Temple was John Temple's wife).

Mr Temple signed the mortgage form at the bank and you took the form to the Temple's home in order to obtain Ann Temple's signature. Ann Temple was happy to sign the form as she was anxious to stay in the family home.

Regrettably, Mr Temple's business fortunes did not improve and as a result the repayment of the loan fell into arrears. Formal demand for repayment brought no response and consequently the bank applied to the courts for a possession order over the family home.

Today, you receive a letter from Ann Temple's solicitor claiming that the bank's mortgage is invalid because Mrs Temple's signature was obtained by the undue influence of the bank and she should have received independent legal advice.

Required

(a) State what you understand by the terms 'undue influence' and 'independent legal advice'.

[4 marks]

(b) On what grounds do you think the solicitor is making his claim? What points would you consider in dealing with his letter? Do you believe that the claim is likely to succeed? Give reasons for your answers.

[16 marks]

[Total marks – 20]

3 At your branch you conduct current accounts for the under-mentioned customers, having obtained the signature of each to the bank's standard mandate. Signing authorities and balances as at close of business last night are shown below:

— Gordon Laurie and Audrey Laurie – joint and several mandate dated 13 July 1971 – both to sign: credit £1,702.

— David Bowman and Susan Bowman – joint and several mandate dated 10 August 1985 – both to sign: credit £400.

— John Hughes and Rachel Hughes – joint and several mandate dated 4 November 1986 – both to sign: credit £417.

— Peter Rolls and Mary Rolls – joint and several mandate dated 6 July 1990 – both to sign: credit £800.

— Freda Thomas – third-party authority for Peter Thomas, her son, to sign dated 3 September 1990: credit £4,002.

Today (15 October 1990) there have been the following developments:

(a) A Mr Anthony Laurie calls and says that his father, Gordon Laurie, died yesterday. In today's in-debit clearing there is a cheque dated 10 October 1990 for £350 in favour of Curtiss Stores Ltd, signed by Gordon Laurie and Audrey Laurie.

[2 marks]

(b) Susan Bowman telephones at 11.00 am and asks you not to pay a cheque for £110 dated 1 October 1990 in favour of Jones Computer Agency. This cheque has been presented in today's in-debit clearing and it is signed in accordance with the mandate which you hold.

[2 marks]

(c) The official Receiver telephones and tells you that a bankruptcy order was made against John Hughes earlier today. In today's in-debit clearing is a cheque for £309 signed by John Hughes and Rachel Hughes dated 7 October 1990. The payee is Kim Bridge.

[2 marks]

(d) Mary Rolls telephones and asks if a cheque for £500 in favour of Teasdale Ltd has been presented. You check your records and see that it was paid on 5 October 1990. Mrs Rolls says that she did not sign this cheque, and she thinks that her husband must have forged her signature.

[5 marks]

(e) Alan Thomas telephones and says that his wife, Freda Thomas, was compulsorily admitted yesterday to a mental hospital for treatment. In today's in-debit clearing is a cheque for £1,117 dated 9 October 1990–drawn by Peter Thomas–payee Walters & Son Ltd.

[5 marks]

Required

State the action(s) which you will take, if any, in respect of each account and the transactions thereon. Give reasons for your answers

[Total marks – 16]

(Autumn 1990)

4   State how you would deal with each of the following situations, and the considerations you would have in mind. Give reasons for your answers.

(a) Last year you provided George Handel with a loan of £10,000 against the security of a guarantee from his father. Today George's father calls at the branch and wishes to know the balances on his son's accounts and how much of his son's loan has been repaid.

[8 marks]

(b) Percy Grainger has a £5,000 overdraft facility at your branch against the security of a guarantee from his uncle, Edward Elgar. Today, with the balance of Mr Grainger's account £750 credit, you receive a letter from Mr Elgar advising you that he wishes his liability under the guarantee to cease as from the end of next month. The guarantee is on the bank's standard form.

[6 marks]

(c) You are lending Arthur Sullivan £17,000 on overdraft against the deposit of a life policy for £20,000 (plus profits) with a signed memorandum of deposit. The policy is due to mature next month and you wish to see the funds used to repay the borrowing.

[6 marks]
[Total marks – 20]

(Autumn 1992)

Q

5   Masterclass Ltd has been your customer for five years, but you know that the company also has accounts with competitor banks.

You recently agreed to lend the company £100,000 repayable over three years, to assist it in building an extension to its existing premises. When you insisted on security, the directors stated that they were anxious to retain a degree of flexibility in case they should need to borrow from their other bankers in the future. Consequently, they offered you either:

(a)   a first mortgage over the company's leasehold factory premises, valued at £70,000 in the company's last balance sheet; or

(b)   the two directors' joint and several guarantee for £100,000; or

(c)   a mortgage over the freehold premises owned by Upper Class Ltd, another company with which the directors are associated and in which they hold all the share capital. Upper Class Ltd trades from these premises, which the directors value at £120,000. This company operates a current account in credit at your branch.

Required

Set out the advantages and disadvantages of each of the securities offered, and indicate any further information you might need to enable you to reach your decision as to which security to take.

[Total marks – 17]

(Autumn 1990)

(Answers are given in Appendix 2, pp. 326–30)

APPENDIX 1

The Code of Banking Practice

Background

The Code of Banking Practice is the result of a number of years of consultation between the financial institutions and incorporates recommendations from, for instance, the banking ombudsman and the Jack Report.

The code's aim is to establish good standards of banking practice which can be followed not only by the banks but also by other financial entities such as building societies and card issuers.

The code was introduced in March 1992 subject to periodical review, which it was anticipated should occur at least once every two years.

Details of the Code of Banking Practice

1.0 Introduction

1.1 The code has been prepared by the British Bankers' Association (BBA), The Building Societies Association (BSA), and the Association for Payment Clearing Services (APACS).

1.2 The code is written to promote good banking practice. Specific services may have their own terms and conditions which will comply with the principles contained in the code.

1.3 The code is in two parts. Part A – 'Customers, their banks and building societies' – is addressed to banks and building societies who adopt the code and offer personal customers ('customers' for short, throughout the code) banking services such as current accounts, deposit and other savings accounts, overdrafts and loans, and various services delivered by the use of plastic cards.

Part B – 'Customers and their cards' – is addressed to banks, building societies and others who adopt the code and provide financial services by means of plastic cards. All such providers are called card issuers in Part B of the code and in this introduction.

1.4 The governing principles of the code are:

(a) to set out the standards of good banking practice which banks, building societies and card issuers will follow in their dealings with their customers;

(b) that banks, building societies and card issuers will act fairly and reasonably in all their dealings with their customers;

(c) that banks, building societies and card issuers will help customers to understand how their accounts operate and will seek to give them a good understanding of banking services;

(d) to maintain confidence in the security and integrity of banking and card payment systems. Banks, building societies and card issuers recognise that their systems and technology need to be reliable to protect their customers and themselves.

1.5 The code requires banks, building societies and card issuers to provide certain information to customers. This will usually be at the time when an account is opened. Information will also be available to customers from branches, if any, of the bank, building society or card issuer. Banks, building societies and card issuers will provide additional information and guidance about specific services at any time on request.

Part A – Customers, their Banks and Building Societies

2.0 Opening an account

2.1 Banks and building societies will satisfy themselves about the identity of a person seeking to open an account to assist in protecting their customers, members of the public and themselves against fraud and other misuse of the banking system.

2.2 Banks and building societies will provide to prospective customers details of the identification needed.

3.0 Terms and conditions

3.1 Written terms and conditions of a banking service will be expressed in plain language and will provide a fair and balanced view of the relationship between the customer and the bank or building society.

3.2 Banks and building societies will tell customers how any variation of the terms and conditions will be notified. Banks and building societies will give customers reasonable notice before any variation takes effect.

3.3 Banks and building societies should issue to their customers, if there are sufficient changes in a 12-month period to warrant it, a single document to provide a consolidation of the variations made to their terms and conditions over that period.

3.4 Banks and building societies will provide new customers with a written summary or explanation of the key features of the more common services that they provide.

3.5 Banks and building societies will not close customers' accounts without first giving reasonable notice.

4.0 Charges and interest

4.1 Banks and building societies will provide customers with details of the basis of charges, if any, payable in connection with the operation of their accounts. These will be in the form of published tariffs covering basic account services which will be available in branches and will also be given or sent to customers:

(a) when accounts are opened;
(b) at any time on request;
(c) before changes are made.

4.2 Charges for services outside the tariff will be advised on request or at the time the service is offered.

4.3 Charges on charges: banks and building societies will disregard the charges to be applied to customers' accounts for any charging period if those charges were incurred solely as a result of the application of charges for the previous charging period. The foregoing shall not apply when customers have effectively been notified in advance of the charges and given a reasonable opportunity to fund their accounts.

4.4 Banks and building societies will tell customers the interest rates applicable to their accounts, the basis on which interest is calculated and when it will be charged to their accounts. These will include the rates applicable when accounts are overdrawn without prior agreement or exceed the agreed borrowing limit. Banks and building societies will explain also the basis on which they may vary interest rates.

4.5 When banks and building societies change interest rates with immediate effect they will publicise those changes by notices in their branches, if any, or in the press, or both.

5.0 Handling customers' complaints

5.1 Each bank and building society will have its own internal procedures for the proper handling of customers' complaints.

5.2 Banks and building societies will tell their customers that they have a complaints procedure. Customers who wish to make a complaint will be told how to do so and what further steps are available if they believe that the complaint has not been dealt with satisfactorily either at branch or more senior level within the bank or building society.

5.3 Banks and building societies subscribing to the code should belong to one or other of the Banking and Building Societies Ombudsman Schemes or the Finance Houses Conciliation and Arbitration Scheme. Banks and building societies will provide details of the applicable scheme to customers using such methods as leaflets, notices in branches or in appropriate literature.

6.0 Confidentiality of customer information

6.1 Banks and building societies will observe a strict duty of confidentiality about their customers' (and former customers') personal financial affairs and will not disclose details of customers' accounts or their names and addresses to any third party, including other companies in the same group, other than in the four exceptional cases permitted by the law, namely:

(a) where a bank or building society is legally compelled to do so;

(b) where there is a duty to the public to disclose;

(c) where the interests of a bank or building society require disclosure;

(d) where disclosure is made at the request, or with the consent, of the customer.

6.2 Banks and building societies will not use exception (c) above to justify the disclosure for marketing purposes of details of customers' accounts or their names and addresses to any third party, including other companies within the same group.

6.3 Banks and building societies will at all times comply with the Data Protection Act when obtaining and processing customers' data.

Banks and building societies will explain to their customers that customers have the right of access, under the Data Protection Act 1984, to their personal records held on computer files.

7.0 Bankers' references

7.1 Banks and building societies will on request:

(a) advise customers whether they provide bankers' references or bankers' opinions in reply to status enquiries made about their customers;

(b) explain how the system of bankers' references works.

8.0 Marketing of services

8.1 Banks and building societies will not pass customers' names and addresses to other companies in the same group, in the absence of express consent.

8.2 Banks and building societies will give new customers at the time they open their accounts the opportunity to give instructions that they do not wish to receive marketing material.

8.3 Banks and building societies will remind customers from time to time, and at least once every three years, of their right to give instructions at any time that they do not wish to receive marketing material.

8.4 Banks and building societies will not use direct mail indiscriminately and in particular will exercise restraint and be selective:

(a) where customers are minors; and
(b) when marketing loans and overdrafts.

9.0 Marketing and provision of credit

9.1 Banks and building societies in their advertising and promotional material will tell customers and potential customers that all lending will be subject to appraisal of their financial standing by the banks and building societies concerned.

9.2 Banks and building societies will act responsibly and prudently in marketing. All advertising will comply with the British Code of Advertising Practice, the British Code of Sales Promotion Practice, and other relevant codes of practice of similar standing.

In particular, banks and building societies will ensure that all advertising and promotional literature is fair and reasonable, does not contain misleading information and complies with all relevant legislation.

9.3 In considering whether or not to lend, banks and building societies will take account of information which may include:

— prior knowledge of their customers' financial affairs gained from past dealings;

— information obtained from credit reference agencies;

— information supplied by applicant;

— credit-scoring;

— age of applicants; and

— applicants' ability to repay, with the aim of avoiding over-commitment by an applicant.

9.4 Banks and building societies will give due consideration to cases of hardship. They will encourage customers who are in financial difficulty to let them know as soon as possible.

10.0 Availability of funds

10.1 Banks and building societies will provide customers with details of how their accounts operate, including information about:

— how and when they may stop a cheque or countermand other types of payments;

— when funds can be withdrawn after a cheque or other payment has been credited to the account;

— out of date cheques.

11.0 Foreign exchange services

11.1 Banks and building societies will provide customers with details of the exchange rate and the commission charges which will apply or, when this is not possible at the time, the basis on which they will be calculated.

11.2 Banks and building societies will provide customers with a fair indication of when money sent abroad on their instructions should normally arrive at its destination.

12.0 Guarantees and other types of third-party security

12.1 Banks and building societies will advise private individuals proposing to give them a guarantee or other security for another person's liabilities that:

(a) by giving the guarantee or third-party security he or she might become liable instead of or as well as that other person;

(b) he or she should seek independent legal advice before entering into the guarantee or third-party security.

Guarantees and other third-party security forms will contain a clear and prominent notice to the above effect.

Part B – Customers and their Cards

13.0   Opening an account

13.1   Card issuers will satisfy themselves about the identity of a person seeking to open an account or to obtain a card, to assist in protecting their customers, members of the public and themselves against fraud and other misuse of the banking and card processing systems.

13.2   Card issuers will provide to prospective customers details of the identification needed.

14.0   Terms and conditions

14.1   The written terms and conditions of a card service will be expressed in plain language and will provide a fair balanced view of the relationship between the customers and the card issuer.

14.2   Card issuers will tell customers how any variation of the terms and conditions will be notified. Card issuers will give customers reasonable notice before any variation takes effect.

14.3   Card issuers should issue to their customers, if there are sufficient changes in a 12-month period to warrant it, a single document providing a consolidation of the variations made to their terms and conditions over that period.

14.4   Card issuers will publish changes to their interest rates in their branches of their stores or in the press or in the statement of account sent to card holders, or by all those methods when such changes are made with immediate effect.

14.5   Card issuers will tell customers the time it normally takes for a transaction to appear on their account and how frequently they can expect a statement.

15.0   Issue of cards

15.1   Card issuers will issue cards to customers only when they have been requested in writing, or to replace or renew cards that have already been issued.

15.2   Card issuers will tell customers if a card issued by them has more than one function. Card issuers will comply with requests from customers not to issue personal identification numbers (PINs) where customers do not wish to use the functions operated by a PIN.

16.0 Security of cards

16.1 Card issuers will issue PINs separately from cards and will advise the PIN only to the customer.

16.2 Card issuers will tell customers of their responsibility to take care of their cards and PINs in order to prevent fraud. Card issuers will emphasise to customers that:

(a) they should not allow anyone else to use their card and PIN;

(b) they should take all reasonable steps to keep the card safe and the PIN secret at all times;

(c) they should never write the PIN on the card or anything usually kept with it;

(d) they should never write the PIN down without making a reasonable attempt to disguise it.

17.0 Lost cards

17.1 Card issuers will inform customers that they must tell their card issuers as soon as reasonably practicable after they find that:

(a) their card has been lost or stolen;

(b) someone else knows their PIN;

(c) their account includes an item which seems to be wrong.

17.2 Card issuers will tell customers, and will remind them at regular intervals on their statement or by other means, of the place and the telephone number where they can give the details of a lost or stolen card at any time of the day or night. Card issuers will arrange for that telephone number to be included in British Telecom phone books.

17.3 Card issuers will act on telephone notification but may ask customers also to confirm in writing any details given by telephone.

17.4 Card issuers, on request, will inform customers whether they accept notification of loss or theft of a card from card notification organisations.

17.5 Card issuers, on being advised of a loss, theft or possible misuse of a card or that the PIN has become known to someone else, will take action to prevent further use of the card.

18.0 Liability for loss

18.1 Card issuers will bear the full losses incurred:

(a) in the event of misuse when the card has not been received by the customer;

(b) for all transactions not authorised by the customer after the card issuer has been told that the card has been lost or stolen or that someone else knows or may know the PIN (subject to 18.4 below);

(c) if faults have occurred in the machines, or other systems used, which cause customers to suffer direct loss unless the fault was obvious or advised by a message or notice on display.

18.2 Card issuers' liability will be limited to those amounts wrongly charged to customers' accounts and any interest on those amounts.

18.3 Customers' liability for transactions not authorised by them will be limited to a maximum of £50 in the event of misuse before the card issuer has been notified that a card has been lost or stolen or that someone else knows the PIN (subject to 18.4 below).

18.4 Customers will be held liable for all losses if they have acted fraudulently. They may be held liable for all losses if they have acted with gross negligence.

18.5 In cases of disputed transactions, the burden of proving fraud or gross negligence or that a card has been received by a customer will lie with the card issuer. In such cases card issuers will expect customers to co-operate with them in their investigations.

19.0 Records

19.1 Card issuers will provide customers with a written record on their statement of account of all payments and withdrawals made. In addition, in many cases customers will be provided with an immediate written record.

20.0 Handling customers' complaints

20.1 Each card issuer will have its own internal procedures for the proper handling of customers' complaints.

20.2 Card issuers will tell their customers that they have a complaints procedure. Customers who wish to make a complaint will be told how to do so and what further steps are available to them if they believe that the complaint has not been dealt with satisfactorily by the card issuer.

20.3 Card issuers subscribing to the code should belong to one or other of the Banking and Building Societies Ombudsman Schemes, the Finance Houses Conciliation and Arbitration Scheme or the Retail Credit Group Mediation and Arbitration Scheme. Card issuers will provide details of the applicable scheme to customers using such methods as leaflets or notices or appropriate literature.

Association for Payment Clearing Services
British Bankers' Association
The Building Societies Association

Glossary of terms

This glossary explains the meaning of words and phrases. They are not precise legal or technical definitions.

Availability of funds Cheques paid into an account are 'uncleared' and they may be returned unpaid by the bank or building society on which they are drawn. Customers may not be permitted to draw against uncleared cheques. Cheques which are not returned unpaid become cleared and form part of a 'cleared balance'.

When returning cheques unpaid (see **Unpaid Cheques** below), banks and building societies have to abide by very strict time-limits. Customers may enquire about the timescale involved to establish which part of their balances are cleared and are therefore available for withdrawal.

Cash paid direct into an account at the branch at which it is held forms part of a cleared balance.

Bankers' references or bankers' opinions An opinion given on request by one financial institution to another about a customer's ability to support or undertake to repay a financial transaction or commitment. A request for such an opinion is sometimes called a status enquiry.

Card notification organisations Companies which will at the request of a card holder maintain a record of all the cards held by the card holder and notify card issuers of the loss or theft of those cards.

Countermand A customer's instruction to a bank or building society to cancel or override a previous instruction to make a payment or transfer of funds, e.g. by 'stopping' a cheque.

Credit reference agencies Licensed companies which hold information about individuals. Banks and building societies may refer to these agencies to assist with various decisions, e.g. whether or not to open an account or to provide loans or grant credit.

Credit scoring A method of assessing risk, based on statistical analysis of previous lending experience and other factors: used, for example, to help in deciding whether a loan should be granted.

Guarantees An undertaking given by a person (the guarantor) promising to pay the debts of another person if that other person fails to do so.

Ombudsman schemes Banks and building societies have separate independent Ombudsman Schemes. The Ombudsmen resolve complaints made by customers against a bank or building society when customers have been unable to resolve such complaints themselves with their bank or building society.

Details are:

Office of the Banking Ombudsman
Citadel House
5–11 Fetter Lane
London EC4A 1BR
Tel 071 583 1395

Office of the Building Societies Ombudsman
Grosvenor Gardens House
35–37 Grosvenor Gardens
London SW1X 7AW
Tel 071 931 0044

Payment Cards A general term for any plastic card which may be used to pay for goods and services or to withdraw cash. A card may be used for more than one function. Common examples are:

Credit card – a card which allows customers to buy on credit and to obtain cash advances. Customers receive regular statements and may pay the balance in full or in part, usually subject to a certain minimum. Interest is payable on outstanding balances.

Charge card – similar to a credit card. It enables customers to pay for purchases, and in some cases to obtain cash advances. When the monthly statement is received the balance must be paid in full.

Debit card – a card, operating as a substitute for a cheque, that can be used to obtain cash or make a payment at a point of sale. The customer's account is subsequently debited for such a transaction without deferment of payment.

Budget card – similar to a credit card but customers agree to pay a fixed amount into their card account each month.

Store card – similar to a budget card or charge card, but issued by particular companies or retail groups for use at their own outlets.

Cash card – a card used to obtain cash and other services from an ATM (Automated Teller Machine/Cash Machine).

Cheque guarantee card – a card issued by a bank or building society which guarantees the payment of a cheque up to the amount shown on the card, provided its conditions of use are followed.

Eurocheque card – a specific cheque guarantee card which can be used either with special eurocheques to pay for goods or services, or by itself to withdraw cash from machines, in the UK and other countries.

Personal customer A private individual who maintains an account (including a joint account with another private individual or an account held as an executor or trustee, but excluding the accounts of sole traders, clubs and societies) or who receives other services from a bank or building society.

PIN – Personal identification number A secret number provided on a strictly confidential basis by a card issuer to a card holder. Use of this number by the customer will allow the card to be used either to withdraw cash from an automated teller machine or to authorise payment for goods or services in retail or other outlets, by means of a special terminal.

Published tariff A list of prices for basic account services provided by a bank or building society.

Security A general word used to describe items of value such as title deeds, share certificates, life policies, etc., which represent property. Under a secured loan the lender has the right to sell the security if the loan is not repaid.

Third-party security Security provided by a person who is not the borrower.

Unpaid cheques A cheque which is not paid, for one of a number of reasons, the most common of which are:

Refer to drawer – This frequently means that there is not sufficient money in the drawer's account. The recipient of the cheque (the payee) should ask the person issuing the cheque (the drawer) why it has not been paid.

Refer to drawer. Please re-present – similar to above, but used when the bank or building society expects money to be available to pay the cheque in the near future and therefore suggests it is presented again for payment.

Post-dated – the cheque cannot be paid because its date is some time in the future.

Out of date – the cheque has not been paid because its date is too old, normally meaning more than six months ago.

Effects not cleared – there is money in the account of the drawer of the cheque but not available as cleared balances, because it is not yet certain that cheques recently credited to the account will be paid.

Words and figures differ – the amount of the cheque written in words is different from the amount written in numbers.

Orders not to pay – the issuer (drawer) of the cheque has instructed his or her bank or building society not to pay the cheque, i.e. to stop payment.

Signature differs – the signature on the cheque is different from that recorded by the bank or building society.

Written terms and conditions Those provisions governing banking services which are produced in written form. They will be expressed in clear and straightforward English but the precise wording of some contracts must, of necessity, be in technical or legal language.

APPENDIX 2

Answers

UNIT 1

Short-answer questions

1 (a) Debtor–creditor.

(b) Principal–agent.

(c) Bailor–bailee.

(d) Trustee–beneficiary.

(e) Mortgagor–mortgagee.

2 *Joachimson* v *Swiss Bank Corporation* (1921).

3 You can divulge your suspicions to the authorities.

4 Drug Trafficking Offences Act (1986).

5 No.

6 A court order, e.g. a PACE order.

7 20 December 1997.

8 Limitations Act 1980.

Multiple-choice questions

1 (b)

2 (c)

3 (a) (b) (c) (d) (e)

4 (a) (c) (d)

Revision questions

1 The question concerns the bank's duty of secrecy.

As a result of the *Tournier* case, banks can divulge details with regard to their customers' accounts in the following circumstances:

(a) by express or implied consent of the customer;

(b) where the interests of the bank require it;

(c) where there is a duty in the public interest;

(d) under compulsion of law.

In this question we have a situation affecting a valued customer who is a personal friend. The following procedure can be recommended:

(a) Ask E Ring Jewellers to bring Dai Monde to the telephone.

(b) Identify your customer by asking shrewd questions. (This should not be too difficult as he is a personal friend.)

(c) Request his permission to answer the question raised by E Ring Jewellers.

(d) If this is forthcoming, advise E Ring Jewellers that if the cheque was in your hands and in order then it would be paid.

(e) If E Ring Jewellers are unhappy with this reply, speak to Mr Monde again and suggest an immediate transfer of cleared funds using the CHAPS system (covered later in the course), from his bank account to the bankers of E Ring Jewellers. If he is agreeable, advise E Ring Jewellers what you intend to do and take action immediately.

2   The question concerns the closure of an unsatisfactory account which has a credit balance.

In *Prosperity Ltd* v *Lloyds Bank Ltd* (1923) it was established that reasonable notice must be given of closure of a credit account. 'Reasonable notice' will vary, dependent upon the circumstances of the customer.

In this question, Jukes would appear to have been given reasonable notice, and he is wrong in his assumption that a bank can only close an account with the customer's agreement.

The action that the bank should take when the period of notice expires is as follows:

(a) Advise Jukes to collect any balance and return any unused cheques and plastic cards.

(b) Place any future credits which are received in a suspense account. Advise Jukes to call and collect the funds.

(c) If any cheques are received drawn on Jukes' account:

(i) pay any cheques which are correctly drawn and have a valid cheque card number on the reverse;

(ii) either return all other cheques marked 'Account closed', or pay all cheques until any credit balance is exhausted and then return all subsequent cheques, marked 'Account closed'.

(d) Ensure that no further cheque-books are forwarded to Jukes.

UNIT 2

Short-answer questions

1   £15,000.

2   Consumer credit licence.

3   Canvassing is an oral attempt by a lender to persuade a potential borrower to enter into an agreement to borrow money from that lender.

4   Section 49 (i).

5   No.

6   Five days.

7   CCA 1974 s.50 states that it is illegal to forward literature to minors which invites them to borrow money, obtain services on credit or to apply for advice or information on borrowing or obtaining credit. You should therefore decline to take up the suggestion of your member of staff.

Multiple-choice questions

1   (a)   (b)   (c)

2   (d)

3   (a)   (b)   (c)   (d)

4   (b)

5   (a)   (c)

Revision questions

1   Banks are not subject to s.145(8) Consumer Credit Act 1974 when providing status enquiries. Because of this, banks do not have to allow their customers sight of any opinions which they may give. Their customers also have no right to alter any opinion given by their bankers.

You should therefore politely refuse Joe King's request.

2   The question concerns action to be taken when a borrower defaults on a regulated agreement.

Under the Consumer Credit Act 1974 a bank cannot make an immediate demand for repayment. It must initially issue a pre-demand default notice. If following this the borrower does not remedy the situation, the bank can call up the total amount of the lending, providing at least seven days have passed since the issue of the default notice.

Thus, relating the above to the question, you should explain to your assistant that under the Consumer Credit Act 1974 a demand for repayment cannot be made immediately.

You should instigate the production and issue of a pre-demand default notice to Peter Gill. This would contain details of the amount involved and the date upon which demand would be made if the repayments were not brought up to date.

Diarise the date when the lending has to be called up if the current position has not been remedied.

Past examination question

As the amount of the borrowing is less than £15,000, the agreement will be regulated under the Consumer Credit Act 1974.

The agreement will detail the terms of the loan and the security involved. It will also show the total charge for credit.

An advance copy of the agreement will be sent to the potential borrower marked 'Copy of Proposed Credit Agreement containing notice of your rights to withdraw. Do not sign or return this copy'.

No approach should be made by the bank to Mr and Mrs Boothman for seven days unless they ask for advice.

Once this period has elapsed, the bank should sign the agreement and send it, together with a copy, to each party. Completed copies of the mortgage forms should also be sent to Mr and Mrs Boothman.

Mr and Mrs Boothman then have a further eight days in which to consider the agreement, which runs from the date that the documents have been posted to them.

The agreement becomes effective when the customers sign and return the documents within the consideration period.

Copies of all documents will have been given to both Mr and Mrs Boothman. This type of regulated agreement is non-cancellable.

UNIT 3

Short-answer questions

1   Yes.

2   (a)   By the express revocation of the donor.
    (b)   On the expiry of the time period for which the power of attorney was given.
    (c)   By the death, bankruptcy, or mental incapacity of the donor.

3   The attorney can act once the enduring power of attorney document has been registered by the Court of Protection.

4   The rule in *Clayton's* case states that where a customer does not allocate a specific amount paid in to meet a particular payment to be paid out of an account, then the first sum paid in extinguishes the first sum paid out.

5   The 'continuing security' clause.

6   Under s.245 Insolvency Act 1986, a floating charge will be void if a company goes into liquidation within 12 months of the giving of the security, unless it can be shown that it was solvent at the time. The floating charge will be good for new borrowing. Therefore, all debts

created by cheques paid after the date of the charge will be secured and the remaining unsecured balance will be gradually repaid by credits paid in.

Multiple-choice questions

1   (c)

2   (a)

3   (b)   (c)

Past examination questions

1   The question concerns the wrongful acceptance of a direct debit entry on a customer's account when a customer has already cancelled her instructions pertaining to making such payment.

   In *Joachimson* v *Swiss Bank Corporation* (1921) it was established that a bank must act in accordance with its customers' written instructions when making payments.

   In this question, the bank has clearly not acted in accordance with a customer's written instructions.

   The bank should therefore:

   (a)   apologise to the customer;

   (b)   re-credit the sum to Lady Good's account;

   (c)   amend any charges which may have resulted from the wrongful payments of the direct debit;

   (d)   contact Mayfair Stores, explaining the position and requesting a refund. (All organisations which participate in the direct debit scheme provide an indemnity to the banks to refund sums which have been debited in error).

2   The question concerns powers of attorney. It is normal banking practice for banks' usual form of third-party authority to be completed in such situations, as otherwise problems could arise on the donor's account if a bank was bound by the original power of attorney document.

   In this scenario the bank has failed to take a third-party authority. It should therefore have examined the contents of the power of attorney given by Black and also have taken a copy of the document, as it will be bound to act in accordance with its contents.

   If it is a specific power of attorney, only certain transactions named in the document can be carried out by the donee on behalf of the donor.

   Under the Powers of Attorney Act 1971 a general power of attorney normally enables the donee to carry out any transactions that the donor can.

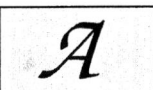

(a) The bank will be able to provide the list to Mr White if

    (i)   his authority originates from a general power of attorney or

    (ii) his authority originates from a specific power of attorney which clearly states that such information can be provided by the bank.

If either (i) or (ii) is not the case, then such a request would have to be declined as any such disclosure would be a breach of the bank's duty of secrecy.

(b) As Mr White is only acting as an agent for Mr Black, he will attract neither rights nor liabilities under the contract.

As such, Mr White's credit cannot be deemed to have suffered due to the non-payment of a cheque which he signed in his position as agent. He would therefore be unable to sue the bank for wrongful dishonour in his own name.

However, Mr Black could have a right of action against the bank due to wrongful dishonour of the cheque. It will depend upon the nature of the authority given to Mr White as to whether he could commence legal proceedings against the bank on Mr Black's behalf.

The bank should apologise to Mr White for the error and carefully refute Mr White's claim for compensation.

The bank should offer to contact the payee, explain the error and confirm that this should in no way reflect upon the creditworthiness of Mr Black or the integrity of Mr White. Such action should safeguard Mr Black's creditworthiness and would help to limit any damages awarded against the bank if Mr Black decided to take legal action.

(c) Mr Black is entitled to determine the power of attorney whenever he wishes. The bank would seek Mr Black's instructions concerning payment of any outstanding cheques which bear Mr White's signature. This is because once a power of attorney has been revoked, any cheques presented bearing the donee's signature will not be honoured by the bank unless it holds instructions to the contrary. The bank would also request the return from Mr White of any unused cheques from the special cheque-book.

UNIT 4

Short-answer questions

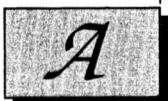

1   Stop the account, allowing no further payments (s.75 Bills of Exchange Act 1882).

2   Jane Parker and Norman Parker.

3   (a) The death of Jack Lill.

      (b) The regaining of his mental faculties by Jack Lill.

4 A partnership is the relationship which subsists between persons carrying on a business in common with a view to profit (s.1 Partnership Act 1890).

5 Stop the partnership account and lodge a claim in Cooper's estate.

6 Yes. Contracts for the purchase of necessaries.

7 The bank should examine the club rules and the trust deed to ensure that there will be no problems in taking such security.

8 Yes.

Multiple-choice questions

1 (b)

2 (b) (c)

3 (b)

4 (b)

5 (c)

6 (g)

7 (a) (e)

8 (c)

9 (b)

Past examination questions

1 *Principle*
The question concerns the retirement of one partner and the appointment of a new partner, and the procedures to be followed by the bank in view of this.

Relate
Is retiring partner to continue being liable for partnership borrowing?

Whatever the answer, no action will be necessary concerning loan account as effect of *Clayton's* case irrelevant as no fluctuating balance.

If retiring partner to be released from liability, is bank agreeable and prepared to rely on other partners?

Is new partner, Mr Taper, to be liable for old partnership's debts? If so, signed acceptance of liability to be obtained.

What is to be the name of the new partnership? Obtain completion of new mandate for office account and clients' account, ensuring that specimen signature of new partner obtained.

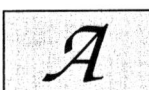

Trustee account – is retiring partner to resign as trustee?

Is Mr Taper to be appointed?

If this is the case, a copy of the trust deed authorising this should be seen.

Security

112 High Street — Is the property to be transferred into the names of the new partnership?

If this is the case, a new charge form will be needed. However, if property not to be transferred into the names of the new partnership, current charge form will cover change in constitution of partnership although new partner could be asked to show his agreement by signing this form.

17 Hazel Way — No action is necessary if retiring partner to continue being liable.

If retiring partner to be released from liability, will bank agree to release mortgage?

If yes, begin procedure to release CI charge.

If no, but presuming bank prepared to release from loan liability, have security recharged using third-party form as no direct liability for debt in future (unlikely situation).

2 *Principle*

The question concerns executors becoming trustees and authority to delegate.

Relate

Executor's account has been open in excess of two years. In view of the amount of time which has elapsed and the payment of income to beneficiaries, executors would now seem to be trustees.

Although executors can delegate, trustees cannot, unless designated in the trust deed. Bank should therefore check will.

If delegation not allowed, new trustee should be appointed.

Alternatively, set up standing order payable to beneficiaries or allow Alice Craven to operate income account against an indemnity from William Roberts. Statements to be sent to Roberts at regular intervals for ratification.

Power of Attorney Act 1971 s.9 is only permissible for a 12-month period. Delegation to be co-trustee not allowable.

UNIT 5

Short-answer questions

1   Refuse to cash the cheque.

Explain to the presenter that alteration of an 'order' cheque to a 'bearer' cheque requires drawer's signature as confirmation.

Suggest that Mr Smith pays the cheque into his bank account so that it can be cleared in the usual way. Alternatively, he should contact Mr Brown for the alteration to be confirmed. (Obviously, in the latter case, Mr Smith would have to await Mr Brown's return from holiday.)

The reason for this action is that the presenter of the cheque is a stranger and as he does not have adequate identification with him, the bank could find itself liable if this person is not the true owner.

2   *Brown* v *Westminster Bank Ltd* (1964).

3   *Greenwood* v *Martins Bank Ltd* (1932).

4   Take an indemnity from Mr Rich in case the original draft is presented for payment, particularly by a holder in due course.
Issue a replacement draft to Mr Rich.

5   No. *Whitehead* v *National Westminster Bank Ltd* (1982) confirmed that if there are insufficient funds on the due date to meet a payment, there is no further obligation for the bank to its customer in respect of that particular instalment.

Multiple-choice questions

1   (a)   (c)

2   (c)

3   (a)

4   (d)

5   (b)

Revision question

Examine the instructions contained in the letter, ensuring that there are no discrepancies between the details contained in the letter and those of the cheque which was debited the day before, e.g. does the cheque number agree?

Ascertain whether the fate on the cheque has been given to the collecting bank. If the fate has not been given, using the late returns procedure, telephone the collecting bank and advise non-payment ('Payment countermanded by order of drawer') before 12 noon. Re-credit customer's account.

If the collecting bank has already been advised that the cheque has been paid, and the bank had paid cheque in error, re-credit customer and debit suspense account. Ascertain whether there is a dispute between Williams and Maguire and Jones which can be resolved. If not, see if you can claim goods under doctrine of subrogation.

If the bank is at fault, apologise and follow one of the procedures given above depending upon the circumstances. If the bank is not at fault, advise customer that you regret that you can do nothing.

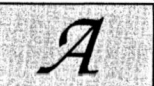

UNIT 6

Short-answer questions

1   *E B Savory and Company* v *Lloyds Bank Ltd* (1932).

2   *E B Savory and Company* v *Lloyds Bank Ltd* (1932).

3   *Orbit Mining and Trading Co Ltd* v *Westminster Bank* (1962).

4   Where companies are members of the same group and suitable authorities/indemnities have been provided by the companies concerned.

5   A holder in due course is a holder who has taken a bill, complete and regular on the face of it, under the following conditions:

   (a)   That he or she became the holder of it before it was overdue, and without notice that it had been previously dishonoured, if such was the fact;

   (b)   That the bill had been taken in good faith and for value, and that at the time the bill was negotiated he or she had no notice of any defect in the title of the person who negotiated it (s.29(1) Bills of Exchange Act 1882).

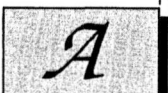

6   A cheque is issued to a payee, and not negotiated. Therefore, a payee cannot be a holder in due course. This was confirmed in the case of *R E Jones* v *Waring and Gillow* (1926).

Multiple-choice questions

1   (b)

2   (a) (b) (d)

3   (d)

4   (b)

5   (b)

6   (c)

7   (a)

8   (c)

9   (c)

10   (c)

Past examination questions

1   (a)   The question concerns the position of a collecting banker when sued for conversion. The bank has collected a cheque for someone other than the true owner.

Section 4 Cheques Act 1957 protects the collecting bank provided it collects the cheque:

(i)   for a customer;

(ii)   in good faith;

(iii)   without negligence.

Was Carter a customer? He did not have an account and therefore cannot be classed as a customer, as held in *Ladbroke* v *Todd*. He did, however, use the bank's services for some of his personal requirements, e.g. provision of traveller's cheques. Thus he could be said to be a customer under the doctrine laid down in the case of *Woods* v *Martins Bank*. Good faith can be presumed on the part of a bank.

On the face of it, the bank acted without negligence, since it appeared that the cheque was payable to Alan Carter whom the bank had known for four years.

Thus, providing that the bank's contention that Carter was a customer is not defeated in court, the bank should be protected.

In addition to the above, under s.29 Bills of Exchange Act 1882, the bank would be a holder in due course because it took the cheque:

(i)   complete and regular on the face of it;

(ii)   without notice of any defect in the title of the presenter;

(iii)   for value (the bank cashed the cheque for Carter);

(iv)   in good faith.

As a holder in due course, the bank is entitled to the proceeds of the cheque and is not liable to anyone.

The only way that the bank's position could be undermined would be if the cheque had been restrictively crossed, e.g. 'not negotiable'. In such a case the bank could not obtain a better title than that of the transferor, i.e. Alan Carter.

(b)   The bank's reply would acknowledge receipt of the solicitor's letter. It would request details of how the theft had occurred and would also ask for details about the crossing on the cheque. It would

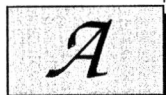

conclude by stating that a full response would be given once all the facts were provided.

2   The question concerns action to be taken when a bank allows its customer to draw against an uncleared cheque which is subsequently returned unpaid.

Action to be taken
The bank should be able to set itself up as a holder in due course under s.29 Bills of Exchange Act 1882. However, to retain its rights as a holder in due course the bank must retain the dishonoured cheque (*Westminster Bank* v *Zang* (1965)). The bank should debit the cheque to a suspense account.

Brian Speed should be advised of the cheque dishonour and asked to pay in to cover the value of the unpaid cheque. If the customer fails to repay, the bank should take steps to give notice to the drawer of the cheque of the bank's position as a holder in due course and request payment.

If the drawer fails to meet his obligation the bank will have to seek restitution through the courts.

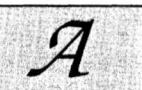

UNIT 7

Short-answer questions

1   A payment card is any form of plastic card which can be used to withdraw cash or to pay for goods.

2   A PIN is a confidential personal identification number which enables a cardholder to use a card to obtain cash from an ATM.

3   The Banking Ombudsman.

4   (a)   Loss or theft of a card.

    (b)   Where their PIN is known to a third party.

    (c)   Where an unknown transaction appears on the customer's account.

5   If the supplier of goods or services enters liquidation and payment was made by credit card, the card holder can seek recompense from the credit card company concerned.

6   Three days.

7   Clearing House Automated Payments System is a method by which sterling transfers are effected between banks through their gateways using the British Telecom switching service (PSS).

8   Truncation is a process whereby cheques physically stop at the bank where they are paid in and details of them are transmitted by special terminals to the relevant banks concerned.

Multiple-choice questions

1   (c)

2   (b) (d)

3   (a) (d) (e)

4   (a) (e)

5   (b)

6   (c)

Past examination question

(a)   Ask customer pertinent questions:

    — Has PIN been divulged to a third party?

    — Were details of PIN kept with card?

    — Was PIN written down where other people could see it?

    — If written down, was PIN disguised?

    — Is customer certain that she did not make withdrawal?

    — Could friend or member of family have used card?

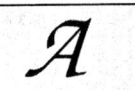

(b)   Ask for return of card and written confirmation that information can be given to the police if necessary.

(c)   Obtain information from branch where cash dispenser sited as to time and date of transaction. Check where customer was at that time. (If customer had forgotten carrying out the withdrawal, this could remind her!)

(d)   Bank's reaction will depend upon customer's response to questions and such considerations as the value of the account. Generally, claims are rejected due to customers being in breach of the terms and conditions of the issue of the card e.g. divulging PIN to a third party. If, however, a customer has not been guilty of negligence or fraud, she is only liable for a maximum of £50. Thus, if this was the position with Mary, some form of refund may be appropriate.

UNIT 8

Mock examination

1 (a)   The bank holds a mandate which requires both parties to sign any withdrawal instructions.

       Even though funds paid into the account appear to have been provided by Miss Bradly, they cannot be released to her against her sole signature. To allow this would lay bank open to a claim from

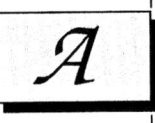

Mr Smith, if Miss Bradly's explanation is countered by her ex-fiancé.

Thus the bank must advise Miss Bradly that:

(i) it cannot comply with her request;

(ii) Miss Bradly should attempt to contact Mr Smith and obtain his written instructions that the balance of the account can be released to her.

As Miss Bradly needs the funds in the account for a holiday, bank may wish to consider granting her an overdraft/personal loan. This will, of course, depend upon her financial standing and also whether the bank is satisfied with Miss Bradly's explanation concerning the account.

(b) Where no mandate is held by a bank in these circumstances, the bank should allow withdrawals from the joint account only with the written authority of both account holders. Thus, the position would be exactly the same as regards the account.

(c) Even if credits to the account had been by internal transfer from Miss Bradly's current account, any withdrawals would still have to be carried out in accordance with the mandate held, i.e. instructions given by both signatories.

The bank may be better disposed to provide Miss Bradly with an overdraft/personal loan in the interim, as it can clearly see that Miss Bradly's explanation is substantiated by the evidence to hand.

2 (a) Cheque numbers 100278 and 100478 should not be paid. The reasons given for non-payment for both cheques would be 'Out of date'.

Although cheque number 400110 is dated 3 January 1990 and therefore appears to be 'out of date' it would seem that Mollie New has issued this cheque from her current chequebook and has merely dated it '1990' instead of '1991'. In such circumstances, at the beginning of a new year, banks will normally pay such cheques, providing it is clear that they have been issued in the current year. Cheque number 100278, although bearing the same date as cheque number 400110, does not appear to have been issued from the current chequebook and would not therefore meet the aforementioned criteria. Thus, to pay this cheque would clearly have placed the bank in a position whereby it might have had to refund to Mollie New.

(b) The question concerns the paying of cheques bearing forged drawer's signatures.

Section 24 Bills of Exchange Act 1882 states that a forged signature is 'wholly inoperative'.

Thus Mr Forest's belief that 'a forged signature is no signature' is correct. However, based upon the surrounding circumstances, the bank would use the maxim of estoppel as a defence. *Greenwood* v *Martins Bank Ltd* (1932) established that the defence of estoppel would be upheld where a customer became aware that forged cheques were being presented on his or her account but failed to advise the bank.

In this scenario, Mr Forest's actions very much mirror the *Greenwood* case. Mr Forest's failure to examine his bank statements has no direct bearing, as the case of *Tai Hing Cotton Mill Ltd* v *Liu Chong Hing Bank* (1985) confirmed that a customer was under no obligation to examine his bank statements.

In view of the above, the bank would cordially refuse to refund.

3 (a) The question concerns the authorising of a third-party minor to operate a parent's account.

The customer will have to complete a bank's third-party mandate which will authorise his son to operate the account. Special attention must be paid as to whether John is to be allowed to overdraw the account, as specific instructions would be required for this. A specimen of John's signature should be obtained.

John's position as a minor does not affect his role as attorney of his father's accounts, as he will be acting on behalf of his father who has full contractual capacity.

Thus, providing that the bank is satisfied as to John's ability, he can operate his father's accounts once the necessary mandate has been completed.

Other matters which the bank may wish to bring to Mr Silver's attention are as follows:

(i) John will not be able to delegate his powers unless Mr Silver gives specific express instructions to that effect.

(ii) During Mr Silver's absence, the bank could pay any bills due by standing order, which would remove some of the work which John would otherwise have to deal with.

(b) The question concerns a dispute between parties to a joint account.

When a bank holds a mandate, which allows for either account holder to sign, either signatory can 'stop' a cheque even if that person did not originally issue that cheque.

A bank will continue to comply with such mandate instructions until:

(i) they are cancelled by either or both of the account holders, or:

(ii) the bank is aware of circumstances which would create problems in the operation of the account under such a mandate.

In relating the above to the question, it can be seen that it was quite in order for George Ruskin to place a 'stop' on the cheque issued by Mary Ruskin.

It is quite clear that there is a dispute between George and Mary. This would have the effect of determining the mandate currently held. Thus, the bank must advise both parties to the account that it will only act upon instructions signed by both George and Mary.

The 'stop' on the cheque will therefore remain in effect unless both parties give instructions for it to be cancelled.

The bank should try to arrange a meeting with both parties so that the future operation of the account can be resolved.

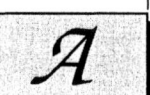

4   (a)   The question concerns the revocation of a fraudulent payment instruction.

The situation is similar to that regarding a forged signature on a cheque. As such, the bank would have no authority to make the payment – s.24 Bills of Exchange Act 1882. However, as the former accounts clerk had been an authorised giver of CHAPS payment instructions, it would seem that he was still the apparent agent of Avast plc and as such the company would be estopped from denying his authority.

Under the rules governing CHAPS, payments are said to be 'unconditional, guaranteed and irrevocable'. Thus, once a CHAPS payment has passed through a bank's 'gateway' it cannot be revoked. As such, Friendly Bank would be unable to comply with Mr Block's demands to revoke the payment instructions.

As regards Mr Block's demand not to debit Avast plc's account, the agreement between Friendly Bank and the company will contain an indemnity to the bank which will cover the bank's position if it should act upon fraudulent payment instructions which appeared to be valid. Thus, the bank would still be able to debit the amount to the company's account, provided that all normal procedures had been complied with.

(b)   This question concerns when a payment is said to be completed.

As noted previously, a CHAPS payment cannot be revoked when it has passed through a bank's 'gateway'. It is not necessary for the payment to be credited to Duff Ltd for Duff Ltd to have an accrued right to the payment as opposed to Chum Bank (*Royal Products Limited* v *Midland Bank Limited* (1981)). Also, even if Duff Ltd have not been advised of receipt of the payment, it is still due to the company (*Momm* v *Barclays Bank International Ltd* (1976)).

Thus, because the payment is due to Duff Ltd, Chum Bank is obliged to credit that company's account.

5   The question concerns the actions taken by a bank when learning of the admittance of a customer to a mental hospital.

Bank should initially have ascertained whether Alan Barker was a voluntary or compulsory patient and whether he was able to continue to manage his affairs.

A Court of Protection Order under the Mental Health Act 1983 should have been obtained and exhibited to the bank before any dealings with Mr Barker's account. Receipt of such an order would determine all mandates held.

Once this had been seen, the balance of Mr Barker's account should have been transferred into an account entitled 'Receiver of Alan Barker'.

As regards the balance of the joint account, this can only be dealt with by Helen Barker and the receiver (who could, of course, be one and the same person).

The circumstances outlined in the question resemble those in the case of *Scarth* v *National Provincial Bank Ltd* (1930), where it was held that under the doctrine of subrogation the bank was protected as the funds from the patient's account were used for the payment of his debts.

In an earlier case, *Re Davies, Banks & Co* v *Beavan* (1912), it was held that payments for 'necessaries' were valid again under the doctrine of subrogation.

Thus, it would appear that providing payments were due to meet Mr Barker's debts or to pay for 'necessaries', then the bank is protected. (This, of course, assumes that the bank has had sight of the Court of Protection Order.)

If the bank has not acted in accordance with the above, then the bank may have to reimburse Mr Barker, but it could seek compensation from Mrs Barker.

UNIT 9

Short-answer questions

1   No. The bank should only act on the instructions of its customer i.e. George Apple.

2   The surviving party and the executor/administrator of the deceased's estate.

3   The bank's investment management service is normally confined to customers who have a minimum of £25,000 to invest. However, its own personal financial advisers may well give advice on certain investments, e.g. an income bond.

Multiple-choice questions

1   (b)

2   (a)

3   (d)

4   (a) (c)

Past examination questions

1   The question relates to bank procedures with regards to supervision of third parties who may have access to a customer's deed-box.

Mr Dorrington's instructions to the bank did not authorise removal of any items from his deed-box by his secretary. A bank official should therefore have been present with the secretary while she listed the contents of the deed-box and should have ensured that no items were removed.

Provided that the bank acted in accordance with its normal procedures, should the matter be referred to the courts, it is likely to be able to refute Mr Dorrington's claim of negligence.

Obviously, if there has been a breach of the bank's normal procedures, then the bank may wish to compensate the customer 'out of court'. In such circumstances, it would probably require some form of evidence of the existence of the missing bracelet.

Mr Dorrington could, of course, claim from his insurance company for the loss. However, this would not help the bank's position, as the insurance company would counter-claim from the bank if the bank had been negligent in its procedures.

2   The question concerns the release of balances held on a deceased customer's accounts without the production of letters of administration or grant of probate.

The Administration of Estates (Small Payments) Act 1976 enables banks to release the balances on a deceased customer's accounts provided that the value of the deceased's estate is below £5,000.

In view of the above, the bank should take the following steps:

(a) Request sight of death certificate and note in records.

(b) Stop William Cowper's accounts. Any cheques presented for payment subsequently should be returned marked 'drawer deceased'.

(c) Identify Mrs Browning and obtain a status report from the branch where her account is held as to her ability to meet any contingent liability which might arise once the balances of her father's accounts are released to her.

(d) Ensure that the bank holds no will in safe custody.

(e) Ascertain whether funeral expenses have been (or will be) paid by Mrs Browning.

(f) Providing that the bank is prepared to release the balances to Mrs Browning, the bank should take an indemnity from her in case any subsequent claim is made against the bank with regard to the balances in question.

(g) Once the above procedures have been carried out, the balances of her father's accounts together with any accrued interest can be transferred to Mrs Browning's account as requested.

UNIT 10

Short-answer questions

1 The sums must be:

   (a) certain and clearly ascertained;

   (b) due between the same parties;

   (c) due in the same right.

2 *National Westminster Bank Ltd* v *Halesowen Presswork and Assemblies Ltd* (1972).

3 Garnishee summons.

4 Immediately.

5 This is to ensure that should the judgment debtor maintain accounts at branches of the bank of which the judgment creditor is unaware, any monies in those accounts will also be attached by the garnishee.

6 *Choice Investments Ltd* v *Jeromnimon; Midland Bank Ltd Garnishee* (1980).

7 To prevent the dissipation of assets prior to court proceedings being heard.

8 The sequestrator appointed by the court.

Multiple-choice questions

1 (a) (b) (c)

2 (c)

3 (b)

4 (b)

5 (a) (b) (c)

6 (b) (c)

7 (c)

8 (a) (c)

Past examination questions

1   The question asks about the bank's right of set off when monies are deposited with it for a specific purpose.

    When the bank is aware of the specific purpose, a resulting trust is created. This was established in the case of *Barclay's Bank* v *Quistclose Investments Ltd* (1968).

    In this question, especially as the funds are to be held in a separate account, the bank has notice of the trust. Thus the bank would have no right of set off against the deposit account in liquidation.

    If the bank refused the directors' request, bad publicity would arise. Thus the bank must agree, but must take precautions.

    The security of £70,000 fully covers the current account limit. Hence there is little danger to the bank, provided that its computer is programmed *not* to show the deposit account balance as a set off. No interest set off between the accounts should be allowed.

    The bank should take reasonable precautions when it allows transfers out of the trust account (*Barclays Bank plc* v *Quinecare Ltd and Another* (1988)). However, as the directors have brought the matter to the bank's attention there seems to be little danger of fraudulent withdrawals.

    Action
    Open the account, obtain the directors' written confirmation of the purpose, and advise them that the bank will not allow set off.

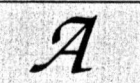

2   This is a garnishee order *nisi* which attaches cleared credit balances at the time when it was served at the branch, unless the customer has implied or express permission to withdraw against uncleared effects, in which case these are attached also (*Jones and Co* v *Coventry* (1909); *A L Underwood Limited* v *Barclays Bank* (1924); *Fern* v *Bishop Burns* (1980)).

    As both Robert and Thelma Pearson are named in the order, all sole and joint accounts, both private and business, are picked up.

    Trust account balances, including the clients' account balance, will be attached (*Plunkett* v *Barclays Bank* (1936)). However, the bank may explain to the court that they are trust funds and the court could then exclude them from the order.

    Deposit account balances will be attached (Administration of Justice Act 1956). Foreign currency balances with a UK bank are also attached (*Choice Investments Limited* v *Jeromnimon* (1980)). They should be notionally converted at the rate prevailing on the day that the order was served.

    Account balances caught under the order may be frozen or transferred to a suspense account until the order becomes absolute, at which time the moneys must be paid over to the court.

The bank will obviously exercise its right of set off in ascertaining the amounts due under the order.

If it is assumed that only cleared funds are attached, the following would be the case:

Partnership account	Cr £ 718.42
Partnership clients' account	Cr £3,216.84
Joint current account	Nil
R Pearson (net)	Cr £ 409.43 *
T Pearson	Nil
Joint dollar deposit account	Cr $1,500 *
Re Kim's deposit account	Cr £ 129.19

* Either of these two balances could be set off against the joint current account debit balance of £206.11.

UNIT 11

Short-answer questions

1 A letter of comfort is a promise to be liable for a third party's debts. Such a promise will only be a moral obligation, unless it is worded to show the intention of being legally binding.

2 Sections 151–8.

3 Section 330.

4 No. Section 334, as amended by s.138(b) Companies Act 1989, allows companies to make loans of up to £5,000 to a director.

5 Yes.

6 Yes. Section 338, as amended by s.138(c) Companies Act 1989, only allows loans to directors of money lending companies up to a maximum of £100,000 except in the case of bank directors, when there is no maximum.

7 The question asks whether an account can be opened for a private limited company prior to incorporation formalities being completed.

It is normal banking practice not to do so if the account is going to be operated prior to incorporation. This is because the company would not be liable for any transactions, as legally it would not exist prior to incorporation. Under s.35 Companies Act 1985, Mark Mason as director of the company would be liable, but the bank could find itself in court as

an accessory as it would have been aware of the situation concerning the account.

The bank should therefore tactfully decline its customer's request and explain the position to Mr Mason. As an alternative it could be suggested to Mr Mason that he open an account with an appropriate designation, e.g. 'M Mason (New Business Account)', which could be operated until the incorporation formalities were completed.

8 The bank can safely open an account for receipt of share application moneys. However, no withdrawals can be made, with the exception of the return of subscription moneys which may arise if a share flotation is oversubscribed.

Multiple-choice questions

1 (a)

2 (c)

3 (c) (d)

4 (b)

5 (c)

Revision question

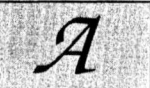

(a) Ascertain whether the new subsidiary company is to be a plc or a private limited company.

(b) Obtain sight of the company's certificate of incorporation and note the company's registered name, number and its date of incorporation.

(c) If the company is a plc the company's trading certificate should be seen by the bank.

(d) The bank will arrange for the company to pass a resolution appointing the bank as its bankers and also to complete the standard bank mandate form. This will give details of authorised signatories on the account.

(e) Take an authority from the company to divulge information to its auditors.

(f) The company must be licensed under the Consumer Credit Act 1974, as it will be providing credit for the purchase of consumer electrical goods. The bank should have sight of the licence and should note its details in its records. This is particularly important to the bank, as if the company is not properly licensed, the credit which it provides will not be legally enforceable against the borrowers. If the company was thus unable to obtain repayment from its clients, this could affect the company's ability to repay any borrowing from the bank.

(g) Agree commission and interest rates which are to be applied to the account.

(h) Fix frequency of statements.

(i) The account can be opened prior to incorporation, but only credits for the purchase of the share capital can be credited to the account, and no disbursements can be made prior to incorporation, except for the refund of subscription monies if the share flotation is oversubscribed.

Past examination question

Banks generally encounter letters of comfort when dealing with a group of companies. If a bank was approached to provide finance for one member of the group, the parent company could offer a letter of comfort as security for the loan. However, the bank must be careful as to the wording of such a letter, as if it is only a moral promise it is not legally binding (*Kleinwort Benson Ltd* v *Malaysia Mining Corporation Berhad* (1988)).

In order for a letter of comfort to be legally binding, it must be phrased to show the intention to create a legal obligation, and consideration must be evident, e.g. the granting of a loan. This was confirmed in *Chemco Leasing S.p.A* v *Rediffusion Ltd* (1987).

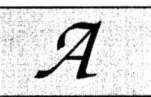

UNIT 12

Short-answer questions

1 Allow the partnership account to continue to operate. Any cheques presented which are signed by Simmons must be adopted by other partners, or returned marked 'Refer to drawer – bankruptcy order made against Simmons'.

2 Yes, provided that the bank is not prepared to merely rely upon the financial standing of the remaining partners. The bank should stop the partnership account in order to fix the liability and to prevent the rule in *Clayton's* case operating against the bank's position. A new account could be opened for the remaining partners.

3 Yes. The account would be allowed to continue, as the bank is well secured by assets charged by a partner other than Simmons.

4 Yes. The account would be stopped. A new account would be opened for the remaining partners. The security given by Simmons could be realised and the proceeds used to repay the partnership debt. Any surplus proceeds would be paid over to the trustee in bankruptcy. Obviously, the bank would also have a claim against the remaining partners.

5 No; however, the bank may decide to exercise its right of appropriation.

6 Stop the account to fix the guarantor's liability. Contact Jim Williams. Ascertain whether alternative security may be available for the loan.

Multiple-choice questions

1   (b)

2   (b)   (c)

3   (b)   (c)

Past examination questions

1   (a)   John Douglas has not divulged that he is an undischarged bankrupt and has traded in a name other than the one under which he was adjudicated bankrupt. He has obtained credit in excess of £250, contravening s.360 Insolvency Act 1986.

In addition, Douglas has charged after-acquired property (inherited shares) to the bank when they do in fact vest in the trustee in bankruptcy, s.307(3) Insolvency Act 1986.

Under s.307(4) the bank's position will be safeguarded providing that when it took the charge:

(i)   it acted in good faith,

(ii)   for value,

(iii) without notice of bankruptcy.

The bank should now take the following steps:

(i)   Stop the account.

(ii)   Return any cheques marked 'Refer to drawer'.

(iii) Advise the official receiver of its position and claim protection of s.307(4) Insolvency Act 1986.

(iv)   Interview the customer concerning the situation.

(b)   Discharge from bankruptcy is normally automatic after three years have elapsed since the bankruptcy order. However, this depends on the circumstances surrounding the bankruptcy and can be as short as two years or as long as five years.

2   (a)   A preference is said to have taken place when a person, who is subsequently made bankrupt, has carried out a transaction which places a creditor/surety in a better position than that creditor/surety would otherwise have been in.

(b)   The criteria which must be met in order for a trustee in bankruptcy to claim that a preference has taken place are as follows:

(i)   A desire to prefer must exist, except in the case of an associate, when such desire can be presumed.

(ii)   The preference must have occurred within six months prior to the presentation of a petition (two years in the case of an associate).

(iii) The person who carried out the preference must have been insolvent at the time, or have become so as a result of the preference.

These criteria are laid down in s.340 and s.341 Insolvency Act 1986.

(c) The clerk is concerned that Mr Abel may be creating a preference in favour of either the bank or his mother.

If the latter is the case, the trustee can recover any payment made to the bank.

However, a preference seems unlikely in this situation: Mr Abel is a valued customer, a partner in a profitable business, and meeting loan repayments as arranged. This is hardly the profile of a man on the verge of bankruptcy!

The explanation concerning the sale of inherited shares seems plausible and there seems to be no intention to prefer.

Any insistence by the bank on retaining the guarantee and share certificates in case a preference should arise would only create problems with a valued customer who would no doubt consider transferring his account elsewhere.

The bank should, therefore, send the letter as requested together with the share certificates. A receipt should be obtained for these certificates.

The guarantee should be placed with obsolete bank security forms.

UNIT 13

Short-answer questions

1   (a) Compulsory winding up.

(b) Members' voluntary liquidation.

(c) Creditors' voluntary liquidation.

2   Return cheque marked 'Refer to drawer – petition presented', unless such a disposition has been agreed to by the court, in which case a validation order issued under s.127 Insolvency Act 1986 should be exhibited to the bank before the cheque can be paid.

3   Politely refuse the directors' request and explain that you can only act upon the instructions of the liquidator of the company.

4   A transaction at an undervalue is an asset which is either given as a gift or sold for less than its true money or money's-worth value.

5   Where the transaction took place with a connected person.

6   When a debtor desires to place a person in a better position than would otherwise have been the case, to the detriment of others, and insolvency occurs, a preference is said to have taken place.

7   A 'shadow director' is a person on whose instructions the directors will normally act. This definition does not include people acting in their professional capacity, e.g. accountants, solicitors, bankers.

8 'Wrongful trading' is where a director or shadow director allows a company to continue to trade, even though it is insolvent or is unlikely to avoid becoming insolvent.

9 'Fraudulent trading' is where a company enters liquidation and that company has been trading with the intent to defraud creditors.

10 The court can order such a director to make contributions to the company's assets.

11 s.213 Insolvency Act 1986.

12 s.214 Insolvency Act 1986.

Multiple-choice questions

1 (a)

2 (e)

3 (a) (b)

4 (c)

5 (e)

6 (b) (See *Re Unit 2 Windows Ltd* (1985), Unit 12).

Past examination question

The question concerns the claim by the liquidator of Kidtoys Ltd that the bank's debenture was invalid (a) as a voidable preference and (b) as a transaction at an undervalue.

The circumstances in this question very much mirror the *Re M C Bacon Ltd* (1989) case.

(a) *A voidable preference*

Preferences are covered by s.239 Insolvency Act 1986 for companies. This states that where a company desires to place a person in a better position than would otherwise have been the case, to the detriment of other parties, and insolvency arises, then a preference can be stated to have taken place. Such an act must have taken place within six months of the onset of insolvency, which the liquidator must prove. In the *Bacon* case it was held that it is possible for a bank to provide assistance to a company in financial difficulty and take security, provided that the company was only motivated by proper commercial considerations. 'Desire' is the key word when relating to preferences, the judge saying that 'a man can choose the lesser of two evils without desiring either.'

In the case in question, if the company had not given the debenture then the bank would probably have called in the borrowing. Therefore, 'desire' is not evident in this situation and the liquidator's claim of a voidable preference would be defeated, as it was in the *Bacon* case.

(b) *A transaction at undervalue*

Section 238 Insolvency Act 1986 covers transactions at undervalue. These are said to occur where:

(i) the company makes a gift or otherwise enters into a transaction on terms that provide for the company to receive no consideration; or

(ii) the company enters into a transaction for a consideration the value of which, in money or money's-worth, is significantly less than the value, in money or money's-worth, of the consideration provided by the company.

Such transactions can be attacked by the liquidator if they have taken place within two years prior to the commencement of insolvency.

In similar circumstances in the *Bacon* case it was held that by charging its assets, the company had merely appropriated them to meet the liabilities due, which, whilst adversely affecting the rights of other creditors in the event of insolvency, did not diminish their value. The company had parted with nothing of value and the value which the company had received in return was incapable of being measured in money or money's-worth. The transaction appeared to be in good faith and for the benefit of the company and for the purpose of allowing the company to continue its business. The liquidator's claim would not therefore succeed.

UNIT 14

Mock examination

1 (a) When a company enters compulsory liquidation, it is stated to begin from the date of the petition. Any disposition of the company's assets between the date of the petition and the date of the winding-up order by the court will be void against the liquidator, unless such transactions have been sanctioned by the court (s.127 Insolvency Act 1986).

In this question, it would seem that the bank had been unaware of the petition, even though it would have been advertised in the *London Gazette*. (NB personal bankruptcy petitions do not have to be gazetted whereas company liquidation petitions do.) Mathon's status as a company provides grounds for the liquidator's claim, although the bank may be able to have some of the disbursements ratified retrospectively by the court.

(b) Wrongful trading is where a director allows a company to continue to trade even though he or she knew, or should have known, that there was little chance of the company avoiding liquidation (s.214 Insolvency Act 1986). A director who is found guilty of wrongful trading may be ordered by a court to contribute to the assets of the company. A director who can show that his or her actions were

merely to minimise loss to the company and creditors may be able to avoid being found guilty of wrongful trading.

(c) The bank will give the information requested once the liquidator has been appointed by the court. Such disclosure does not breach the bank's duty of secrecy.

2 (a) A petition is a written request to a court that a bankruptcy order be granted against a debtor.

Grounds for the presentation of a petition are as follows:

(i) The existence of an outstanding unsecured debt of £750 or more.

(ii) The non-satisfaction of a statutory demand by a debtor.

(iii) Where a judgment or other execution against a debtor has not been satisfied.

(iv) Where there are grounds for a criminal bankruptcy under the Criminal Justice Act 1972 or the Criminal Courts Act 1973.

A debtor may present his or her own petition in the event of being unable to pay debts.

Where a debtor is unable to comply with the terms of an individual voluntary arrangement, the supervisor can present a petition.

(b) Stop the customer's accounts under advice to the customer. Return the cheques marked 'Refer to drawer – bankruptcy petition presented'.

(c) As the bank had no knowledge of the petition when the cheques were presented for payment, and provided it acted in good faith it is likely that the court would ratify such payments should a claim be made by the trustee in bankruptcy.

(d) The answer would be the same as for (c); as regards credits, it will be protected from the claims of the trustee in bankruptcy provided it acted in good faith and for value.

3 (a) In *Re Unit 2 Windows Ltd* (1985) it was established that where a company enters liquidation and has maintained a number of overdrawn accounts and one account with a credit balance, then this credit balance must be set off on a pro-rata basis, notwithstanding that some of these debit balances may relate to preferential liabilities.

In *National Westminster Bank* v *Halesowen Presswork Assemblies Ltd* (1972) it was established that a bank has an immediate right of set off upon the liquidation of the company.

Applying the decision in *Re Unit 2 Windows Ltd* (1985), £12,000 would be applied against the debit balances on the current and loan account and £6,000 to the wages account.

As it is not possible to set off a credit balance against a contingent liability, the bank would submit the following claim:

Preferential   £14,000

Non-preferential   £28,000

Contingent   £50,000

(b) The bank should first examine the bond to establish whether it is conditional or unconditional and whether the Town Local Authority has a valid claim. If it does, the bank will have to pay out. As it had not taken a counter indemnity it would not have an automatic right of recompense. However, discussions should be held with the liquidator to establish whether he or she would accept a claim in the liquidation with regard to this even, without the existence of a counter-indemnity.

4   (a) When banks accept items in safe custody they are only responsible to the depositor.

In view of this, delivery of any item can only be allowed upon receipt of the depositor's authority.

Although the share certificates held may belong to Jane Trasker, they cannot be released to the person purporting to be her without the authority of Mr Trasker. (There may be more than one Jane Trasker!)

The bank is in an unenviable position because it clearly cannot give up the certificates, nor, because of its duty of secrecy, can it divulge any facts concerning the whereabouts of the certificates.

The normal course of action would be to obtain some document of authority from Mr Trasker. However, if as Mrs Trasker says, Mr Trasker cannot be contacted and is away for six months, little can be done unless a power of attorney has been granted by Mr Trasker to a third party enabling that person to deal with his affairs while he is away. The bank should check its records to see if it holds such a document, in which case authorisation from that party would suffice. If no such authorisation materialises, then the bank must decline Mrs Trasker's request.

(b) It is the bank's normal procedure to advise customers that they should ensure any items deposited in safe custody against loss or damage. If Phil Attlee had failed to follow this advice then any loss would have been his own fault.

The one possible exception to this would be if the vault had been flooded previously and the bank had taken no steps to prevent this happening again. In such an instance the bank would be considered to have been negligent and would therefore be liable.

It would seem unlikely that the bank would not have taken action if flooding had occurred before.

5   The serving of an unlimited garnishee order *nisi* has the effect of freezing all cleared funds held by the bank at that time. Banks normally will either stop the customer's account and open a new one, or transfer the cleared balance to a suspense account and allow the original account to continue.

Assuming that the bank will stop the account and open a new one for its customer, the cash part of the bank giro credit should be credited to the old account and the uncleared part of the credit should be credited to the new account. This also presumes that the customer does not have permission from the bank to draw against uncleared effects, because if the customer does, then the garnishee order would also attach to these uncleared effects (*Fern* v *Bishop Burns* (1980)).

At that time the garnishee order merely freezes the credit balance and need not be paid over to the court until the garnishee order is declared absolute.

As a director of Custard Pies Ltd is at the bank counter, the opportunity should be taken to discuss the situation and to agree what should happen regarding future banking arrangements. Obviously if nothing is agreed, and the cheque which the director wishes to cash is drawn on Custard Pies Ltd, then the bank will have to refuse payment.

As regards the two cheques in today's in-clearing, presuming that nothing has been agreed with the director/Custard Pies Ltd, they will be returned marked 'Funds attached by garnishee order'.

As regards the special presentation of the cheque, the decision as to whether the cheque is paid depends upon whether the presenting bank has already been advised verbally that the cheque has been paid. If it has, the cheque would be debited to the original account and its amount deducted from the credit balance which will be eventually forwarded to the court once the garnishee order has been made absolute. However, if the fate of the cheque has not been advised, it should be returned to the presenting bank marked 'Funds attached by garnishee order'. As the cheque has been cancelled by one of the clerks, it should also be marked 'cancelled in error'.

UNIT 15

Short-answer questions

1 (a) All moneys clause.

(b) Continuing security clause.

(c) Repayment on demand clause.

(d) Power of sale clause.

(e) Additional security clause.

(f) Conclusive evidence clause.

(g) Consideration clause.

(h) Successor clause.

(i) Priority protection clause.

2   It could be pointed out to Mr Edwards that the 'all moneys' clause in the security forms which he signed specifically excludes s.93 Law of Property Act 1925. As such, the bank has the right to retain all security held until all the borrowing has been repaid.

3   As in Q2, the 'all moneys' clause in the security form means that the security given covers all moneys owing, including the balance on the loan account. In addition, mention could be made of the 'continuing security' clause which means that the security continues to cover any future borrowing even if the borrowing for which the original security was given has been repaid. You should therefore tactfully decline to release the security.

4   The Law Society.

5   (a)   As the solicitors are known to the bank, no status enquiry need be carried out.

    (b)   The deeds will be delivered to the solicitors against their receipt and undertaking to hold the deeds to the bank's order and to return them immediately if requested to do so.

    (c)   The solicitors will return the deeds to the bank following completion of their inspection.

UNIT 16

Short-answer questions

1   The certificate will show particulars of the charge and the date of delivery to the registrar of companies.

2   A form containing amended details signed by the company and the bank will be sent to the Registrar of Companies.

3   *Siebe Gorman & Co Ltd* v *Barclays Bank* (1979).

4   (a)   Yes.

    (c)   A first equitable charge.

5   Yes.

6   A floating charge will crystallise under the following conditions:

    (a)   Appointment of an administrative receiver.

    (b)   The company ceases business or enters liquidation.

    (c)   There is a breach of the terms of the debenture.

7   When a retention of title clause is included in a commercial contract, the legal title to goods does not pass to the purchaser until the goods have been paid for. As these goods, once paid for, will be covered by a floating charge, it can be seen that where stock has been obtained under

a contract containing a retention of title clause, the value of the floating charge will be seriously affected.

8   A floating charge holder who receives notice of a petition to appoint an administrator will have at least five days in which to appoint an administrative receiver (Insolvency Rules 2.6 and 2.7), which will prevent the appointment of an administrator.

Multiple-choice questions

1   (b)   (f)   (h)

2   (c)

3   (b)

4   (b)

5   (a)   (b)   (c)   (d)   (e)

6   (b)

7   (b)

Revision question

Advantages of a fixed charge

As a bank has a fixed charge over an asset, it prevents the company concerned from disposing of this asset either by sale or by way of legal mortgage without the permission of the bank.

If a company enters liquidation then the bank will be repaid from the proceeds of the sale of the security which it holds ahead of any other creditor. This should be compared to the proceeds from the sale of assets picked up under a floating charge, which must be used to satisfy preferential creditors before the indebtedness of the floating charge holder can be considered.

Assets covered by a fixed charge tend to be easier to value than those covered by a floating charge.

Book debts and other debts when turned into cash have to be paid into the bank as they are covered by a fixed charge.

Fixed charges do not suffer from the provisions covered by s.245 Insolvency Act 1986 as floating charges do, whereby the latter can be invalid except for future advances if a company commences winding-up procedures or a petition for an administrative order is made within 12 months of its creation if the company was insolvent at the time that the charge was created.

Advantages of a floating charge

A floating charge will pick up any assets now or in the future which are not covered by a fixed charge.

When a floating charge crystallises on the occurrence of a prescribed event, the free use of the assets by the company is curtailed and the bank has full control of them.

If an application is made to the court for the appointment of an administrator, a floating charge holder can defeat this process. There is a period of five days during which time the holder may appoint an administrative receiver, which would automatically prevent the appointment of an administrator – Insolvency Rules 2.6 and 2.7. The appointment of an administrator would prevent the bank exercising its rights as regards the disposal of assets covered by its fixed and floating charges. By appointing an administrative receiver these assets can be disposed of so that the bank can be repaid, although the rights of preferential creditors to proceeds from assets covered by a floating charge should not be ignored.

UNIT 17

Short-answer questions

1 No. When a bank instigates its power of sale over unregistered land and has surplus proceeds, it must search at the Land Charges Register to ensure that there are no subsequent mortgagees. If any do exist, the proceeds will be paid to them against their receipt. If there are no subsequent mortgages, the surplus proceeds can be paid to Neil Ames against his receipt.

2 The value of a sub-mortgage is based upon the amount outstanding on the original mortgage and decreases pro rata with the repayments made under this mortgage.

3 No.

4 (a) Have the land certificate written up to date.

   (b) Conduct an official search at the District Land Register.

   (c) Obtain an office copy of the register.

5 Obtaining an office copy of the register.

Multiple-choice questions

1 (b)

2 (c)

3 (c)

4 (c)

5 (c)

6 (c)

7 (b) (c) (d)

Past examination questions

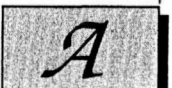

1 The question asks about the value of searching when taking a second mortgage over registered land. The land referred to in the question must be registered land, as only registered land has a title number.

Registered land
All searches against registered land must be made at the appropriate District Land Registry.

When taking a second mortgage the bank would expect to see the first mortgage recorded on the search. The bank will have a period of 30 days from the date of its search in which to register its second mortgage at the District Land Registry. Provided this deadline is met, the bank's second mortgage will have priority over any other mortgages which were not revealed by the search.

Unregistered land
When dealing with unregistered land, banks search at the Land Charges Register.

First mortgages of unregistered land normally have possession of the deeds and their priority depends upon retention of those deeds. Mortgagees who have the deeds cannot register their mortgage at the Land Charges Register.

The search at the Land Charges Register will ensure that the bank has priority over any other mortgagees who have not registered and who do not have possession of the deeds.

However, the bank must register its own second mortgage before the period of protection expires, i.e. before 30 April.

In practice, with second mortgages of unregistered land, banks will always search at the Land Charges Register after their mortgage has been registered there, to ensure that only the bank's mortgage is shown.

Conclusion
Miss Gordon has searched in the wrong place and must search at the District Land Registry.

2 *Sale of old factory*

(a) Status report on solicitors acting for the company, unless they are known to us.

(b) Customer's authority addressed to the solicitors regarding disclosure of information and requesting them to join in the bank's undertaking.

(c) Request confirmation from solicitors of price and of exchange of contracts.

(d) Solicitors to complete bank's undertaking, in standard form for Law Society protection:

   (i) To hold the deeds to the bank's order.

(ii) To remit the net sale proceeds to the bank on completion.

(e) Send the deeds to the solicitor and diarise for sale proceeds.

(f) On receipt of sale proceeds, release the two mortgage forms, duly receipted, to the solicitors. These forms will be part of the chain of title.

> (Note: If deeds are owned by a sole trader they are left in his name to save expenses on incorporation; the bank will require two charge forms, one signed by the previous individual owner and one completed by the company.)

Purchase of new factory

(a) Have factory professionally valued.

(b) See evidence that Mercury will provide £60,000 loan.

(c) Obtain solicitor's undertaking on standard form, for Law Society protection, to use any funds received from customer or bank to help acquire a good title to the property. Also obtain solicitor's confirmation that the company will execute a second mortgage in favour of the bank when the property is transferred into the customer's name.

(d) On completion of the second mortgage, the solicitor or bank must:

   (i) Register the charge at Companies Registry within 21 days in accordance with s.398 1985 Companies Act.

   (ii) Register at Land Charges Registry as a class C(i) puisne mortgage.

   (iii) Give notice to first mortgagee and confirm the amount owing (£60,000) and obtain acknowledgement.

   (iv) Confirm that fire insurance is adequate. Give notice to insurance company. Insurance to take effect from date contracts exchanged. Obtain acknowledgement.

   (v) Remit funds to the solicitor or pay the company's cheque in favour of the solicitor.

UNIT 18

Short-answer questions

1 (a) Surrender the policy if its value is greater than the borrowing.

   (b) If the policy is nearing its maturity date, the bank may decide to continue to meet the premiums and then obtain repayment from the maturity proceeds.

   (c) The bank may decide to convert the policy into a paid-up policy, in which case it will retain a reduced value until the maturity date.

2 No. The beneficiary must be named.

3 If the beneficiary is a minor, the bank would not take an assignment over the policy as it would be difficult to enforce (Minors Contracts Act

(1987)). If the beneficiary is an adult then an assignment can be taken over the policy providing that the proposer and beneficiary of the policy were prepared to execute the bank's form of assignment. This assumes that normal precautions, e.g. independent legal advice to avoid undue influence, were taken.

4   (a)   The policy could be declared invalid.

   (b)   The amount to be paid out under the policy could be reduced.

5   Martin Jax Ltd.

Multiple-choice questions

1   (a)

2   (c)

3   (b)

4   (b)

5   (a)

6   (a)   (b)

Specimen examination question

The question concerns whether the bank acted correctly when it realised a life policy after it had made demand and had not received any response.

Standard Chartered Bank Ltd v *Walker and Walker* (1982) states that a bank must act reasonably and must not sell at a particularly unfavourable time.

Providing the bank was not aware that Henry Hepworth had gone to Australia and had forwarded its correspondence to his last known address, then the bank can be said to have acted reasonably. The bank's charge form would specifically exclude s.103 Law of Property Act 1925, which requires three month's notice to be given before a security can be realised. The charge form will normally state that realisation on the policy can be made once a set number of days have elapsed. This is usually seven or 14 days.

It is unfortunate that the bank surrendered the policy after the life assured had died. However, the bank was not aware of this at the time and it would be pertinent to advise Ian Hepworth to contact the assurance company to ascertain whether the full capital value can still be paid. If it can, then the bank should intimate that it would assist Mr Hepworth, if possible, in order to obtain the residue due under the policy. However, the bank should not accept any responsibility for Mr Hepworth's position concerning the policy.

As can be seen from the above, the bank has acted reasonably in respect of the situation with Henry Hepworth and it can therefore refute the claims made by his son.

Past examination question

(a) Policy is a trust/settlement policy and not an endowment policy as first envisaged.

(b) Thus, both the proposer and beneficiary under the policy will have to join in the bank's assignment.

(c) As Laura Budd is providing security for her husband's borrowing, she will need to receive independent legal advice (*Barclays Bank plc* v *O'Brien* (1992)) in order to avoid the possibility of a claim of undue influence.

(d) The borrowing is a regulated agreement under the Consumer Credit Act 1974.

(e) The bank's charge form will contain details of the amount of the loan.

(f) A copy of the bank's charge form and the executed agreement must be given to both Billy and Laura Budd.

(g) Notice of the assignment will be given to the assurance company by the bank.

UNIT 19

Short-answer questions

1 No. The borrowing is made within the terms of the Consumer Credit Act 1974, which prevents negotiable instruments like bearer bonds being pledged as security.

2 (a) Difficult to value.

(b) Difficult to sell.

(c) Sale of shares may be restricted.

(d) There may be restrictions regarding the giving of such shares as security.

(e) The company may have a prior lien over the shares.

3 Failure to ensure that American or Canadian securities are in good marking names could affect their saleability in the event of the bank having to realise its security.

4 No. It is not possible for National Savings Certificates to be transferred into the name of the bank.

5 The bank can serve a 'stop notice' on the company through the Supreme Court. The company must then notify the bank of any attempt made to deal with those shares. The bank then has eight days in which to obtain a court injunction or restraining order to prevent the transaction going ahead.

Multiple-choice questions

1   (b)

2   (c) (d)

3   (a)

4   (b) (c) (d)

5   (a) (c) (d)

6   (b)

7   (a)

Revision questions

1   The question concerns the duty of care owed by a bank to a guarantor to sell mortgaged shares at a specific time in order to avoid a fall in value of the mortgaged shares.

In the case of *China & South Sea Bank Ltd* v *Tan* (1990) it was confirmed that a mortgagee of shares is not obliged to sell these shares, but if they are sold, then it must be for the best price obtainable at that time. It was also established that if the mortgagee also holds a guarantee for the principal debt, the mortgagee owes the guarantor no duty of care to sell at a particular time in order to avoid a depreciation in the value of the mortgaged shares.

The question therefore is related to the *Tan* case, in that the bank took the decision not to sell the shares at a particular time. Applying the principles confirmed in the *Tan* case, the bank had no duty of care to the guarantor to sell at a certain time to avoid a depreciation in the value of the shares.

The bank should therefore deny liability to the solicitor and insist on Brian Powell meeting his guarantee liability in full.

2   (a) The question asks about the position of an equitable mortgagee when faced with a prior equitable claim.

Equitable mortgages are subject to prior equities, thus the bank's security is void, if the facts are correct. It is too late to convert the equitable mortgage into a legal one once the facts are known (*Coleman* v *London County & Westminster Bank Ltd* (1916)).

(b) If the bank had taken a legal charge over the shares and had registered them in the bank's nominee name, then the bank would be able to realise its security provided that it had no knowledge of any prior equity when it originally took its charge.

Past examination question

(a) (i) *Mrs Frost*
— Mrs Frost's signature was forged and is therefore inoperative on the security and stock transfer forms.
— Mrs Frost must be returned to the same position that she was in prior to the forgery being perpetrated.

(ii) *The local solicitor*
— Unless he was aware of the fraud being perpetrated, he would not be liable.
— His professional services were merely used to provide independent legal advice to the bogus Mrs Frost and to explain the nature of the document to her.
— In witnessing the bogus Mrs Frost's signature, the solicitor was only confirming that she had signed having received independent legal advice.
— The solicitor would not be expected to verify Mrs Frost's identity.

(iii) *The company registrars*
— Cannot be held liable.
— *Sheffield Corporation* v *Barclay* (1905) and *Yeung Kai Yung* v *Hong Kong and Shanghai Banking Corporation* (1980) confirmed that the transferee warrants that the signature of the transferor is authentic. Consequently, the transferee is liable to indemnify the company should any loss arise out of the bogus transfer.

(iv) *The bank*
— The bank is liable.
— Its only course of action would be against Mr Frost and his female accomplice, if they can be found.
— Bank was negligent in not checking Mrs Frost's signature with the specimen held in the bank's records.

(b) — Bank's legal department should advise police of deception.
— Bank should contact company registrars and arrange for shares to be transferred back to the name of Mrs Frost. All costs will be borne by the bank.
— Cancel bank's guarantee form.
— Apologise profusely to Mrs Frost and confirm that steps have been taken to restore her former position.
— Unless £30,000 can be traced, it will have to be written off.

UNIT 20

Short-answer questions

1 (a) Stop the account.

(b) Prove in the bankruptcy for £18,000 as an unsecured creditor.

(c) Make demand on Robert Rees for £18,000 and, when received, place to a suspense account (*Re Sass* (1863)).

(d) It will depend on what payment the bank receives from the bankrupt's estate as to whether it will use the funds provided by the guarantor for repayment.

(e) Any funds left from the guarantor's contribution after the bank has been repaid will be returned to the guarantor.

2 The bank will refund the £10,000 to the guarantor.

3 Arrow and Bow will not be liable under the guarantee. *National Provincial Bank of England Ltd* v *Brackenbury* (1906) confirmed that all joint and several guarantors must sign the bank's guarantee before it becomes effective.

4 *James Graham & Co Ltd* v *Southgate – Sands and others* (1985) confirmed that all joint and several guarantors are released from their liability where one of the signatures has been forged on the guarantee. Therefore, Brice, Briggs and Bragg are released from their guarantee liability.

5 Advise the guarantor that his guarantee is currently relied upon for £5,212.

Multiple-choice questions

1 (c)

2 (b) (d)

3 (c) (d)

4 (a) (b)

5 (c)

Revision questions

1 (a) *Barclays Bank plc* v *Khairia and Another* (1991) confirmed that a bank has no duty to explain the clauses in a guarantee to a customer of another branch of that bank. Therefore, Mr Atkinson is still liable under the guarantee.

(b) *Barclays Bank plc* v *O'Brien* (1992) confirmed that where a married woman provides security for her husband's debts, the bank must ensure that she understands the nature of the transaction which she is entering into. In view of the possibility of undue influence by the husband it is also advisable that the wife receives independent legal advice. In this instance, Mrs Bassett merely signed the form, without an explanation of the nature or extent of her liability being provided by the bank's security clerk. It is therefore likely that the guarantee could not be enforced against Mrs Bassett.

(c) This situation mirrors the background to the *Cooper* v *National Provincial Bank Limited* (1946) case. Here it was held that the bank was under no obligation to divulge that the customer's husband was an undischarged bankrupt and had signing rights on the account. Therefore, Mr Clough would still be liable under the guarantee.

(d) Mr Dalglish's claim is based on the rule in *Clayton's* case working to his benefit. However, as the guarantee is in standard form it will include a clause which will protect the bank's position, even if it fails to stop the principal debtor's account. This is known as a *Cond* clause, named after the case which agreed the validity of such a clause *(Westminster Bank v Cond* (1940)). Thus Mr Dalglish would still be liable.

(e) Mr Evans is stating that the bank by its actions in both word and deed led him to believe that he was signing other than what he actually signed and as such he is not liable. *Lloyds Bank plc v Waterhouse* (1990) mirrors the situation described and the court found for the defendant. Therefore, providing the facts are confirmed, Mr Evans will not be liable.

2 The principle involved concerns the liability of a guarantor of a holding company's debts for the liabilities of the holding company's subsidiary.

The case which relates to this situation is *Bank of Scotland v Wright* (1990). In this case it was stated that a guarantor of a holding company's liability to a bank could also be liable for the debts of the holding company's subsidiary if the guarantee was intended to secure an inter-available facility as between companies in the group, and not merely a direct facility to the holding company.

As can be seen from the facts of this question, the personal guarantee was given as security in respect of a group facility. Thus the ruling in the Wright case would be upheld. (In any case, it was stated by the judge that as the liability of the subsidiary company had crystallised and that each company's guarantee liability had been called upon prior to the demand being made on Wright, the indebtedness of the holding company included the indebtedness of the subsidiary company.)

The bank was therefore correct in its demand made on Choo for £205,387.

UNIT 21

Short-answer questions

1 Letter of pledge.

2 Yes. A letter of pledge does give a bank a power of sale.

3 Barry Griffiths is acting as trustee for the bank with regard to the goods. The bank can therefore take control of the goods and sell them in order to obtain repayment of the produce loan. The trustee in bankruptcy will be unable to lay claim to the goods or to the ultimate proceeds (s.283 (3) Insolvency Act 1986).

4   No. The debtor may be prepared to waive this clause, particularly if no funds exist to be set off. However, further enquiries would have to be made initially. Failure to take any action could erode the whole of the moneys due.

5   The priority of agricultural charges is determined by the date when they were registered at the Agricultural Credits Department of the Land Charges Registry.

6   No. The search merely identifies any prior charges.

Multiple-choice questions

1   (b)

2   (a)   (i)   (b)   (iii)

3   (b)

4   (a)

5   (b)   (c)   (d)   (g)

6   (b)

Revision question

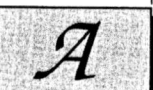

Section 8 (5) Agricultural Credits Act 1928 states that if a farmer becomes bankrupt on a petition presented within three months of the creation of a fixed or floating agricultural charge then, unless he can be proved solvent when the charge was created, the charge is valid only for money lent after its creation.

If the farmer was solvent on 1 March, then the charge is valid.

If the farmer was insolvent at the time when the charge was created then the charge will only be valid for £15,000. The bank will have to claim as an unsecured creditor for the remaining £20,000.

Past examination questions

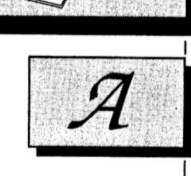

1   (a)   The bank would have originally made a produce advance to the partnership with the imported tinned fruit being pledged as security.

Procedure for perfecting the security

(i)   Partners sign letter of pledge.

(ii) Carry out status reports on suppliers, supermarket chain and warehouse-keeper.

(iii) Have the goods warehoused in the bank's name.

If the goods are imported by sea the bank will require a complete set of clean bills of lading, blank endorsed. The bank's agent can use the documents to obtain a warehouse-keeper's warrant showing goods warehoused in bank's name.

If goods come by air, the airway bill should show the goods consigned to the bank.

(i) Goods to be insured at customer's expense.

(ii) When time comes for delivery to the supermarket chain, the customer must complete a trust receipt. This will state that the customer will retain the goods and the sale proceeds received from them, in trust for the bank.

(iii) The bank then issues a delivery order for the customer so that the goods can be taken from the warehouse and delivered to the ultimate buyer.

(iv) Diarise when proceeds are due to be received.

(v) Banks will normally lend on loan account for ease of control.

(b) In *Lloyds Bank* v *Bank of America NT & SA* (1938) it was held that where the customer is in breach of his trust and pledges the goods to another lender as security, contrary to his undertaking in the trust letter, the new lender will take priority if acting in good faith. Presumably the same will apply if the warehouse accidentally releases the goods.

However, the bank could claim full compensation from the warehouse-keeper.

The German supplier appears to be referring to retention of title clauses in the underlying contract, which means that the title to the goods does not pass from the seller until payment has been made. Such clauses were held to be valid in the *Aluminium Industrie Vaassen BV* v *Romalpa Aluminium Ltd* (1976) case.

The bank should have ensured that the underlying contracts did not contain such clauses; as they have not done so, it would seem that the bank's claim on these particular consignments would lose priority to the German seller providing that they can be identified. The bank should examine the underlying contract in order to establish whether 'Romalpa' clauses are included here.

2 — Check to see whether interested directors can vote on the giving of the security, as the decision in the *Victors* v *Lingard* case could invalidate the charge if this is not the case. If necessary the company should amend its articles of association by special resolution and confirm that everything is in order.

— Either check the memorandum of association of the company or, relying upon s.35 Companies Act 1985, obtain confirmation from the company or its legal advisors that the assignment does not contravene the powers of the company.

— Examine the contracts for the precise terms.

— Diarise to establish outstanding amounts each month.

— Search at Companies House to ensure that there are no prior charges.

— Make status enquiries on other parties and diarise for regular renewal.

— Have bank's standard form executed. This should contain details of the contracts concerned.

— Register particulars of the charge at Companies House within 21 days of creation (s.398 Companies Act 1985). (This is not strictly necessary (*Siebe Gorman* case), but banking practice is to carry this step out as precaution.)

— Give notice to the other parties.

— Forward the irrevocable authority of the company to the other parties confirming that all moneys due should be sent direct to the bank. Obtain an undertaking from the parties concerned that they will comply with this.

Benefits

— If the company goes into liquidation, the bank will be entitled to the proceeds of the contract, even if the due date of payment is after the liquidation.

— The bank can monitor the customer's sales on a regular basis and the creditworthiness of the purchasers concerned.

— The customer cannot open another bank account elsewhere and divert the proceeds to it.

UNIT 22

Mock examination

1   (a)   A 'shadow director' is a person on whose instructions directors will normally act. Excluded from this definition are people acting in a professional capacity, e.g. accountants, solicitors, bankers.

(b)   'Wrongful trading' is where a director allows a company to continue to trade even though it was insolvent or was unlikely to avoid insolvency. 'Wrongful trading' is covered by s.214 Insolvency Act 1986.

(c)   (i)   Check branch records and memorandum cards concerning what is supposed to have taken place between the former branch manager and the company.

(ii)   Obtain the former branch manager's views on the situation.

(iii)   It is not unusual for a branch manager to attend a board meeting; providing only advice of a professional nature was given, all should be well.

(iv)   There is nothing untoward for a branch manager to discuss with a company director which cheques should be paid and which should not.

(v) The liquidator's comment concerning the balance sheet would carry little weight as it would only recently have been available and it would be unlikely at the time that it was certain that the company was trading in an insolvent situation. It must be ascertained from the directors when they realised the company's dire financial position and whether they took any steps to prevent it.

The above considerations would have to be looked at before the bank would respond to the liquidators' claims. Obviously if the bank/Mr Smith were acting in a professional capacity and giving advice accordingly, the liquidator would be unlikely to succeed with his claim.

2 (a) *Undue influence*
— Applies where a stronger party induces a weaker party to enter a contract he/she would not do otherwise.

— 'Manifest disadvantage' of a person influenced must be shown for transaction to be set aside for undue influence.

— Undue influence is presumed in certain relationships, e.g solicitor/client; in the past this has not been presumed for husband and wife, although this premise has been somewhat clouded by the decision in *Barclays Bank* v *O'Brien* (1992).

Independent legal advice

— Advice given, usually by a solicitor, independent of the bank, to a person signing a legal document.

— So that he/she understands the meaning of the document and the implications of the liability.

(b) Solicitor is probably basing claim on decisions in *Lloyds Bank* v *Bundy* (1974) and *Barclays Bank* v *O'Brien* (1992).

In the *Bundy* case undue influence was held to exist where there was an inequality of bargaining power between customer and bank.

However, for transaction to be set aside for undue influence there must be 'manifest disadvantage' of the person influenced (*National Westminster Bank* v *Morgan* (1985)).

In the circumstances given, this would seem unlikely as Ann Temple was keen to remain in the family home and the transaction averted possession proceedings by the building society. Therefore the solicitor's claim *re* undue influence based on the *Bundy* case would be unlikely to succeed.

The decision in the *O'Brien* case stated that where a married woman gives security for the liabilities of her husband she must receive independent legal advice, otherwise the security given will be invalid. Independent legal advice was not given in Ann Temple's case and therefore it would seem that the solicitor's claim would succeed, based on the outcome of the *O'Brien* case.

3 (a) Pay the cheque. Delete Gordon Laurie's name once death certificate exhibited.

(b) Return cheque marked 'Payment stopped – written confirmation awaited'. Ask Susan Bowman to confirm stop instruction in writing.

(c) Stop account. Return cheque marked 'Joint account holder in bankruptcy proceedings'. Await joint instructions of Rachel Hughes and Official Receiver regarding disbursement of account balance.

(d) — s.24 Bills of Exchange Act 1882 states that a forged signature is wholly inoperative.

— Obtain cheques from day's work. Compare signature with specimen held. Consider whether the defence of estoppel would be permissible here.

— If a bank has no viable defence, refund £500 to account.

— Contact Peter Rolls with a view to reimbursement.

— If not forthcoming, consider doctrine of subrogation and advising police via the bank's legal department.

— Advise bank staff of problematic situation regarding the account.

— Obtain further instructions from account holders regarding their future use of the account or otherwise.

(e) — Identify Alan Thomas.

— Compulsory admittance to a mental hospital will determine the bank's mandate.

— Return cheque marked 'Insufficient mandate'.

— Obtain copy of court of Protection Order and establish how balance on Freda Thomas's account is to be dealt with.

4 (a) — The loan is a regulated agreement.

— Under s.107 Consumer Credit Act 1974, upon payment of a fee, a guarantor can obtain details of the amount outstanding on the loan and the total amount repaid.

— However, customer's father cannot be advised of balances on other accounts without his son's authority (*Tournier* v *National Provincial & Union Bank of England* (1924)).

— Guarantor should be advised of the above.

(b) — Bank's standard form of guarantee will normally require three months' notice to be given to the bank before the guarantor's liability is determined.

— Advise guarantor of this and explain that payments will continue to be allowed to be made out of the account during the determination period.

— Contact Grainger and advise him of situation. Ascertain whether he still requires overdraft facility. If not, guarantor may be released from his liability.

— If Grainger still requires facility, is alternative security available?

— Bank would retain guarantee, in case there should be a later claim for preference.

— When guarantee is determined, advise guarantor of his liability, if any. If the account is overdrawn, stop it and open a new one for Grainger.

(c) — Obtain claim forms from assurance company.

— Obtain Sullivan's signature to these and his authority addressed to the assurance company to forward the proceeds to the bank.

— Send policy and completed forms to assurance company.

— Diarise for receipt of proceeds.

— When proceeds arrive, credit customer's account.

— Cancel overdraft limit. If premiums were paid by standing order, cancel it.

— If Sullivan refuses to co-operate with the bank, the bank will have to apply to the courts for a court order to ensure that the policy proceeds are paid to the bank.

5 (a) *Advantages*

— Direct security – not third party.

— It is likely that, as the extension is being made to the company's existing premises, it will fall under the first mortgage.

— There are no occupancy rights problems as there would be if domestic property was involved.

Disadvantages

— The premises are leasehold, which is a reducing asset as regards security valuation.

— Covenants contained in leasehold document could create risk of forfeiture if breached.

— If mortgagee entered into possession, it could be bound by clauses contained in leasehold documentation.

— If bank has to realise its security, it may need to pay any rent arrears from the sale proceeds.

Further information required

— Terms of lease need to be examined with regard to onerous clauses, forfeiture rights, period of lease still to run.

— Will extension be built on land covered by the mortgage?

— What is the current market price of the security offered?

— How accurate is the balance sheet valuation of the property?

— Is property adequately insured?

(b) *Advantages*

— Easy to take.

— Ensures directors' commitment to the success of the company.

— Value of the security is fixed.

— Bank is protected by the strength of the bank's guarantee clauses which remove most of a guarantor's common-law rights.

— As a third-party security, the bank would not have to take it into account in submitting its proof in the event of the company going into liquidation.

Disadvantages

— Difficult to realise.

— If the director's additional assets are tied up in the company, then should the company fail, the directors may not be able to meet their guarantee liability.

— If the directors are a good connection for the bank, over and above the company's account, the bank may be reluctant to enforce the guarantee if it would put such a connection in jeopardy.

Further information required

— What assets outside the company do the directors have?

— Can they meet their guarantee liability? Status enquiries may need to be taken.

(c) *Advantages*

— Very few, except that if the directors' valuation can be confirmed, it would cover the proposed borrowing.

Disadvantages

— There must be commercial justification, for the transaction to be valid (*Charterbridge Corporation Ltd* v *Lloyds Bank* (1969)).

— If this security were realised, it could lead to the demise of Upper Class Ltd, leading to unemployment and a devastating effect on local businesses which relied on the company for their livelihood. This could create bad publicity for the bank.

— The giving of the security could later be considered as a transaction at an undervalue (s.238 Insolvency Act 1986).

Further information

— Is commercial justification evident?

— Is the company able to give such security according to its memorandum and articles of association?

— How have the directors arrived at the property valuation? Is it based on a recent professional valuation?